the BEAUTIFUL generation

the BEAUTIFUL generation

ASIAN AMERICANS

and the

CULTURAL ECONOMY

of FASHION

Thuy Linh Nguyen Tu

DUKE UNIVERSITY PRESS

DURHAM AND LONDON   2011

© 2011 Duke University Press

All rights reserved

Printed in the United States of America on acid-free paper ∞

Designed by Heather Hensley

Typeset in Scala by Keystone Typesetting, Inc.

Library of Congress Cataloging-in-Publication Data appear on
the last printed page of this book.

To my mother

CONTENTS

ACKNOWLEDGMENTS

This book would not have been possible without the time, energy, and imagination of many friends, colleagues, and kind strangers. It is a pleasure to be able to acknowledge them here. I want to begin by thanking all the designers who allowed me to talk with them, hang around their shops, and learn from them. Knowing what I now know about the demands of their work, I am even more amazed that they could find so much time for me. Without their generosity, I would not have this story to tell.

The seeds of this book were planted many years ago, but they really grew in conversation with the wonderful colleagues, at different institutions, who have read, heard, or talked about these ideas with me, including Christine Balance, Luz Calvo, Derek Chang, Beth Coleman, Iftikhar Dadi, Maria Fernandez, Wen Jin, James Kim, Nhi Lieu, Christina Moon, Viranjini Munsinghe, Mimi Nguyen and Minh-Ha Pham (and their spot-on blog, Threadbared), Jeffrey Santa Anna, Barry Shank, Julie Sze, Elda Tsou, K. Scott Wong, Shelley Wong, and Judy Wu. Thanks to all their insights, this project became much more than I alone could have imagined.

I am indebted in particular to the faculty of the Department of Social and Cultural Analysis at New York University. I joined the department just as I was completing this manuscript, and I can think of few places where I could have learned from more dynamic scholars. Arlene Davila, Julie Elman, Jennifer Morgan, Crystal Parikh, Anne Rademacher, Sukhdev Sandhu, Nikhil Pal Singh, and Caitlin Zaloom all took time to read drafts, talk through ideas, or to sneak off for a drink. Thank you for the direction and the diversion. Andrew Ross has seen this work in many different forms and has shaped it in many different ways. It is difficult to acknowledge his many contributions, but I hope that he will recognize some of them in these pages.

Ken Wissoker saw this manuscript in its most embryonic form and championed it even when it required some great leaps of faith. I thank him, and Leigh Barnwell, for guiding me so gently through the editorial process. I am also grateful to the anonymous reviewers for engaging so carefully and generously with my work, and to the Mellon Foundation and the Woodrow Wilson National Fellowship Foundation for supporting this project. Thanks also go to Eva Hageman, my research angel, for scouring the library for images, tracking down permissions and footnotes, and for making my life just plain easier. She pulled this book together when I needed it most.

The years of writing this book were some of my loveliest and some of my most challenging. For sharing in all of those times, I thank Jungwon Kim, Victoria (Graci) Brown, Mary Chan, and Lorraine Paterson. My sister-friend, Alondra Nelson, saw it all, heard it all, and spared no amount of wisdom, good humor, and love. Our fifteen years of friendship (and counting) has been a constant joy to me. Logan Hill has seen me wrestle with this project longer than anyone. He endured countless conversations, dozens of drafts, foul moods, and crises of faith—all with great patience. I thank him for his sharp editorial eye, his unwavering enthusiasm, and for inspiring me with his love of writing.

My family would be the first to say that they have no idea what I spend my time doing. I am pleased to finally have something to show them, and to have this opportunity to thank them. I owe so much to my sister, Ai Linh, who always gave me more than she ever had, and to my brother, Duy Linh, who helped me to laugh at everything. My dad, who spent most of his time in this country working on an assembly line, shaped my worldview—and this project—in ways I am only just beginning to understand. Finally, my greatest gratitude goes to my mother, Thi Thi, who always dreamed the best for me, and to my daughter, Myha, who is my best dream.

FASHION, FREE TRADE, AND THE "RISE OF THE ASIAN DESIGNER"

On December 11, 1990, U.S. officials charged into a nineteenth-century, brick, walk-up apartment building at 247 Mulberry Street in New York City and arrested John Gotti Sr., the suspected leader of the Gambino crime family. Home of the Ravenite Social Club where Gotti and his associates ran their organized crime business, the building stood in the heart of a small residential neighborhood stretching no further than the few blocks running along Elizabeth, Mott, and Mulberry Streets, on the northern edge of New York's Little Italy. After Gotti's arrest, the Ravenite building was sold to the investment group Allied Partners, which immediately knocked down the walls of its cramped rooms and replaced its bricked-up windows with a glass storefront. Before long, they had transformed the notorious social club into a bright new retail space. On February 23, 1999, the date of the auspicious lunar new year's eve, the handbag designer Amy Chan opened her first store in the old Ravenite building. After she hung her logo—a lucky number eight—over the door and made her feng shui adjustments, the only hint of the social club left was the cracked black-and-white tiled floor, where New York's iconic Italian gangsters made their last stand.

Chan's appearance at 247 Mulberry was a sign of changes to come, not just for the Ravenite building but for the whole neighborhood. Shortly after her arrival, a host of other designers began replacing its old tenements and boarded up storefronts with shiny new boutiques. Over the course of just a few years, they transformed it into the shopping mecca now known as Nolita. Among those who joined Chan were Anna Kim, Margie Tsai, Elaine Kim, Kazuo Nakano, and Jennifer Wang—second-generation Asian American women who, like so many of Nolita's pioneers, were eager to try their luck in one of the city's oldest industries: the clothing business. The prevalence of these women in Nolita and nearby in the also rapidly changing East Village was such that in 2000 *The New York Times* dubbed the area from the Lower East Side to Tribeca a "Little Seoul in the making" in honor of the "hip little fashion shops owned and supplied by young Korean-Americans, the daughters of immigrants who have moved on from the greengroceries and dry cleaners of their parents' generation and entered the fashion world."[1]

These shops provided a kind of visual proof that the same newspaper's speculation just five years before was right—we were seeing what the *Times* dubbed the "Rise of the Asian designer." Citing the prominence of figures like Anna Sui, Vera Wang, and Vivienne Tam, and the burgeoning number of Asian students at institutions like the Parsons School of Design, the *Times* had announced in 1995 that "Asians, whose nimble hands have for decades sewn in factories in the United States and Asia," had now also "become an emerging force in design."[2] The paper did not make clear whether these conditions were causally linked or merely coincidental, but its emphasis on a narrative of transformation hinted that something historic was in the making.

The *Times* was right in this instance. At the beginning of the twenty-first century, Asian Americans, whose presence in the fashion industry had previously been virtually nonexistent, seemed to be thriving in that field. Their clothes were being regularly featured in the pages of *Vogue, Harper's Bazaar, Elle, W, InStyle*, and other door-opening fashion publications. They were winning an unusually high percentage of the prestigious fashion awards, particularly the recently established prizes for new designers. As of 2007, Asian American designers had won eleven of the forty-one Ecco Domani Fashion Foundation awards; they were ten of the forty finalists for the coveted CFDA/Vogue Fashion Fund prize.[3] They even nabbed a few of the most coveted honors, including the Swarovski Award for Womenswear, awarded by the CFDA (the Council of Fashion Designers of America), which went to Philip Lim in 2007, Doo-Ri Chung in 2006, and Derek Lam in 2005 (between 2003 and 2006, this award was known as Swarovski's Perry

Ellis Award for Womenswear). In 2009, Jason Wu won what amounted to a prize when Michelle Obama, after much suspense and speculation, chose to wear his dress to the inaugural balls. And, in perhaps the clearest indication of their status, Asian Americans were tapped to head up major design labels (Peter Som for Bill Blass) and to design capsule collections for mass-market firms (Richard Chai and Thakoon Panichgul for Target).

At approximately the same time that Asian American designers were emerging as a force on Seventh Avenue, fashion enthusiasts were becoming enthralled with another trend. During the 1990s, Asian chic—or "the utopian and euphoric embrace of elements of particular Asian traditions that have now come to stand in for an undifferentiated Asia," as the anthropologists Carla Jones and Ann Leshkowich have characterized it—captured the sartorial imagination.[4] So-called Asian shapes, fabrics, iconography, and colors pervaded the sartorially high and low, appearing on both the couture runways of Yves Saint Laurent and Gucci and the mass-market racks of Urban Outfitters and Target. Celebrities and socialites donned kimonos, cheongsams, and *salwaar-kameez* for the red carpet. Magazines and newspapers filled their pages with countless "East meets West" photo shoots, fashion layouts, and advertising campaigns. In that decade, Asian chic dominated the fashion landscape.

These twin developments presented a rare convergence between the popular appetite for Asianness—which has certainly come around before—and the presence of Asian designers—novel by all accounts. In the popular press, these developments inspired myriad stories about the Asian invasion of fashion, none of which addressed such basic questions as: What accounts for this historically unprecedented rise of the Asian designer? What effect did the presence of these designers have on the industry? How did they fit into an economy of Asian chic? How did they interpret its signs?

This book began in part as my attempt to answer those simple questions. But while it was prompted by my interest in the fashion industry, it was driven by my broader curiosity about the changing role of culture in the new global economy. As many scholars have said, in the last few decades, we have seen culture expand from a form of social expression or a way of life into an important mode of economic production.[5] From the erection of museums to stimulate tourism to the institution of biennales to spur art sales, culture has increasingly been seen as an economically productive enterprise that is crucial to regional and national development. In recent years, investments in these cultural enterprises have grown, as scholars, policymakers, and politicians have asserted their faith in the ability of this sector to drive innovation, economic development, and global competition.

The historical moment when design became an Asian American practice and when fashion reembraced the signs of Asian culture coincided with this shift toward what has been called a cultural or creative economy. During this time, efforts to financialize culture fostered the creation of a range of new industries, fueled by youthful ingenuity and prioritizing creativity and innovation. These industries, fashion prominent among them, were touted as prized sites of creative work, offering purportedly fulfilling, flexible, and potentially profitable jobs to which young entrepreneurs rushed and around which an entire "creative class," as Richard Florida has called them, emerged.[6] Member of this class were often self-employed, bore unusually high financial risks, enjoyed few benefits of secure employment (like regular wages or health insurance), and generally deferred any real wages for their labor until (if) they finally hit the jackpot.[7] But if they could endure those conditions, then they could achieve the dream—worth dreaming—of creative and autonomous labor.

Who are these creative types who can do creative work? According to boosterists like John Eger, they are primarily Americans who have been made fit by a culture with "tolerance for dissent, respect for individual enterprise, freedom of expression," and a national belief in "innovation as the driving force of the economy, not mass production of low value goods and services."[8] What he fails to add is that they are also young, unencumbered by the demands of children and families, and willing to accept long hours and little security in part because their personal situations permit them to do so. In certain sectors, like fashion, they are also primarily female, workers who have traditionally been slotted into precarious and flexible employment and whose presence here can be considered a continuation of, rather than a break with, the gendered division of labor. Indeed, the neoliberal values of free-market competition and personal flexibility, of individual risk and sacrifice that are a hallmark of these creative industries have long been a part of the reality of women's work. In this sense, occupations such as fashion design are gendered not just because women do them, but because they require a model of self-discipline and insecurity that is a fundamentally gendered model.

Yet, while Asians in America have long taken up precarious work, they have not figured prominently in the ranks of this creative class. Historically constructed as smart but unoriginal, Asians' alleged imaginative limitations have largely marginalized them in knowledge industries. In those rare fields where they are prominent, such as the high-tech industry, their roles are quite circumscribed. Most work as mid-level programmers and systems analysts, involved, as one industry publication put it, in the "laborious, labor-intensive 'legwork'" distinct from "the design, marketing, and creative end."[9] Purported to be inherently efficient, methodic, and geeky, Asians are seen as well-suited to the technical needs of knowledge work. But, coming from a culture that "prizes rote memorization over creativity," they are considered ill-equipped to handle its creative demands.[10]

Given this history, Asian Americans' overwhelming presence in fashion design, a premier site of entrepreneurial creativity, is something of an anomaly. (This is largely what makes their rise so newsworthy.) In examining this rather exceptional presence, I hope to offer greater insight into how culture and economy have become intertwined for this constituency—in particular, how Asianness has become a resource in this creative economy, and how the economic terrain has worked to shape what we have come to know or claim as Asian American. How are those communities formed across linguistic, social, religious, and national differences? Why do people divided by ethnicity, class, gender, sexuality, and migration histories and settlement patterns come to see themselves as having a common identity or allegiance? How and when does this shared identity get activated? These questions have long animated the field of Asian American studies, and scholars have posited that alliances among Asian Americans are built through histories of struggle, by willful performance, and out of political necessity.[11] In my observation, they are also generated through relationships of material exchange. My inquiries into this nexus of culture and economy have shown that for this constituency, collective identities—across differences of class, nation, and so forth—are forged and claimed materially, in the sharing of resources, and provisionally, in those moments of exchange.

This investigation, then, is framed by the understanding that, as many scholars have pointed out, Asian American culture always bears the traces of its material conditions.[12] But for me, that materiality has to be a central site of analysis, rather than simply a context for understanding the cultural text. In this work, I bring together modes and units of analysis that may at first appear unconnected—the apparel trade in Asia, advertisements in *Vogue*, the family life of sewers, images of Mao—in order to show how the material and the symbolic, the cultural and the economic, are in fact linked. Situating fashion design within the broader contexts of globalization, labor history, and racial formation, I demonstrate that industrial labors and creative productions are intertwined, and that innovation emerges not just through the "weak" networks forged between creative types—as many have suggested—but through the dense connections that extend across class and occupational locations, national and generational lines, and between those deemed to be creative and those dismissed as merely functional.[13]

The realm of fashion offers a particularly useful site to investigate these variegated connections. As a symbolic object, fashion is subject to the same demands that guide other cultural practices. But because it operates on both the material and immaterial realms—designers are concerned with both the design and the production of their garments, the two being inseparable—it is also governed by other pressures and liberties that link together these often severed domains. Fashion thus provides a useful departure point from which to observe the intimacies between the realms of creative and noncreative, art and labor, Asia and America, and so on which are at the heart of this book.

Tracking these constitutive threads—between design as an Asian American practice and Asianness as a fashionable commodity—required me to delve into multiple sites and to employ multiple approaches. The first part of the book relies primarily on an ethnographic mode and is dedicated to questions of material production: how Asian American designers have come to this work, and how they understand its nature. Between 2001 and 2008, I spoke informally to dozens of designers, design students, fashion curators, and fashion publicists, and formally interviewed nearly thirty designers who have their own labels. I spent countless hours with them in their shops and studios, on their factory visits, at their fashion shows, and attended numerous industry events without them. These observations allowed me to consider how designers constructed narratives about their work—how they defined skills and expertise, the origins of technical knowledge—and how they understood their relationship to the garment workers who produced their goods.[14]

In the second part of the book, I investigate problems of aesthetic production—how the fashion industry has framed ideas of Asianness, how Asian American designers fit into this economy—and I rely heavily on modes of visual analysis. I analyzed over 500 issues of fashion magazines, spanning the years between 1995 and 2005, to determine how ideas of

Asian chic were constructed during this period. I poured through writings about these designers and scrutinized the clothes they designed, the images they bore, the methods used in their construction, the look, the feel, and, most important, the relationship of these clothes to the body.

By separating these two modes of analysis, I do not mean to suggest that material and aesthetic productions are distinct and do not fundamentally rely on each other. In fact, I hope to show quite the opposite. I hope in this work to bring to the foreground the ways that aesthetic productions rely on labor, capital, and other material resources and, moreover, to show that processes of immaterial labor mirror and are linked to other forms of work—industrial and entrepreneurial among them. This is reflected in my approach in each part of the book, which considers the aesthetic and material always in relation to each other. Material exchanges are framed by ideas about culture; symbolic creations are informed by their conditions of production.

The story I attempt to tell here, about the art and labor of Asian chic, is necessarily a fractured and incomplete story. Change is endemic to fashion. Designers come and go; styles burst on the scene and fade away. New York's industry too continues to shift, as sewing factories regularly close in the face of overseas competition, and as rising rent and labor costs in the city makes it less hospitable to young designers.[15] If culture is ever-changing, it changes perhaps fastest in fashion. This book is thus only a partial picture of the second-generation Asian Americans[16] who entered New York's fashion industry beginning in the 1990s—a snapshot of a beautiful generation that is always in formation. The men and women who animate it do not represent a coherent group or movement. While many know each other, having sometimes worked together in the early phases of their careers, they do not identify themselves as a cohort. But what they do share is a professional and cultural milieu; a collective desire to create objects of beauty and fascination; and, perhaps most important, a common migration history that shapes their work in strikingly similar ways.

This professional milieu is largely dominated by women. Though it is difficult to establish precisely the gender ratio in this industry, even a cursory glance at the designers listed in the CFDA will show that women are well represented. (One estimate suggests that in comparable fashion centers like London, women outnumber men approximately ten to one.)[17] Within the apparel trades, female workers have long been a prominent part of the labor force, domestically and internationally. While the latter work is deemed unskilled and the former creative, with all the differences in value that such designations entail, in a sense they are both "women's work"— framed by gendered assumptions about, in the first case, their interchangeable and dispensable nature and, in the second, their frivolous and casual character.[18]

The clothing industry is in this sense a feminized industry, utilizing feminized labor to create objects for primarily female consumption.[19] Yet, despite their centrality to both its production and consumption, women have not consistently occupied its positions of power. The great majority of female workers still occupy its lowest paid ranks. And within the upper echelons, prized positions at major couture houses still routinely circulate among a few men. Female designers generally take up positions in mass-market firms (such as the Gap), as employees and increasingly as part-time workers, or struggle to establish their own label. Under the forces of neoliberalism, this overwhelming female presence has enabled not collectivity but greater and greater individualization, as women are continually asked to master new skills and to assert the uniqueness of their talents and their brands. And even as female designers are disciplined into becoming appropriate producing subjects—flexible, despecialized multi-taskers—they also help discipline other women into becoming appropriate consuming subjects, able to keep up with fashion and responsive to its calls. The Asian Americans at the center of this story are not immune to these forces. But their ethnicized and racialized histories have altered these gendered dynamics. As children of immigrants (and sometimes immigrants themselves), these designers occupy a complex position: they are incorporated within the nation but exist largely outside of its imaginary; they are central to New York's industry but are situated (and situate themselves) as a bridge to Asia's markets.[20] Positioned at a remove from U.S. national culture (and from American fashion), they have formed and imagined intimacies that challenge what we might call the fashion industry's logic of distance.

This logic, which seeks to delink fashion design from garment manufacturing and to render the two as distinct practices, is constituted by various discourses, produced at multiple sites. These sites include the marketing industry (which fetishizes clothing into abstract ideas—freedom, romance, luxury, etc.—in order to distance it from the labor of production); the global economy (which sees fashion design and garment production as distinct forms of labor—the former as creative or informational white-collar work and the latter as manufacturing, blue-collar work); international trade (which regulates garments as a good and their design as an intellectual property); scholarly treatments (which considers one through studies of labor and the other through studies of art and culture); and designers themselves (who frequently maintain an imaginative and social distance from the people who produce their goods).

The emergence of Asian American designers in the industry throws these neat partitions into disarray, for their very presence, I suggest, has been built on an architecture and aesthetic of intimacy. Asian American designers have been able to navigate the demands of the fashion industry in part by engaging in small, sporadic acts of exchange that allow them to access important resources and, in doing so, to transform what are usually considered market relations into intimate relations (of kin or culture). Moreover, they have exploited these objects of our most intimate fascination to generate an aesthetic that prioritizes connections and affiliations—between past and present, nation and diaspora, garment and body. These are acts of intimacy not just in the sense that they are private—though certainly they rely on and reconstruct the private domains of the family, with all its attendant problems—but also in the sense that they acknowledge proximity, contact, and affiliation between domains imagined as distinct.

My focus here is on these designers—their histories, discourses, imaginations, and creations. As such, I give little attention to the various ancillary sectors that drive fashion as an industry, such as marketing, merchandising, retailing, or modeling. And, though I am particularly interested in the way designers think and talk about garment work and workers, this book is not about the garment industry. The wealth of scholarship on that topic has been invaluable to my project, but my aim here is not to produce a workplace history. Rather, it is to consider how those workplaces are imagined by this generation, and the implication of those ideas for our understanding of how and where Asian American culture is made.

FREE TRADE AND THE EMERGENCE OF ASIAN FASHION

How did this beautiful generation come to be? What accounts for the "rise of the Asian designer"? The answer depends in large part on how one understands the term. As I discovered, there were some important differences between the *Asian* students filling up classes at Parsons and the *Asian American* designers turning downtown into a "Little Seoul." These differences had less to do with ethnic identification—which in this milieu was certainly vague and difficult to establish[21]—than with matters of historical motivation. Asian and Asian American designers came to New York through different routes, paths that were shaped differently by state policies, cultural markets, and labor formations. While this book focuses on Asian American designers, there are lessons to be learned in exploring where these routes diverge and where they intersect. In what follows, I provide a brief outline of the political and economic forces that have contributed to the increased circulation of Asian designers in the West. I offer this broad sketch as a global context for my local study, but also as a way to highlight a key assertion of this book: that these designers' fates were tied in different ways to the same institution—the global garment trade.

In 1994, just a few years before Amy Chan showed up on Mulberry Street, members of the World Trade Organization (WTO) began the Uruguay Round of negotiations and made a decision that would have major repercussions on the entire system of clothing production—and on the visibility of Asian designers in New York. Representatives passed the Agreement on Textiles and Clothing (ATC) with the intent of gradually eliminating all quotas on the apparel and textile trade. The ATC would in effect phase out the Multi-Fibre Agreement (MFA), which had governed the worldwide textile trades since 1974 through a comprehensive system in which a precise quota was set for every single product for every one of the WTO's member nations. Originally created to protect European and U.S. domestic industries from low-cost production sites in developing countries, the MFA inadvertently allowed some developing nations to build up their textile and clothing industries by sheltering them from global competition and granting them (limited) access to wealthy Western markets. While the MFA was in effect, garment production expanded across the developing world as nations sought to take advantage of this market access, generating in the process the global supply chain that we have today, in which a single buyer might make purchases in as many as eighty different countries.[22]

Though the demise of the MFA did not lead to full liberalization—regional and bilateral agreements, such as the one the United States signed with China in 2005 to limit Chinese exports to America, have now become the norm—it nonetheless signaled the beginning of a new era. No longer limited by quotas, buyers can now theoretically consolidate their sources to one or two sites and limit contracts only to those suppliers offering the highest quality products at the lowest price, and in the shortest amount of time. (This last factor has become particularly important in recent years, as consumer cycles have greatly shortened, expanding from four seasons of clothing to about sixteen.)[23] The prospect of this free-trade future generated no small amount of anxieties among garment producing nations. In Asia, the least developed countries like Bangladesh worried about their ability to compete with the massive production capabilities of places like China and India. For their part, China and India, which were expected to gain most from trade liberalization, feared the loss of their industry to areas with lower labor costs like Vietnam, as rising wages (especially in China, which continues to suffer labor shortages in certain sectors) threatened to diminish their competitiveness.

In the years since the announcement of the phaseout of the MFA, suppliers have worked to raise efficiency and improve quality by undergoing what is known in the industry as product upgrading and process upgrading. What this entails, largely, is the adoption of new technologies to reduce inconsistencies in the quality of a garment; to a lesser extent, such upgrading also involves new practices, like the use of cellular manufacturing systems to improve the speed of production, especially of smaller batches of goods. With the aid of the state and international investors, manufacturers have poured tremendous amounts of money into new machinery and technology training. In India, for instance, they have already begun a multibillion-dollar push to replace the country's 1.8 million power looms with new, shuttle-less looms, 1 million of which will be installed by 2010.[24] Between 1996 and 2005, manufacturers in Vietnam spent $2.5 billion to replace obsolete machinery and revamp plants.[25]

However, these changes are only a partial or short-term solution to the demands of the post-MFA market, since they help firms only to make low-cost garments better and cheaper, keeping them competitive primarily at the level of assembly work, or CMT (cut, make, trim). But if the impending free market heightened anxieties about competitiveness, it also sowed discontent about the limitations of this low-yield production. As nervous leaders began strategizing about how to contend with the open market, they repeatedly stressed the need to "move up the value chain," urging manufacturers to expand beyond their assembly operations to a fuller range of services—including, most significantly, designing and branding.

Designing and branding reside at the highest and most profitable end of the global apparel commodity chain.[26] These functions have traditionally been the reserve of Euro-American firms, whose locations in the culturally rich West enables them to access the variety of cultural resources—

including media outlets, marketing organizations, technologically skilled workers, and globally visible youth cultures—that are crucial to the production of style-sensitive, branded goods. Despite their extensive manufacturing networks, very few Asian firms have been able to take up these high-end tasks, which require detailed knowledge of primarily Western consumer markets and trends, and access to the cultural apparatus that can turn a product into an image. In the era of free trade, Asian government leaders increasingly saw access to this sector as the key to gaining long-term advantage, meaning long-term profit. If their manufacturers could master these upper-level tasks, they would have the unique opportunity to integrate the entire production chain—designing, sourcing, assembling, and selling—within a single site.

At the beginning of the twenty-first century, Asian nations began to put in place policies that they hoped would make this possible. In 2001, for instance, Vietnam issued its "Speed up Strategy for 2010," a white paper that outlined its plans to focus on the upstream sector by increasing governmental support to those manufacturers producing their own brands.[27] India had issued a similar white paper a year earlier, stating that its Office of Textiles would "focus attention on the development of the branded sector."[28] In 2004, Yi Xiaozhun, China's vice minister of commerce, summed up the strategy of these nations when he told the press—partially to allay the fears of China's nervous neighbors—that his country's manufacturers had been given "a clear signal" to move up the value chain "so that they don't compete against the low-cost t-shirts of Bangladesh."[29]

These types of mandates—directed not just at garment manufacture but at a range of industries—reflect a widespread commitment to a new model of development that privileges "creativity" and "innovation" as the keys to global competitiveness. As manufacturing or outsourcing economies continue to face downward pressures, more developing countries are investing their hopes in creative or knowledge-based economies. The impact of these directives will not be fully known for some time.[30] Michael Keane has argued, for instance, that China's attempt to shift from a "made in China" to a "created in China" model has so far not been successful, in part because policy changes have not been accompanied by widespread structural reforms.[31] My sense is that shifts up the value chain will be slow and uneven. While government leaders in Asia have been boldly calling for all sorts of ambitious upgrades, individual companies have been cautious about taking on the additional risks that these moves up the apparel chain require. Although China, primarily Hong Kong, had seen a significant growth in fashion-led garment production, as of 2007, 90 percent of Vietnam's manufacturing firms were still operating largely at the CMT level.[32]

But many Asian states, particularly newly industrialized countries, have already begun to invest in the infrastructure that would give their policies some teeth. In the past decade, they have poured tremendous resources into fostering the growth of their fashion industries. Each year, consultants —corporate executives at fashion companies, curators of fashion museums, and deans and teachers at fashion schools like the Fashion Institute of Technology (FIT) and Parsons—are retained at extraordinary costs to instruct city and regional governments on how to turn their urban centers into so-called fashion cities. In addition, state agencies have spent billions to create such institutions as design schools, in order to train students for their national fashion industries. Thailand's Bangkok International Fashion Academy, for instance, was formed in 2005 as part of an initiative by the country's former industrial minister to turn Bangkok into a fashion city. Sri Lanka, with a grant from the Asian Development Council, has just built its first fashion school at the University of Moratuwa. India's National Institute of Fashion Technology, begun in 1986 by the ministry of textiles as a society, has now become an independent school, with branches across the country. In China, there are several state-run design schools in each major city, which enroll an estimated 100,000 design students each year.[33] To meet the rising need for fashion education, students have also been flocking to private institutions such as Raffles Design Institute, a for-profit school with fourteen branches in China, India, Vietnam, and Thailand.

Over the last few decades, these schools have helped give birth to that novel creature, the Asian designer. Though design and creative input into the production of clothing certainly existed long before, the designer, as a disciplinary and professional category, is of a much more recent vintage.[34] Xie Feng (Jefen), one of China's premier designers, noted: "When I was in college in the early Eighties, you couldn't even major in fashion. It wasn't part of the culture at all."[35] Now China graduates about 20,000 new designers each year, about as many designers as there are currently working in the entire United States. India's situation is very similar to China's. According to the anthropologist Parminder Bhachu, the Indian design economy has been radically altered by professionalized designers trained in state-sponsored design schools. Not long ago, Bhachu writes, Indian designers were "few and far between." By the late 1990s, she observed, there was "a flood" of designers.[36]

In addition to training these designers, nations have also taken on the responsibility of showcasing their skills. In the last decade, fashion weeks have blossomed all over Asia, in Bali, the Philippines, Thailand, Hong Kong, India, Korea, and China—funded and organized by state agencies in order to attract foreign and local buyers. Hardly the celebrity-studded events that fashion shows have become in the United States, these programs are often attended by government officials and are staged less to promote not just individual designers but the idea of a national craft tradition more generally. At the 2005 Beijing Fashion Week, for instance, organizers showcased wedding dresses made by NE TIGER hailed as China's first luxury brand. Organizers stressed that these garments were crafted using a centuries-old "seamless" weaving method, once reserved for the emperor's robes. Made of yun brocade, historically used only for Chinese royalty, each dress reportedly took a dozen masters 800 hours to finish. These types of over-the-top creations are flaunted by organizers because they demonstrate the country's long craft tradition and highlight Chinese workmanship in a domain dominated by European couture.

Despite this insistence on the strength of their expert workforce, government and industry leaders know that local training and showcasing alone will not establish Asian designers in the international fashion market. This requires acceptance in the world's fashion centers, where a garment's value is ultimately determined.[37] In an effort to increase these brands' cultural cachet, state and industry leaders have set up various initiatives to augment the presence of Asian designers in the West. China, Japan, and Korea formed the Asia Fashion Federation in 2003—Singapore and Thailand were admitted in 2007—to "disseminate Asian fashion to Europe and the United States" through regional conferences, promotional activities, and research initiatives that they hoped would "strengthen marketability and improve the international design of Asian products."[38] China has held several exhibitions in Berlin, Paris, and New York, showcasing its national talent. Korea has instituted the World Designer Promotion Project, which funds Korean designers to participate in fashion weeks in New York and Paris.

The circulation of these designers in the West requires a delicate balance between an ability to internationalize and a capacity to represent the national. If the goal is to move up the value chain—transforming Asia from the world's factory into its catwalk—then the promotion of these designers must be attended by a rearticulation, or rebranding, of Asianness itself. The idea of Chinese fashion, Korean fashion, and so forth must become as commonplace as other place-based signifiers, whether French couture, Swiss watches, or Danish furniture. The historian Antonia Finnane has shown that this delicate balance has produced some persistent tensions for Chinese designers, particularly when the government demands that designers incorporate Chinese sartorial traditions in their work—to showcase the "glorious history of Chinese clothing." These directives are emblematic, Finnane writes, of the desire to achieve "success in the international arena while simultaneously encouraging an obsession with the essence of Chinese culture."[39]

At the spring 2008 New York Fashion Week shows, I could see these tensions clearly when I entered the booth set up by the Seoul Metropolitan Government to announce its upcoming Seoul Design Olympiad 2008. Inside this small, makeshift room filled with huge pictures of Seoul, guests were given information about a twenty-one-day event organized to promote Seoul as a world design center. They were also given a so-called look book of collections by Korean designers (two of whom were actually then showing in Bryant Park). Amid all this display of Korea's innovative design talents, young Korean women dressed in traditional *hanboks* were bustling about, offering visitors brochures and the opportunity to have photos taken with them.

The contrast between Seoul as a site of new, hip internationalism and Seoul as the domain of hanbok-laden tradition demonstrates the tensions inherent in these efforts to promote Asian fashion. In order to show that they are capable of producing fashion, these nations must demonstrate their capacity to be modern. (After all, according to most theorists and observers, fashion—as opposed to clothing or costume—is characterized by change and is limited to those societies that are technologically and epistemologically capable of change, growth, and modernization. To be in fashion is to be modern.)[40] But in order to establish their unique contribution (and their competitive niche in the global market), they must emphasize their national markers and ethnicized traditions.

Among the many efforts to increase the visibility and presence of Asian designers in the West, some of the most effective have been partnerships with U.S. educational institutions. Since the 1990s, Parsons has formed a series of affiliate schools in Asia that represent a complex mix of mutually reinforcing governmental, economic, and educational interests. These include the Kanazawa International Design Institute, founded in 1991 in Japan; the Samsung Art and Design Institute (SADI), built in Seoul in 1995; and the Center for Advanced Design (CENfAD), created in Kuala Lumpur in 1996. Though these schools operate independently, they all follow the Parsons curriculum and, most significantly, allow qualifying students to transfer to the Parsons Manhattan campus after two years. Technically funded by private businesses, these affiliates have strong governmental ties. For instance, Datuk Effendi Norwawi, who headed the Encorp Group when it started Kuala Lumpur's CENfAD, became Malaysia's minister of agriculture the next year, and remained in the government until 2008; his daughter is the executive director of the school.[41] SADI, funded largely by the electronics giant Samsung, was founded after the company began receiving the low-interest loans and tax exemptions offered by the Ministry of Trade, Industry, and Energy to "officially recognized design companies."[42]

For business and government leaders, these schools train the specialized workforce required to "upgrade" their nations' garment industries.[43] For Parsons, the affiliates burnish the university's brand name and produce significant income. The school collects a yearly fee from each affiliate ($250,000 from the Kanazawa school, and $280,000 from SADI), as well as tuition from students after they come to New York.[44] For many students, these partnerships offer them a prestigious education and make it possible for them to visit the United States—and even to stay there.

This affiliate arrangement was a significant catalyst for the well-publicized boom in Asian students at places like Parsons. Currently about 40 percent of the students in the school's fashion department are Asian, primarily from Japan, Taiwan, South Korea, Malaysia, and China—places where Parsons currently has affiliates or has significant interest in fostering new affiliates.[45] (While there are no guarantees of admission, students from these affiliates are accepted at a very high rate; everyone who applied from CENfAD's first two classes was allowed to transfer to Parsons.)[46] Though these numbers represent a boon to the school, and a source of pride for its partners overseas, they have also produced some tensions. A student who transferred from SADI to Parsons told me that instructors there often grumbled about the high number of Asian students, claiming that many were not qualified. Yet when I attended Parson's senior show in the spring of 2008, I noticed that over half the students selected to present their designs and to receive the top awards were Asian students. The faculty comments, then, seem to say less about the ability of the students than about the tensions produced locally by deals brokered internationally.[47]

Many students who came to the United States to study have stayed on, sometimes to start their own labels, but mostly to work for large clothing companies. Those who have returned home come back to showcase their work at fashion week and sometimes eventually to set up shop in New York. Asian designers trained in their home countries also make an appearance at the shows and in the various exhibitions that help to draw attention to their countries' burgeoning fashion industries. The movement of these bodies between Asia and America—sanctioned and supported by state and business interests in response to the challenges of the global garment trade—has contributed to the increased visibility of Asians in New York's fashion industry.

While New York design programs were enrolling record numbers of Asian students, young Asian Americans were setting up fashion boutiques in the city's gentrifying neighborhoods. Predictably these two constituencies were casually conflated in popular accounts of the supposed Asian invasion of fashion, eliding their myriad divisions in terms of nationality, citizenship, migration history, and ethnic identification. These distinctions are important not as a matter of border marking—the lines between Asians and Asian Americans are certainly not fixed—but as a way of understanding the differing forces that have contributed to the so-called rise of the Asian designer. Asian and Asian American designers came to the industry by different paths. The latter were not, for instance, beneficiaries of investments made by Asian governmental and business interests. They were mostly children of immigrants and had found their way to fashion after detours through liberal arts colleges and unrelated careers. Yet the stories of these two groups intersect. If Asian designers' arrival in New York underscores the intimate relationship between the developments of Asia's fashion industry and the demands of the garment trade, Asian Americans' emergence as a force in design reflects similarly intimate though much more informal ties to the local garment industry.

THE BEAUTIFUL GENERATION

Though New York is now commonly seen as a fashion center, it was not so long ago that this city, much like Bangkok or Beijing, had to struggle to prove its fashion worthiness. Because the U.S. apparel industry originated in the ready-to-wear sector, it had little in the way of a couture tradition or local design talent. Until well into the 1950s, the industry took all its cues from Paris. Retailers and manufacturers hopped on a transatlantic flight each season to buy and copy the latest looks. Schools like the Pratt Institute (established in 1888) and Parsons (established in 1897) modeled themselves after French fashion schools. At Parsons in the 1920s, most of the instructors were French, and students spent all their time sketching French designs; the school even established a branch in Paris where students could spend their second year. Back then, one manufacturer admitted, New York's industry was "not so interested in making something good, as [in] making it cheap."[48]

Difficult as it is to remember, there was a time when, as Dorothy Shaver, a member of the influential Fashion Group International, noted, "the word 'American' and the word 'designer' had not even been introduced to each other."[49] The very same conditions that are seen as obstacles to Asia's ability to upgrade—the lack of designers, a reputation as the producer of cheap goods—once characterized the U.S. industry as well. To move up the value chain, cities like New York built schools like FIT (which described itself as "an MIT of fashion") to train a generation of designers. They fostered homegrown publications, such as *Harper's Bazaar* and *Vogue* (whose very name identified fashion with France), which gradually began to promote the idea of an original American fashion.[50] They instituted fashion weeks in places like New York to rival those of Paris, London, and Milan. One need not look too closely to see that these strategies parallel the formula that Asian countries are following today.[51]

The transformation of New York into a fashion city required an erasure of its history as a garment town. Once synonymous with low-cost immigrant tailors and copied couture, it is now famous for DKNY, Condé Nast, and Bryant Park Fashion Week. But garment production has certainly not disappeared. Rather, it has become something of a poor cousin to fashion, an acknowledged but often forgotten kin.[52] By the time Asian students began showing up at Parsons and Asian Americans began turning downtown into a "Little Seoul," fashion had become one of New York's biggest businesses, pulling in an estimated $30 billion per year. Its garment industry, on the other hand, was suffering from intense overseas competition—a result of the same free-trade demands that sent Asian students to New York—soaring domestic real estate prices, organizational restructuring, and workforce fluctuations. Since at least the 1960s, the development of the fashion industry in New York has been accompanied by a simultaneous underdevelopment of the city's apparel industry. While the U.S. Bureau of Labor Statistics projects a 1 percent growth in jobs for fashion designers between 2008 and 2018, it projects a 15 percent decline in jobs in the apparel sector. The bureau characterizes apparel as "among the most rapidly declining occupational groups in the economy."[53]

While it has become easy to forget the centrality of apparel to New York's fashion history, the links remain unbreakable. The tents of Bryant Park are still filled with samples produced locally, in factories that skirt the line between workshop and sweatshop. Young designers still buy fabric and buttons on 37th Street and put in their orders on 39th. Part of the aim of this book, then, is to think these through together and to ask how designers imagine and talk about their relationship to the domain of production. If apparel manufacturing has become a distant cousin to fashion design, for the Asian Americans who are at the center of this book, these connections were much more intimate. For many of them, their very presence in fashion has been informed by their deep and close ties with those working in its cognate industries.

When I first began my research, in 2001, I was of course curious about why there had been such growth in the numbers of Asian American designers. I came up with several plausible explanations: the door-opening effects of the so-called Japanese three (Rei Kawakubo, Issey Miyake, and Yohji Yamamoto), whose success made "Asian designer" a conceptual possibility; the expansion of consumer interest in high-fashion, or style-sensitive, branded clothing, which increased the market for designer goods; the general growth in the number of "young designers" in New York, supported by an industry looking for new labels as established names like Calvin Klein and Ralph Lauren were edging into retirement.[54] But when I asked my sources how they personally came to this work, they spoke far less about these developments than about the influence of their relatives, many of whom had worked in the garment industry or its associate trades, as sewers, tailors, and dry cleaners. About 50 percent of the designers I interviewed had at least one family member with this history. Of the six most prominent young Asian American designers working today—Thakoon Panichgul, Alexander Wang, Peter Som, Derek Lam, Doo-Ri Chung, and Philip Lim—half (the latter three) claim this history.

For many of these designers, clothing is literally a family business. In contrast to the alumni of FIT, Parsons, and Central Saint Martins—of the

University of the Arts London—who dominate the world of New York fashion, many of the designers I interviewed did not train formally or extensively at fashion schools. Most took some classes, but few completed a degree; some never attended fashion school at all. They learned instead by watching their mothers, fathers, aunts, sisters, and cousins sew, cut, and knit—and by doing it themselves from an early age. This knowledge was passed around and handed down through familial networks. For these designers, the time spent in a garment factory or a dry-cleaning shop, whether they were there by choice or compulsion, functioned as the informal training and inspiration for their careers.

The familial context served as many designers' jumping-off point, enabling them to start their work and shaping their understanding of it in important ways. But families offered more than just knowledge. They gave designers material benefits, including financial assistance and, equally important, unpaid help. The same parents and siblings who taught these designers how to sew, cut, and imagine often lent their expert hands to making their goods. Many designers told me that in their early days, producing a collection became a family affair, with mothers, sisters, aunts, and uncles all helping out, and with homes turned into factories.

These accounts are remarkable because they trouble common assumptions about the nature of creative work. Fashion design, as a vaunted creative profession, is typically understood as distinct from the craft or labor of sewing. But in the work and lives of many Asian American designers, these forms of labor are contiguous, performatively and spatially, and actually resemble less the occupations of the new economy than those of the far less shiny ethnic entrepreneurial economy. As I demonstrate in chapter 1, young designers starting their own businesses have leaned on the same familial and social networks that Asian immigrants have historically used so effectively to establish their entrepreneurial niches. (The Korean green-grocer is a much-studied example.) These networks have given young designers access to money, labor, contacts, and information—resources that have been crucial to their work, especially in the early days and particularly among those who lacked the professional training and networking afforded by a formal education. Equally important, these networks have also fostered in the designers different conceptions of the labor of sewing (as central, not marginal, to fashion design) and of the sewer (as expert, rather than unskilled) that challenge traditional ideas about the sources of expertise and knowledge.

Of course, not all designers have fashion "in their blood," as these children of sewers often characterize the significance of their familial histories. But even for those without that legacy, the family still occupies a central role in their work. Like most designers in New York, Asian Americans rely on the local garment industry to produce their goods—an industry that has come to be dominated by Asian and Latino workers. The relationship between these groups is primarily an economic one: contractor to client, worker to boss. But, as I reveal in chapter 2, designers have extended these relationships far beyond the realm of economic exchange. They do so, I argue, by constructing and performing a narrative of kinship, one that transforms Asian sewers and contractors into "uncles" and "aunties" who "help out" Asian American designers because they are "their girls."

This discursive production of kinship allowed designers to forge intimacies with their contractors and sewers and to benefit from these connections. As "their kids," designers were given access to remaindered fabrics at discounted prices, had orders fast-tracked, and often received "the family price" on everything from patterns to production. At the same time, it enabled workers to rearrange the organization of power. As uncles, aunties, mothers, and fathers, they could exercise authority over their "children" in ways that they could not as employees or "helpers." Over the years, I have heard countless complaints from designers that these producers, who are technically their employees, failed to listen to them and treated them, as they said, "like a kid." These tensions were often exacerbated by the gender differences between them, revealing that this performance of "the family" was not free from conflict. These intimacies worked to minimize some conflicts and differences—of, for instance, class positions, citizenship status, and occupational locations—but they could not erase them.

In highlighting these performances of "the family," I do not mean to suggest that Asian Americans are, by dint of their cultural values, inherently more family-oriented. These are discursive and performative productions that, far from revealing any internally coherent or constitutive cultural characteristic, actually demonstrate how contingent, fragile, makeshift—and not a priori—social relationships really are. And I certainly worry about more than just the disconnect between a discourse of familiarity and the continuation of class and other divides. The figurative family is, after all, no more innocent than a real family—an institution that, as many scholars have noted, has often rewarded the reproduction of ethnic, gender, and sexual norms; that has served as labor recruiter for capital's needs; that has colluded with nationalist imaginings; and so on. Coercive as well as comforting, it is an institution in whose name myriad injustices have been enacted.[55] Yet while I do not want to romanticize this construction of family, or to minimize its potential for extending inequalities, I do want to consider how it has allowed designers to enter into a type of gift economy—an intrinsically unequal and implicitly coercive system of exchange that nonetheless facilitates and often prioritizes efforts at social connection.

If Asian American designers ever understood themselves as a distinct group, it was in these moments of intergenerational and intra-ethnic exchange—of knowledge, labors, and resources—made possible in spite (and sometimes because) of these actors' occupational, generational, and national differences. It was in the sharing of material resources that designers and sewers could grasp their interconnectedness and forge a sense of collectivity. These informal instances of exchange, between families both figurative and literal, are then also moments of social connection, emerging from the economic terrain but exceeding its boundaries.

Recognizing this helps to shed new light on one of the central questions within the field of Asian American studies: What holds this fragile coalition together? The story of these designers show us that it is, at least in part, the small, voluntary acts of unequal exchange that broadcasts the mutual interdependence of giver and receiver and fosters in each something akin to a commitment. The story demonstrates that through these provisional and fleeting moments of interaction, socially divided constituencies can come to see themselves as connected and to recognize their potentials as collaborators. In this sense, it makes clear that race and ethnicity are social constructs that have material and institutional ramifications, and also that material conditions help to constitute what subjects come to know, or claim, as their race, ethnicity, nationality, and so on.

In shedding light on these moments, I want to show that they have been crucial in fostering a sense of a collective identity among young designers. But more broadly, I want to demonstrate that they have put pressure on the neoliberal values that reduce all rationales to a market logic of wins and losses, and all collectivities to self-interested individuals. Working in a mode of intimacy, Asian Americans' attempts to recognize proximity and affiliation belies the fashion industry's logic of distance and fundamentally challenges the creative economy's ethos of individualism.

If the production of fashion as a material good has been structured by this constitutive split—between sewing and design, the creative and the noncreative—its production as a symbolic good has depended on similar practices of distancing. As I detail in the second part of this book, fashion's embrace of Asian chic during the 1990s relied on the same Orientalist gestures that have historically been used to construct Asia as an unchanging difference. While ostensibly an expression of appreciation for Asian sartorial traditions, Asian chic, I argue, actually functioned to reinforce social hierarchies and to reestablish what Arjun Appadurai has called a "cultural economy of distance."[56] The consumption of these goods and images, far from suggesting an intimacy with the cultures from which they purportedly emerged, both presupposes a cultural remove and enacts a cultural distancing.[57]

In chapter 3, I begin to unpack these dynamics by asking first what we mean by Asian chic. Analyzing over 500 issues of fashion magazines between 1995 and 2005, I examine the discourses of Asianness produced by the designers, advertisers, and editorial writers who contribute to the pages of the mainline fashion magazine. The meanings of Asianness in these pages changed over time, shifting in ways that both dovetailed with political discourses (of multiculturalism, for instance) and contradicted them. But through the establishment of a series of binaries—the modern and the traditional, the designed and the real—these publications collectively worked to foster in the fashionable public a sense of their distance from and superiority to Asia.

Yet, I argue, the resurgence of interest in these elements and motifs should not be seen just as an expression of Euro-Americans' cultural power, of their ability to dictate fashions to the rest of the world and consume all it has to offer. This interest should also be read as the expression of a collective anxiety about America's global competitiveness. At a time when America's economic losses were being tied to Asia's economic gains, Americans were continually reminded not of their distance from the East but of their connections to it. In the face of this inescapable intimacy, Asian chic provided a symbolic resolution to this crisis of competition by offering consumers an Asia imagined to be simultaneously untainted by modernity and at its cutting edge.

Asian American designers who entered the industry during this decade of Asian chic occupied a unique position. While they may have shared the interests, anxieties, and longings that animated American desire for these goods, their consumption and production of these products was far more fraught. What these designers thought about the trend toward Asian chic and how it shaped their experiences was framed by their individual inclinations—political, aesthetic, and so on—and their position in the fashion hierarchy. But though Asian Americans never drove this trend, controlled its command metaphors, or truly profited from it, they were not absent from its production. How did these designers shape the images and ideas of Asianness? How did they fit into this cultural economy of Asian chic?

While Asian American designers certainly contributed to the production of Asian chic, they failed to hew entirely to its economy of distance, struggling at times to forge connections to Asia (and beyond) and to assert the types of transnational intimacies that it precluded. Employing an aesthetic of intimacy, they fashioned a diasporic imagination that challenged the operations of the fashion market even as it was driven by it. Chapter 4 illustrates this by looking at the work of Vivienne Tam, arguably one of the most prominent Asian Americans in fashion and certainly one of the most enthusiastic promoters of Asian chic.

In 1995 Vivienne Tam collaborated with the New York–based Chinese artist Zhang Hongtu to create a collection of shirts and dresses imprinted with reworked images of Chairman Mao. Produced at the height of the 1990s "Mao craze" in China, this collaboration coincided with a much broader debate about Mao, China's political future, and his role in shaping it. Chinese avant-garde artists at this time employed Mao's image to satirize life and politics in a nation undergoing political upheaval and culturally contradictory economic reforms. Across the ocean, Zhang also took up Mao's image, but he did so to reveal the personal, intimate, affective relationship of the artist to this global icon.

Tam's collection brought this image—which was already circulating between the religious and the profane, the high and low, the personal and the political—into the gendered circuits of fashion. By "loosening up" Mao with a bit of fashion, as Tam said, the collection deployed Mao's image within an acceptable discourse of Asianness.[58] Yet even as it rendered Mao as a recognizable visual trope, the collection also exposed his image as an icon of intimate fascination. In doing so, it participated in the ongoing conversations about Mao's legacy and—lying at the intersection of art and fashion, high and low—extended Zhang's critique in ways that revealed the importance of this figure for Chinese in the diaspora. As such, the collection pointed to the possibility that Asian images could, in this cultural economy, be more than just a floating signifier. They could serve as a resource to narrate cultural memories, and to reaffirm the importance of history, here posited neither as time or place, but as a set of questions to be continually repeated.

For most of the Asian American designers I interviewed, however, such images could not be used to articulate their sense of history, culture, and nation. While they were drawn in various ways to Asia, the transnational intimacies they forged could not be expressed through a visual economy alone. So what did Asia mean to these designers? In chapter 5, I take up this question by considering their relationship to this material and symbolic site. In examining these connections, I reveal that Asian Americans' diasporic imagination, while manifested in the terrain of the symbolic, was activated by exchanges made in the realm of the material. Just as they had been encouraged to articulate an ethnic identity by the benefits won and relationships built with garment producers, Asian Americans were similarly persuaded to claim a transnational identity by incentives provided by Asian states and corporations. These subjects forged relationships with Asia in part because they could imagine it as a home, but also in part because they saw it as a burgeoning market.

These material connections were manifested in the symbolic realm not through the use of exotic images and styles, but through a particular approach to design—one that saw clothing as a form of architecture, protecting and enabling the body, rather than dissecting and displaying it. This approach, drawn from the work of avant-garde Japanese designers, became Asian Americans' most important "Asian influence." But while such ideas were introduced to Parisian couture by Japanese designers, they were already circulating in contexts further afield. Tracing their formal affinities to certain forms of Arab clothing, I reveal that the influences that shape Asian Americans' imaginations reaches both to what we know of as Asia and extends to what we have assumed is elsewhere.

This investigation into Asian Americans' participation in fashion design will, I hope, make clear that the various streams, worlds, spheres, and domains that at first appear distinct may in fact be intimately tied.[59] This seemingly simple admission has some important implications for our investments, individually and nationally, in maintaining the boundaries between such accepted categories as producer and consumer, Asia and America, creative and noncreative, material and symbolic. We construct our lives and longings at their intersections, and as scholars we have to think more seriously about how, precisely, they seep into each other, leaving their marks and traces. The accounts I have gathered here help us to see some of these marks, for they suggest that Asian American identities are articulated, performed, and activated at the confluence of material practices (that can help to reassert a ethnic or national identity) and symbolic practices (that can enable a diasporic sensibility). These are not, as some have feared, contradictory impulses.[60] They are, rather, an articulation of the highest hopes for this thing we call Asian American, a national project that can engage with the transnational, a collective imagination that can be a material force.

FASHION'S INTIMACIES

The journey from cloth to clothing, from the hands that sew to the bodies that wear, mapped out in this book is by most accounts a long one. Stretching across multiple nations, modes of labor, forms of presentation, and ways of knowing, the production of fashion is literally a global project. Indeed, many have noted that it exemplifies the most advanced form of globalization. The clothing industry was, after all, among the first to become transnational, and its structures of production, both material and symbolic, are among the most globally dispersed. This story of how children of immigrants became makers of fashion is, then, also a story about how culture is made in the age of globalization—under what conditions of possibility, through whose sacrifice, as an expression of what faith and criticism of what arrangements. In this regard, my account is a testament to that academic and popular truism: the local is always global, the transnational is ever present in the national—and, in this case, what appears as Asian American usually exceeds that category.

From our imported fish to our exported jobs, we have gotten used to the idea that people, goods, ideas, money, and so on move across spaces and geographies. Still, though we hear repeatedly that "the world is flat," as Thomas Friedman's best-selling book announced, we remain unsure about how to address the political implications of this reality.[61] In the world of fashion, the recognition that globalization has been an industry-changing force has offered few answers about how to address lingering challenges like the reemergence of the sweatshop in the global South and in Western cities.[62] Indeed, that recognition seems geared less toward providing answers than toward producing anxieties, worries about how to remain competitive in an altered terrain. In this regard, the stories of Asian American designers might be instructive. For this examination of Asian Americans' participation in the fashion industry allows us to see not just how Asian-ness works in this creative economy but also how those who participate in it can forge ideas, exchanges, and innovations that can help us to think differently about globalization, and the neoliberal values that guide it.

Fashion is a cultural arena that is at once both intensely public and profoundly private, and that marks those boundaries ambiguously. It gives voice to private sentiments and sensibilities by connecting it to the material, performative, visual, and tactile spheres. Fashion as an economic form, however, operates through a logic of distance—through the location of production and consumption, and the material and the symbolic within distinct psychological and spatial geographies. To an extent this is how all commodities are made, as Marx first theorized—through the masking of social relationships as objective relationships. But in the world of fashion, this distance does not function as a disavowal. It is important to know where things are made (Italy or Thailand?), how they are made (by hand or machine?), and by whom (craftsman or unskilled laborer?). Value is assigned based on these considerations. The logic of distance thus works not to mask or deny the labor of clothing production, but to isolate it from the here and now of fashion making—in essence, to situate these endeavors as entirely different enterprises, with distinct physical and social locations.

This presumption of distance and disconnection abets the forces of neo-liberalism by presenting the products of social relationships as the work of individual enterprise. It has helped to maintain the attendant global inequities by obscuring the possibilities for connections—between consumers and producers, North and South, creative and noncreative—that might be mobilized to change them. Because Asian American designers work in what I argue is a mode of intimacy, they strive to acknowledge and forge proximity, contact, and affiliation between domains imagined as distinct. Such acknowledgments should be obvious, especially in a cultural arena where the division between the public and the private is ambiguous, and between the material and the aesthetic untenable. And yet these acknowl-edgments appear infrequently. Like many acts of intimacy, these ties can become quite taut and can pull violently at times. But in highlighting them, I hope to reveal how the logic of distance, despite admissions of intercon-nectedness, can make ghosts out of things and peoples right here in our midst. I hope to show how an aesthetic and an architecture of intimacy might reorient our imaginations and allow us to see how social connec-tions can happen and where coalitions might survive.

As the following pages will demonstrate, while it cannot be said Asian Americans' presence has transformed the fashion's structures of production or feeling, it has exposed the industry's pressure points. The creative kinship structure that these designers employ—for all its erasures, denials, and abuses—makes aunties and uncles out of abstract workers and sutures them to an imaginary that habitually sees them as necessary but as profoundly distant and different. Likewise, Asian Americans' use of Asian political imagery and aesthetic traditions exposes fashion's periodic love affair with Asianness as, paradoxically, less a gesture of embrace than one of distance, reinforcing these elements as removed from and inferior to European aesthetic traditions. If these acts of consumption rely on a "cultural economy of distance," Asian Americans' acts of cultural production rely on the modes and markers of proximity.

The various acts of intimacy marked here are limited, not pervasive. They are improvisational, informal, and frustratingly unsystematic. But bringing them to light can, I believe, reinvigorate discussions about the often hidden circuits that link together the domains of culture and labor, of the material and immaterial, and of the here and there. This study clearly demonstrates that fashion—the very medium that seduces and traps us, that exploits our labors and drives our consumption—can also be the site where we reimagine the lines that divide us.

This story is a long one, taking us from Bryant Park to Beijing, but it is also an intimate one, written through such details as the glass doors and cracked floors of 247 Mulberry Street. After being arrested there in 1990, John Gotti spent the rest of his days in prison. He never saw the transformations that took place in his old neighborhood, but I suspect that he would not have entirely disapproved of these Asian American designers. Gotti could not have foreseen their rise, comprehended the global machinations and personal trajectories that made it possible, or predicted the effects of their presence. He was certainly no godfather to this beautiful generation. But he loved fashion—he was nicknamed the "dapper don"—and understood well the business of family.

Part I

Chapter 1

CROSSING THE ASSEMBLY LINE

SKILLS, KNOWLEDGE, AND
THE BORDERS OF FASHION

In 2005 fashion fans in the United States were treated to two dramatic media events: the release of Douglas Keeve's much-anticipated documentary, *Seamless*, and the return of the hit television show, *Project Runway*. Keeve's behind-the-scenes film examined the harsh realities of the fashion business by following designers as they competed for the first annual CFDA/Vogue Fashion Fund, a prestigious $200,000 prize awarded to one emerging American designer every year. The stakes were high: the money and exposure could make or break a designer's career. Even though the finalists represented ballyhooed, high-end brands such as Habitual, Libertine, and Cloak, none of them had yet turned a profit, despite reams of press coverage and boutiques stocked with their thousand-dollar dresses. (In fact, several finalists closed their businesses the following year.) The documentary—and the prize itself, established to buttress flagging sales after September 11— was a grim reminder of the odds against making it in fashion, talent notwithstanding.

Project Runway, which also followed designers trying to win a fashion prize, was much more upbeat. Broadcast initially on Bravo, with video confessions and celebrity guests, the show was a reality television competition in which designers competed for a chance to present their work during Olympus Fashion Week. Unlike the *Seamless* designers, these contestants were judged solely on their ability to make one-off pieces in a series of television-friendly challenges, occasionally for celebrity clients (like the heiress Nicky Hilton) and often out of implausible materials (like flowers).

Though quite different, these two productions had several similarities. Both presented comparable narratives, dramatizing a series of eliminations before unveiling a winner in the last, nail-biting moment. Both capitalized on fashion's glamour, while promising viewers a gritty glimpse behind the scenes. Both featured a significant number of Asian American contestants—a testament to that group's burgeoning presence in fashion. Three of the ten finalists for the CFDA/Vogue Fashion Fund were Asian Americans (Peter Som, Derek Lam, and Doo-Ri Chung), as were three of the sixteen for *Project Runway* (Diana Kim, Guadalupe Vidal, and Chloe Dao). And the two productions framed their Asian American contestants in oddly similar ways.

In his film, Keeve featured three of the ten finalists for the CFDA/Vogue award most prominently: Alexandre Plokhov (designer for the menswear line of Cloak), the team of Lazaro Hernandez and Jack McCollough (designers for Proenza Schouler), and Doo-Ri Chung (for Doo.Ri). While the director scripted all three contestants as similarly talented and hardworking, Chung's story was given a unique treatment. Unlike the other designers, who were shown toiling in their studios alone, Chung was repeatedly presented in the context of her family. When the judges came to view her collection, they were introduced to her parents, who were lingering shyly nearby. (Chung's workshop was actually housed in the basement of her parent's dry-cleaning store, which, in a dramatic turn, burned down during the filming.) In later scenes, Chung is filmed at dinner with her family; they appear again during her runway show. Chung even confessed that it is her mother who sews the zippers on her dresses.

On *Project Runway*, Chloe Dao, the winner of that season's competition, was presented in a very similar manner. Dao's family too becomes a central part of her story, whereas the families of the other contestants get only passing mentions. When Tim Gunn, the show's resident expert, visits Dao's workshop, he is introduced to Dao's mother, also lingering shyly nearby. Dao still lives with her parents in Houston, where her family emigrated after spending time in a Laotian refugee camp. Dao shows Gunn pictures of her seven sisters; her brand, Lot 8, is named for the eight children. She recounts to Gunn the story of the family's harrowing attempt to escape from the Viet Cong and their subsequent imprisonment in Laos.

He is appropriately shocked, and not surprisingly so, given that his previous meeting with one of the finalists consisted of a trip to the mall. Before he leaves, Gunn poses for a snapshot with Dao's entire family.

Why this strikingly similar representation of Asian American designers? If these types of stories were highlighted only to add color to the show's predictable dramatic arc, why not dig for them among all the designers? In one sense, it would be easy to read this through the lens of Orientalism. By framing Chung and Dao in this way, these productions constructed them as typical model minorities—as children of immigrants who work hard and make good. The families, particularly the shy and obviously self-sacrificing mothers, serve to reinforce the idea of traditional Asian values and to highlight how far such upbringing has taken their now-successful children. The sensational headlines that accompany the press coverage about these designers make this clear. A *Newsweek* article on Chung, for instance, was titled: "Doo-Ri Chung: Rising from the Basement to the Big Time."[1] An *US Weekly* piece on Dao had the headline: "From Refugee to *Project Runway*."[2] In addition to constructing them as Horatio Algers of the fashion world, this framing reiterates the argument that Asian American designers should not be seen as individual geniuses like their non-Asian counterparts, but as a product of their families, histories, and cultures.

Orientalism may well be at work here, but there is more than a little truth that families have played a crucial role in the working lives of Asian American designers. While Chung's and Dao's stories appear anomalous within these media productions, they are in fact quite characteristic of the experiences of many Asian American designers. Like Dao, who admits that sewing came naturally to her because her mom was a seamstress, many Asian American designers got their start by learning from their parents, who often worked on the lowest rungs of the clothing industry. Like Chung, who relies on her mother to sew zippers, many other designers make use of their family's technical skills and borrow freely from their resources.

This familial history led many to describe their path to fashion design as inevitable, a logical result of their upbringing. But this narrative of inevitability belies a much more complex social process in which families served as points of knowledge transfer and of unpaid or low-paid labor. Access to this knowledge was, moreover, framed by larger social forces, and enacted in the context of larger demands, such as to help the family economically or to learn gender-appropriate skills.[3] Motivated not just by desire but also by compulsion and necessity, this informal training structured Asian American designers' work and shaped their understanding of its nature.

Families and other intimate associates revealed to designers the proximity between the labor of sewing and the work of design, making it difficult for them to embrace the divisions—between the first and second generation, mental and manual work, the creative and the noncreative—that have become entrenched in fashion and elsewhere. It encouraged them to see sewing and sewers as central, rather than marginal, to the production of fashion, and as near rather than distant to their own lives and labors. As such, these relationships formed the foundation for what I have a called an architecture of intimacy—a mode of working that acknowledges and forges proximity, contact, and affiliation between domains imagined as distinct.

"IN MY BLOOD"

If *Seamless* and *Project Runway* hinted at the remarkable number of Asian Americans working in fashion, the streets of New York City provided undeniable proof. By the time Chloe Dao and Doo-Ri Chung became fashion news, shops helmed by Asian Americans selling labels bearing their names were cropping up all over New York. As various scruffy residential neighborhoods—in Manhattan's East Village and Lower East Side, and along Park Slope's Fifth Avenue, Carroll Gardens' Smith Street, and Williamsburg's Bedford Street—underwent "boutiquefication" during the mid-1990s, young Asian Americans began taking advantage of the relatively low rents there to launch their design careers. These shops were one of the first and most visible signs of their emergence as a force in design.

But why were so many Asian Americans motivated to pursue careers in fashion at this particular time? Several factors may have contributed to their increased participation during the 1990s. These young designers all came of age after the mid-1980s, a time when, as noted in the introduction, the Japanese three (Rei Kawakubo, Issey Miyake, and Yohji Yamamoto) had already gained international recognition, and when Asian Americans like Anna Sui and Vera Wang were becoming known as top New York designers. These pioneers opened the door for other Asian designers. More importantly, though, this was a time when national and international interest in high-fashion, or style-sensitive, branded clothing was greatly expanding. As the market for specialized goods grew, the number of new, mostly young designers—whose small labels produced a limited quantity of high-end garments—also grew.

These young designers, members of a category that had barely existed in the industry a few decades before, were helped along by a few developments. First was the existence of relatively affordable retail spaces in the city's gentrifying neighborhoods, which kept start-up costs low and allowed designers to sell directly to their customers. Second was the availability of a local labor force that could quickly produce the small batches of highly variable goods required by young designers seeking to enter the contemporary or high-fashion market. Third was the establishment of New York as a fashion center, with the institution of Fashion Week in the 1990s and the concomitant expansion of the design and retail industries. Fourth was the generation gap in fashion's ranks, which required that the industry find new talent in preparation for the eventual retirement of its established designers. (The spate of recently instituted awards offering young designers cash and other support was meant to do precisely this.) Last was the growth in online magazines and blogs, which allowed these new designers to circumvent the gate-keeping forces of the traditional fashion magazines, and the expansion of e-commerce, which allowed them to sell their goods nationally and even internationally.

These factors lowered what economists call the "barrier of entry" into fashion, making it possible for small-scale entrepreneurs to enter the market. But if these young designers were the industry's greatest hopes, they were also its most vulnerable participants. A full 26 percent of the approximately 22,000 designers working today are self-employed; all but one of the designers I spoke with belong in this category.[4] These men and women operate, essentially, as high-risk entrepreneurs—speculators who make goods they are never sure they will be able to sell. They work in very competitive market, which pits them against not just each other but also the major couture conglomerates and mass-market firms that dominate the fashion industry. The U.S. Bureau of Labor Statistics classifies the level of competition for these jobs as "keen"—meaning "fewer job openings compared with job seekers"—and projects the field to grow about only one percent between 2008 and 2018.[5] Turnover is high, and the field is small (there are 22,000 fashion designers in the United States, but only about half work in design; the remainder work in retail, management, and technical services). Though the rash of celebrity labels and how-to books make it appear as if anyone with a dress and a dream can become a designer, few who start actually stay in the business. Young designers work for years without actually turning a profit; many close their doors before ever doing so.

In 2001, I began meeting with some of these designers, many of whom had just set up their shops in the gentrifying neighborhoods of Nolita, the East Village, or Brooklyn. Boutiques at that time were booming, and there was a sense of optimism about the possibilities in this cultural marketplace. By 2008, when I completed my research, many of them had closed up shop—an indication less of their fitness for the job than of the volatility of the business and their vulnerable place in it. But as these designers shuttered their storefronts, new designers were emerging, many boldly entering the more capital-intensive wholesale market.[6] In fact, their presence only seemed to increase throughout the first decade of the twenty-first century.

Given the volatility of this market, why did Asian American designers fare so well, relatively speaking? How did they manage to meet its demands? Lowered barriers of entry provide only a partial answer. The designers I interviewed all agreed that the changes I outlined above had made the industry more hospitable to them and other young designers. But when I asked my sources how they had come to this work and endured its challenges, none talked in any detail about those factors. Almost all spoke, instead, about their relationships with their families.

The women's wear designer Jussara Lee, for instance, told me about growing up in São Paulo. The Lees had moved there during the late 1960s, looking for opportunity and prosperity after the Korean War, but they found instead low-wage work in a garment industry that had become dominated by Koreans. By the time they arrived, Korean immigrants had taken over most of the contracting firms from their Jewish predecessors. These immigrants provided a continuous flow of labor for the industry in Brazil, much as they had done in the United States. The majority of Brazil's garment firms are currently owned and operated by Asians, either Korean immigrants or transnational Asian corporations (which located their businesses in South America because of its proximity to U.S. markets).[7] Arriving in this historical context, Lee's parents found themselves pulled into the industry. "It was as if there was no other choice," Lee recalled, "if you were Korean, you worked in garment."[8]

Both of Lee's parents worked in the garment industry, but in order to take care of their three children, the mother elected to work at home, doing piecework sewing. As is common in these types of arrangements, Lee and her sister were expected to help. "Everyone had to pitch in," she remembered. Lee claimed she was four years old when she began to sneak materials from her mother's bag and to secretly construct her own fanciful outfits. As she grew older and her sewing skills improved, she continued to surreptitiously dissect and reconstruct the pieces of mass-market clothing her mom brought home. She recalled:

> I was a little girl when I observed the power clothing had on people and on myself. While my rich friends would parade around in designer labels that I couldn't afford, I decided the only way to beat the competition was with creativity. So I snatched pieces from my mom's bag of samples, which were mass market, most of the time ugly, cheap-looking clothes, and started to modify them to suit my taste. That's how I started in design.

Recognizing her talents, Lee's mother encouraged her to pursue a career in fashion. In 1980, Lee set off for New York to study design, but she was ultimately disappointed by the teachers whom she described as "frustrated designers" interested only in "servicing the garment industry with technical workers." Lee confessed that she mostly learned about fashion from "the club scene of the late 80s," where she could experiment with clothing in a culture that rewarded creativity. "It wasn't about how expensive your outfit was, it was about how cool it looked." In 1997, nearly four decades after she started reassembling clothes in her bedroom, Lee opened her own boutique. After just a few years, she had won enough of a following to make her line international, selling to Indonesia, Hong Kong, and Japan. True to the changing tides of fashion, however, her business faltered shortly afterward. In 2002, she returned to her sewing roots and opened a boutique where bolts of fabric and boxes of buttons sit alongside her collection, and where she encourages customers to embellish on her designs or to work with her on creating their own.

Just a few blocks from Jussara's former boutique is a sliver of a storefront that once housed the designer Sarah Ma's collection of fragile, handmade dresses. Though her clothes are radically different from Lee's, Ma's path to design was remarkably similar. Ma told me: "I grew up in Seattle, and like everybody else, my mother was a sewer. When I was a kid, you could always tell the children of sewers because they would all have the same clothes—whatever jacket or pants or shirt our moms were sewing at the time. I made my mother teach me how to sew so I could make my own stuff. My mom died before I finished college, so she never saw my store. I don't know what she would have thought—I mean, she wanted me to be a lawyer. But she probably would have gotten a kick out of seeing me on the other side of the assembly line."

Comparable experiences also led the women's wear designers Christina Kim and Elaine Kim, whose families were involved in the garment industry in Los Angeles, to their professions. While the details vary, the stories are much the same. Time and time again I heard about parents, uncles, even grandparents whose labors in the clothing business paved the way for the careers of their offspring. Indeed, it is true of three of the most prominent young Asian American designers working today—Doo-Ri Chung, Philip Lim, and Derek Lam.

This pattern seems to exist in fashion hubs outside of New York, too. In Los Angeles, for instance, the emerging fashion industry (built primarily around casual wear and denim) has been driven by Asian American designers who are the children of manufacturers. As has been well documented, California's apparel industry is dominated by Korean manufacturers and importers. In recent years, as overseas manufacturing has created downward pressures on price, these firms have begun to move toward the contemporary and designer markets, where they compete on quality and style rather than simply on cost. It was their children, the second-generation Korean Americans, who led them there. Peter Kim of Hudson Jeans, Eric Kim of Monarchy, Samuel Ku of AG Adriano Goldschmied, and Seun Lim of James Jeans are just a few of the children who have moved to the "other side of the assembly line."[9]

The designer Thuy Diep's trajectory is typical of their stories. Diep was born in Vietnam into a clothing family; her parents ran a tailoring school and a custom-made clothing shop in South Vietnam. "Many of my memories are not unlike everyone else's, except they're often related to sewing," she says, "[When I was little] I loved to make princess gowns from Mom and Dad's leftover fabrics. When I got a little older . . . my parents would have me and my sisters help with sewing projects." Diep's family emigrated to Ohio following the Vietnam War but soon left for the warmer climes of southern California. Her parents continued to sew. Diep eventually headed off to Brown University and went to work for PriceWaterhouse upon graduation.

She left after a few years, however, to pursue her first love: fashion. Though she obtained a degree from Parsons, Diep says it was those childhood experiences that fed her dreams and "honed her tailoring skills." For these children who ended up "on the other side of the assembly line," familial relationships—and the labor they contributed to their family's economy—served as points of knowledge transfer, providing them with the skills that were crucial to their work. These skills included not just technical expertise such as how to sew and cut but also imaginative facilities—how to piece together something out of almost nothing, how to take some mass-market garment and make it their own.

Chloe Dao, the *Project Runway* winner, similarly recounted that having learned sewing from her mother, she could transform vintage clothing into new garments for herself and her sisters. The famed designer Derek Lam, whose parents owned a business importing clothes from Asia, and whose grandparents ran a garment manufacturing company in San Francisco, attributes this background to his current success in the fashion industry: "As a child I spent a lot of time with my grandparents, and I would always hang out with the seamstresses in the factory. I guess the clothing business is in my blood . . . I was born into it and lived it all throughout my childhood."[10]

These types of accounts were often offered in response to my questions about how my interviewees came to embark on their design careers. Children who "lived it all" pointed to these early experiences as the impetus for their work. Even those who did not grow up with parents in the industry, however, highlighted the familial context as the source of their sartorial knowledge—referring to past experiences watching their mothers, aunts, or cousins sewing, knitting, or simply working with their hands. The milliner Eugenia Kim, for instance, told me in an interview that the talent she has for making phenomenally popular hats "runs in the family." She said:

> My mom used to do these kinds of crafty things at home. She would always be putting something amazing together while she was doing three other things. My mom started to study fashion but she gave it up when she married my dad. It was the fifties in Korea, and that's just what you [did]. I guess I inherited that craftiness from her.

The dress designers Kelima K and Jean Yu similarly told me that they first learned to sew from their mothers. And the jewelry designer Sehti Na noted: "I learned everything from my sister."

Indeed, the familial roots of their fashion education are an important part of the story that many of these designers tell about themselves. The very successful Vivienne Tam, whose father was a tailor, has repeatedly told the fashion press that it was the creative efforts of her mother that fed her design dreams. "Even though we didn't have much money," she said, "my mother would buy scrap fabric and make clothing nobody else had." Tam quickly followed suit.[11] Likewise, Jen Kao writes in an autobiographical statement posted on her company's website: "Perhaps more than any formal education or training it is her family that inspires Kao and informs her collection. In particular, her grandmother, who was born and raised in Taiwan under Japanese influence [sic]. From her, Kao learned the traditional crafts, artistry, and folklore of Japanese culture, as well as an intense love for details and precision."[12]

In emphasizing these sources of inspiration, designers situated their informal education at the center of their work and highlighted its importance over and beyond that of any formal training they received. Certainly the importance of this informal education should not be understated. While Asian Americans are not the only designers who have learned from their friends and families, they may have had to rely on this mode of knowledge sharing more than others.[13] Historically an apprenticeship-based craft, design became much more formal and professionalized in the late 1950s, with the rise of fashion and art schools.[14] Now, designers still typically work as assistants before venturing out on their own, but these assistants are usually plucked from professional schools, which have become in many ways feeders into the industry.

But many of the designers I interviewed did not formally train at fashion schools, which is relatively unusual in a fashion world currently dominated by alumni of FIT, Parsons, and Saint Martins. Some studied at Parsons or FIT, but most only took several classes, and many had no formal fashion education. Unlike most of their fellow designers, they attended liberal arts universities instead of design schools. One interviewee, Yvonne Chu, was a Ph.D. candidate in East Asian studies at the University of Chicago before trading in her books for bags. Another, Jennifer Wang, studied political science and worked in advertising. Though many of them described themselves as "always interested" in fashion, most felt compelled to pursue safer or more practical careers, leading them to obtain degrees in fields such as psychology, anthropology, finance, and biology. Many, like Thuy Diep, began their careers on radically different tracks—in finance, publishing, research, and so on. Fashion school came afterward, if it came at all.

Without those crucial experiences and social connections, designers lacking a formal education have had to rely on other paths of skills acquisition and social networking. For many Asian Americans, the knowledge passed around and handed down was quite crucial, at least in the beginning, for it fostered in them a sense of ease and familiarity with the craft of fashion that made it possible for them to experiment with its forms. It was through casual experimentation, making things for themselves and their friends, that many found their entree into the fashion world. Wenlan Chia, for instance, started her label, Twinkle, when as a fine-arts student she found herself inundated with inquiries about the sweaters she knitted for herself. Eugenia Kim began her fashion career after being stopped by store owners and magazine editors while wearing a hat of her own creation. Wayne Lee was convinced by her colleagues to start a collection when the dresses she wore to work at Barneys became a hit with the staff. None had intentions of pursuing a career in fashion until the garments they made for their own use caught the attention of so many others. It was by chance that they came to try their hand at design, but given their backgrounds, many saw it more as fate.

This discourse of inevitability allowed designers to acknowledge their familial debt, but it also enabled them to naturalize their path to fashion design. For children who grew up in this context, entering the fashion world seemed almost unavoidable. As Thuy Pham (of the label United Bamboo) joked in an interview with me: "You do something enough, you get good at it." But by naturalizing this history with claims that "it's just in my blood," these designers actually obscured the ways that larger social structures framed their process of learning, as noted above. Though designers generally perceived this informal training in retrospect as immensely useful, the experience of it was also quite fraught, motivated at times more by compulsion than desire.

Sewing has long been a skill that women were required to have. This knowledge was historically passed on by older family members and friends to women as a part of their domestic training. In the late eighteenth century, however, its instruction was formalized through the institution of home economics courses in U.S. public schools. This national effort helped to reaffirm sewing as a gendered activity, so integral to women's education that, as one nineteenth-century commentator put it, a "woman who does not know how to sew is as deficient in her education as a man who cannot write."[15] By the 1960s, the practice of home sewing had ebbed significantly, due in great part to the ready availability of affordable clothing made possible by the increasing use of garment outsourcing.

As sewing became less important in the United States, it grew in importance in Asia and other non-Western places where these garments were manufactured. For my older interviewees, who spent some time in Asia, sewing was a skill they were required to learn as part of their training for the home, but also outside of it. Women were expected to employ this skill in the service of their families, but they were also increasingly being asked to use it in the marketplace, as employees of transnational garment firms. This education was, in other words, part of a larger effort to situate women appropriately within the family and the state—not to enable them to pursue creative interests or entrepreneurial profits. Though my interviewees never articulated it precisely in this way, they nonetheless understood the limitations of that training. "We were being prepared to become the perfect housewife," Gemma Kahng, who grew up in Korea, told me. "My mom was always sewing. My sister, too. Starting at a very early age, you had to know these things. I was knitting when I was three years old."

Kahng's comments echo the findings of the anthropologist Parminder Bhachu. In her study of Indian designers in Britain, Bhachu noted that sewing, and the practices of *sina-prona* (sewing and beading) more generally, which provided these women with the skills to enter the clothing trades, was very much a part of their socialization into norms of domesticity. Indeed sina-prona is a metaphor within diasporic Indian communities for the many skills that constitute the making of a good home and a good woman. It is a code for femininity and conventional womanliness, with all the gendered norms and expectations that this implies. Indian women are socialized into the economy of sina-prona to produce, reproduce, and service the family, to maintain the traditions of home in a community displaced from home.[16]

For the younger generation—who were not instructed in this way—many learned by watching, practicing, and sometimes helping with the work that their parents undertook. Jussara Lee acknowledged that her mother's seamstress job was a family responsibility—everyone contributed. Likewise, Diep and her sisters were expected to help with sewing. Unpaid family labor here—as with most immigrant businesses, including restaurants, nail salons, gas stations, and delis—was crucial to the family's survival. But bringing children into this economy was not without its costs. As Lisa Park's study of Chinese and Korean children of entrepreneurs revealed, tensions often arose as children were asked to take on adult responsibilities, and as the boundaries between worker and family member and between adulthood and childhood became increasingly blurred. These children often expressed a sense of loss—of a "normal" childhood—at the same time that they accepted these responsibilities as necessary, and admitted to having learned from the experience.[17] I sense a similar ambivalence in my interviewees. Even as they look back on their past as immensely helpful, and their evolution as inherently natural, the experience was regarded as a matter of necessity, not choice.

The origins of this knowledge, then, must be understood within the broader history of migration and labor. This context shaped not just how skills would be disseminated but who had access to them. It is no coincidence that the majority of Asian American designers are Chinese and Koreans, with Vietnamese trailing behind and Indians following at a distance. This was certainly true among my interviewees but, from my observations of such registers as the list of CFDA members and the coverage by fashion magazines, also of the industry as a whole. This pattern follows from the ethnic distribution of the garment industry, where Chinese, Koreans, and, increasingly, Vietnamese workers also dominate. We can speculate that the proximity of these workers' children to the garment industry, itself shaped by their family's migration histories—when they arrived, where they settled, how ethnic networks enabled or hindered their ability to take up this work—configured in a significant way their conditions of possibility. For migrant populations that entered other networks of labor—taxi driving among Bangladeshis, for instance—their distance, though not absence, from the industry made these skills less accessible to the next generation. In this sense, the category of Asian American designer is fundamentally uneven, shaped by these different ethnic groups' disparate proximities to the apparel industry.

Yet even for those groups adequately represented among designers, what the children gained were not simply cultural practices or traditions that can be easily passed from one generation to the next.[18] Rather, they are what we might think of as inherited resources that are generated by the labors of parents and children working at the blurred boundaries between the private and the public, the domestic and the economic. The transmission of those resources and their translation into new forms of creative expression are never passive, unmediated, or "natural," to use the language of my interviewees. They require work, or "laboring," to use the term of the historian Michael Denning, for they are endeavors that require an active linkage between the labors of working peoples and the creation of new cultural forms.[19] Such interconnectedness, which existed not just in designers' memories of the past but in their activities in the present, made it difficult for them to maintain the clothing industry's logic of distance.

CULTURAL WORK AND ETHNIC ENTREPRENEURS

Though many of the designers I spoke to talked about their career choices with a certain sense of inevitability, in reality their path to fashion was far from predetermined. By constructing their origin stories in this way, these designers both drew attention to and, paradoxically, hid the contributions of their families. While these narratives were meant to highlight the importance of the family in fostering the roots of these designers' creative knowledge, they also relegated those familial influences to the past. In doing so, they glossed over the ways that families continued to serve as a material resource for their creative work.

If the familial context served as a jumping-off point for many designers, it was their families who made such leaps possible. As Keeve's documentary revealed, Doo-Ri Chung's ability to rely on her family's resources—on her mother to sew her zippers, and on her parents' store to house her studio—helped her immeasurably in the early days. In this regard, familial ties offered these designers more than just knowledge. It also offered them material benefits, often in the form of free help.

Wayne Lee's road to the prestigious Ecco Domani Fashion Foundation prize was certainly a testament to this. Lee was born in Vietnam; after the Vietnam War, her family, like Diep's, migrated to the United States, where they settled in Orlando, Florida. And like Diep, Lee dutifully headed off to Vassar to study English and was well on her way to earning a medical degree from the University of California at Berkeley when she decided to quit. Lee moved to New York, where unsuccessful attempts to obtain positions in other fields forced her to take a job as a stock clerk at Barneys, the famed New York department store. She eventually worked her way up to salesperson, then junior buyer. In her time off, she designed her own clothes, "because I had to have something to wear to all these fashion shows, and I couldn't afford the clothes from Barneys." Lee told me she was constantly stopped by strangers asking where to find these garments. Her answer: "Well, my auntie made it."

Lee's family had long been involved in the clothing business. Her grandfather owned a little clothing company in Vietnam; when it closed, he became a tailor. Her mom made all the children's clothes. Her sister was a designer for a corporate label. It was her aunt, though, a seamstress living in the Bronx, who sewed all those dresses Lee wore to Market Week. "We worked on it together. We made clothes together for about a year," Lee recalled. When she decided to launch her own label, she remembered thinking: "There's no way I can do this. I'm not a designer. I don't have any experience. I can't even draw." But what she lacked in knowledge, her aunt more than made up for in skills. Lee's aunt worked with her to create her first eighteen-piece collection. When the orders started coming in, her aunt helped Lee to get them filled.[20] Now that Lee is more established, she uses a factory in the garment district for her production, but it was her aunt, Lee admits, who opened the door for her at a time when her limited skills and resources might otherwise have made her leap into fashion impossible.

Gemma Kahng shared a similar story with me. Though she had studied fashion design at the Illinois Institute of Art in Chicago and had worked for another label before starting her own, she still relied heavily on her family's help. Because her financial resources were extremely limited, she "had to do everything myself. Cut, sew, pattern—everything." Her family, who could all sew, stepped in: "My sister did so much sewing for me. She has this beautiful house and she turned the basement into a little sewing factory for me. My mom sewed, too. Her garage became my warehouse." Kahng went on to build a multimillion-dollar fashion business and became one of the premier designers of the early 1990s.[21]

Tales like these abound. Friends' and relatives' lending a hand to make the first collection is certainly a common story among almost all designers. But for those with access to such a knowledgeable and willing workforce, able to offer hours of labor without pay, familial contributions were more than just ad hoc and ancillary. They constituted a central source of material assistance, the presence of which forces us to rethink the image of the independent creative entrepreneur and the equally unencumbered model minority achiever—exemplary neoliberal subjects both.

Family participation in these businesses has ranged from unpaid help to financial investments and formal employment. Selia Yang's brother, for instance, took out a loan to help her start her business; he and his wife now work for the company. Shin Choi's brother-in-law helped her to obtain a line of credit to start her company, and her husband was its first employee. Alpana Bawa's sister has been integral to her business, at first just helping out, then becoming an employee. In this sense, families were never just sources of inspiration—bracketed off and relegated to the past—but also of continuing investment. As Doo-Ri Chung admitted, "I couldn't have done what I did without them [my parents]. It's not just the money. Money is important, yes, but my mother helped me sew, my father picked up the clothes from the production house. They fed me. It's little things like that . . . My parents became my co-workers, as opposed to Mom and Dad."[22]

Family help of the kind Chung describes cannot, as she said, be reduced to money, but it does have monetary worth. Family labor has been proven to be crucial to the maintenance of small businesses because relatives' help can radically reduce operating costs. Families and friends tend to work for less than market wages, tend to be more reliable, and are more susceptible to moral pressures (for instance, to work longer hours and to defer payment during lean times).[23] Though I was not told how much designers' families were paid for their labors, my interviewees characterized this labor as always more valuable than any wages used to compensate relatives. Bawa admitted to me, for instance, that though her sister plays an important role in the company, she is "still not getting paid what she should be for everything that she does."

How should we characterize these efforts by family members to help young designers out? Is this equivalent to the labor that many children have contributed to their family economy, and through which some learned the skills to begin this trade? These kinds of questions are not easily answered and depend a great deal on how one views the uniqueness of kin relationships. Some scholars have argued that an element of altruism exists within the household that distinguishes it from other forms of social obligations.[24] In that view, labor performed within the context of the family is not bound by the rules of the free market. But the existence of moral obligations does not preclude the possibility that economic aspects are embedded within familial exchanges, or that, as many feminist scholars have pointed out, unremunerated labors have disadvantaged certain members of the family more than others.

In raising these issues I do not mean to suggest that familial contributions—made by children helping out parents or vice versa—are somehow inherently exploitative, but only to emphasize the material value of these efforts and, more generally, the continuing importance of familial relationships to these enterprises. I do so in order to reveal not just the hidden labors that have made Asian Americans' creative work possible, but the structural similarities between this work and that of their parents' generation.

If ethnic entrepreneurialism is characterized by a particular reliance on the family as a source of labor and capital—"a family mode of production," as Roger Waldinger, Howard Aldrich, and Robin Ward have called it—then these endeavors bear more than a passing resemblance to the more traditional ethnic businesses.[25] Scholars have posited that what makes certain ethnic groups particularly adept at business ownership, or high in ethnic entrepreneurship, is their ability to utilize or passively benefit from various ethnic resources, including family and co-ethnic labor, informal credit, shared knowledge and expertise, and social support. Asian immigrants—Koreans in particular—have had such a high rate of business ownership precisely because they have been able to rely on families and peers for knowledge, contacts, and even capital to start their businesses.[26]

Families here have also served as an important source of skills transmission, paid and unpaid labor, and financial support. And, like other ethnic enterprises, these fashion businesses have also been able to rely on the labors (and largesse) of members of the designers' ethnic groups. As I discuss in the following chapter, Asian American designers, like most young designers in New York, must work with Asian sewers and manufacturers to produce their goods—if only because of the sheer dominance of Asians in the industry (70 percent of clothing in New York City is made in Asian-owned shops). These manufacturers have turned out to be something of an ethnic resource, providing Asian American designers with a range of accommodations—from lower prices and fast-tracked orders to informal credit—that have been invaluable to their work.

In this sense, the development of these young designers' fashion businesses repeats some of the patterns of other immigrant businesses. As such, it might not be inappropriate to characterize their work as a form of ethnic entrepreneurship. Thinking of it in this way might provide an explanation for Asian American designers' relative success in the industry that goes beyond both the Darwinian narrative of survival of the fittest and the racialized logic of model minority achievement. "Success" for Asian Americans has long been understood, in fashion and elsewhere, as a product of their innate abilities and indomitable work ethic. Tracing these networks of support allows us to see how social ties, rather than cultural proclivities, have worked to open up some opportunities for Asian Americans, even as others become foreclosed to them.

If the arrival of Asian Americans in the fashion industry can be read as evidence of their having moved on or up from the sweated work of their parents' generation—"once the nimble fingers that sewed in factories," they have now become a "force in fashion," as *The New York Times* put it—that mobility has been facilitated by parental and other familial investments, both formal and informal.[27] When popular publications like the *Times* explain the increased presence of Asian Americans in fashion by stating quite simply that "the storefront ethic is in their blood," they fail to see how family and ethnic resources, far more than any inherent cultural characteristics, have given the designers a leg up in an industry where they enjoy few other advantages.[28] Perhaps more important, these publications fail to see that the risk and sacrifice that are endemic to the work of the designers' parents' generation have also taken root in their own.

No doubt fashion design looks on the surface quite different from the far less glamorous forms of immigrant businesses—greengrocers or dry cleaners, for instance. And I would venture to guess that none of my own interviewees would see their work in precisely this light. After all, fashion design belongs squarely within the ranks of creative or informational work—those valued and vaunted occupations prized as skilled, and reserved for the educated and the innovative. These good professions are by definition not the undesirable positions picked up by immigrants eager for work and lacking in other options. Creative jobs and the creative economies to which they belong have indeed become one of the most eulogized in recent years, purportedly able to provide young people with creative, fulfilling, flexible work at the same time that they can generate enough revenue to save the U.S. economy even as manufacturing and "unskilled" work continues to rush offshore.[29]

But as many scholars have pointed out, there are hidden costs to this creative haven in a heartless world. For instance, the flexibility that is touted as one of its greatest virtues—the ability to telecommute, to escape traditional work schedules—has often resulted in an increase in the amount of time people spend working. Moreover, most of the creative workers in cultural industries, including fashion, are self-employed, which means they bear unusually high financial risks and, as a result, push themselves to work beyond reasonable expectations or legal limits. While there are many benefits to these careers—such as control over the time and place of labor—they rely on a self-disciplining model of work that is rationalized by the promise of autonomy and creativity.[30] In this regard, while creative work's potential for reward is certainly greater, and its types of work activities differ qualitatively, the demands and risks associated with some forms of creative and some forms of noncreative work are quite similar.[31]

This suggests that the types of financial uncertainty and of sacrifices (even, from a strictly economic viewpoint, exploitation) of self and family are as much a part of this work as they are of the work of many immigrant occupations. And like many of those occupations, designers enjoy few benefits of secure employment, such as regular wages and health insurance. The fashion designers I interviewed were all self-employed (though a few had financial backers), eking out a living but not yet turning a profit. Industry insiders all claim that it takes a new label approximately seven to ten years to actually make money. But since small labels have a notoriously high turnover rate, most close before ever making any money.

Yet rather than railing against these conditions, designers accept them as simply the rules of game, agreeing to defer any real wages for their labor until they finally hit the jackpot. They also accept the volatility of the market. They assume, for the most part, that change allows for new ideas to emerge, and that the most talented will inevitably last the longest. This neoliberal ethos is typical of most creative industries, but in fashion it is rationalized as a natural effect. After all, fashion is defined by change. As Heidi Klum, the host of *Project Runway*, reminds designers each week: "In fashion, one day you're in, the next day you're out."

If designers did not generally see or talk about their work as precarious and self-exploitative, they nonetheless understood that this creative labor demanded far more than creativity alone. Although they certainly saw their jobs as fun, rewarding, and even glamorous, the work was to them first and foremost "a business." They referred to it always in those terms, and they spoke constantly about its demands: the long hours, the stress, the risks. None of them believed that a designer could make it on creative talents alone; business acumen was considered a survival skill. The designer Charles Chang-Lima went so far as to claim that he considered himself "more a businessman than a fashion designer." He explained in our interview:

> For me, to design is a piece of cake. I can solve a design problem in a few seconds. But to struggle with the business is another thing. What if someone gives you a $100,000 order and you only have $1,000 to pay the rent? That's a problem that's harder to solve. This is just a business. It happens to be involved with clothes so people think it's glamorous. But I could be selling a car and it would be the same thing. I still need to build the car, sell it—same thing.

Though these sentiments are a bit extreme in their disavowal of some of the more glaring differences between industries and occupations, they do express a commonly held notion that, in the end, as Gemma Kahng said and countless others reiterated, fashion "is a business like any other business."

Asian American designers are certainly not the only ones who see that creative work can be as demanding and as ho-hum as any other business enterprise. Few designers would deny these realities, though certainly the fashion industry works, like other creative industries, by promising that it is always more than just business. Yet while Asian Americans' experiences in this regard may not be unique, the meanings they have made of these experiences are quite distinctive.

My purpose in linking the work of these Asian American designers to other ethnic enterprises and to other forms of insecure work has not been to show that they are equivalent. Rather, it has been to suggest that the structural similarities and, even more important, the interconnections between them have sutured Asian Americans closer to the immigrant generation. The familial relationships that inspired some Asian Americans to enter the fashion industry have also been crucial in sustaining their presence within it. This link has fostered in them a different understanding of its divisions—of class, ethnicity, skills, and knowledge—and have encouraged them to see the labors that constituted it in very different terms.

LOCATING CREATIVE KNOWLEDGE

Though Asian American designers recognized that they had learned useful skills from their families, they did not always paint that process of knowledge transmission in rosy hues. Sometimes this learning had occurred in spite of, rather than because of, their parents' help. When Thuy Diep's parents came to visit before her New York Fashion Week show, for instance, the designer enlisted their help in assembling her collection. But Diep recalled that her father proved to be a recalcitrant worker. "I'd tell him to put something together one way," Diep said to me, "and he'd argue and say you can't do it like this. It won't look professional. He'd constantly argue with me."

Diep criticizes her dad for being overly technical, "to the point where it cripples him." Her mother, she said, is more forward thinking, able to appreciate the look of a garment and not just its technical qualities. But after finishing Parsons, Diep returned home to her dad, spending six months in

Los Angeles to "relearn from him." He was a strict teacher, pushing her to be technically proficient but discouraging any experimentation with her forms. "There is a danger of being so technical," she griped, pointing out the various limitations to his approach. But her criticism was tempered by the concession that "as a designer you need to know these techniques, so you can understand how to take that kind of knowledge and move it forward."

Interviewees who talked about learning from their parents often presented the experience in this grudging manner. Thuy Pham told me quite frankly that though his mother was a seamstress, he "didn't learn anything from her." Yet his dismissal was followed by this telling account: "My mom, she can tell when she looks at my collection when the design is getting more complex. She'll say 'Oh, your skill is getting better. There's more detailing.' She has a good eye. She gets it. She can look at something and really see how it's put together." While Pham may say he learned nothing from his mother, he still recognizes her technical knowledge. It is his mother, he claims, who doesn't care much for his work. Pham told me he was considered the "black sheep" of his family, and that his parents were very disappointed when he gave up his architecture degree to pursue fashion: "In the beginning, when I started making clothes, I was very poor. So they didn't think that was a good idea." But now that he is a fairly established designer? "Well, they don't really care that I'm called a 'designer.' To [my mom] it's not a big deal at all."

The designer Philip Lim has a similar perspective about his seamstress mother. Lim admitted that she was not happy when he stopped his studies in finance to pursue a fashion career: "She sewed to give us an education, opportunities she didn't have. She didn't want me to end up making clothes too." Still, Lim counts her among his most important influences, and the driving force behind his ethos of quality, not cost: "There was always integrity behind everything she made—whether a $3 garment or a $300 garment—at every step of the way. That's my mind frame too."[32]

Having a good eye and doing things with integrity are not usually the way designers characterize sewers or their work. Certainly, we can attribute remarks like these to Lim's and Pham's well-intentioned desire to respect, if not romanticize, their parents' difficult labors. But in their choice of words, they were also recognizing the crucial knowledge that their mothers possessed. And behind these jabs at parental pressure, there lurks a suspicion—or maybe a fear—that perhaps their work is not so different after all. At the very least, there is an implicit recognition that these forms of labor are related, rather than distinct.

This stands in sharp contrast to the perspective of most designers. In her study of young British fashion designers (small-scale cultural entrepreneurs who resemble the designers discussed here), Angela McRobbie observed that most worked hard to distance themselves from the image of the sewer because "they saw this as a threat to their skills [and image] as designers." They wanted to protect their professional identities and to frame their creations as art; some even went so far as to deny that they could sew at all. None of the designers she interviewed had visited a factory or workshop, even when it was clear that they were just a few miles away. There seemed to be "very little need on the part of the designers to make any contact with the women who were doing their making up."[33] Though McRobbie admitted that this tendency was "as much the outcome of a rigid, class-based and hierarchical division of labour as it is the fault of the young designers," it nonetheless reveals the designers' tendency to maintain a firm division between fashion and its fabrication.[34]

Asian American designers' familial history makes it clear that for them, fashion design and sewing are intimately connected, sharing a point of origin. However, this common origin has been hidden by the process of commodification, in which the tacit knowledge involved in creating clothing has become codified, standardized, and ultimately deskilled—made replicable by less-skilled people or machines within a complex division of labor.[35] This process necessarily entails a continual splitting up of manual and mental tasks, which over time erases the shared ancestry of creative work and its supposedly noncreative counterparts.

As has been the case with many other goods, the commodification of clothing has resulted in an entrenched division between the head and hand tasks of design and construction, respectively. This process of splitting has only been further reaffirmed by the forces of globalization. The clothing industry was among the very first to employ a transnational mode of production. Over the decades, it has perfected this system, enabling it to divide up design and construction across separate regions and continents. Though design is technically the first step in the production of a garment, it is imaginatively and spatially distinct from the work that follows. In the West, developed nations trade on their technically skilled workforce and their cultural capital to monopolize the more valuable services—like design—and send the labor-intensive manufacturing work to developing countries around the world.[36]

This distinction between clothing's cultural production and its manufacturing production has been reinforced by various international trade organizations and arrangements. For instance, developing nations are often told—by the International Monetary Fund, the World Bank, and other institutions—that garment production, which requires little start-up money and draws on their most abundant resource, labor, is a first and necessary step toward industrialization. These nations are encouraged to pursue this path through various loans, incentives, and trade agreements.[37] But in doing so, they are also forced to accept and reinforce their position in the high-low fashion divide. As Lise Skov has explained, in sites of mass production the distinctions between manufacturing and design are well guarded. In Hong Kong, for example, there is little to no aesthetic input on the part of local manufacturers and workers; to the extent that design services are required, they are provided by expatriated Western designers, whose design knowledge is safeguarded from local producers. Skov concludes: "Great care was taken to establish an industrial system that was geared to satisfy overseas buyers' demand for reliable and standardized manufacturing to any given specification. In the process, local tastes and design skills were gravely devalued."[38] Under this system, the United States and Europe are reaffirmed as fashion centers, and local design skills remain grossly underdeveloped.

Although much effort has gone into trying to reinforce these divides, it has not been entirely successful. As I previously noted, developing nations in places like Asia have increasingly rejected them, pouring money into building their own fashion industry—establishing schools, trade shows, and exhibits—in order to get their piece of the fashion pie. These boundaries, moreover, were always porous. Buyers have always transferred some knowledge to their manufacturers in the production process, if only to ensure that products meet their specifications. As the demand for goods of greater distinction and quality has increased, buyers have had to also increase this level of interaction and training. Many large firms now have designers based in overseas locations so that they can work with manufacturers. They have a vested interest, in other words, in transferring to these manufacturers some limited aesthetic knowledge. Their products depend on it.

For their part, manufacturers have been eager to absorb this information. Knowledge transfers happen in all types of garment production, but they are more prevalent in designer fashion, which often requires more complex assembly and more detailing. I have been told by my interviewees, some of whom produce their clothes overseas, that manufacturers have taken on their relatively small orders precisely because they want access to this sector. They enter into partnerships with these young designers because of the design knowledge that they believe they can gain. Increasingly, manufacturers in China and India are seeking out designers to produce their own lower-priced lines, offering to do the production in exchange for their design skills.

The boundaries between design and construction are even less clear in Western cities where fashion is made. In places like New York, where various sectors of the industry—retail, design, textiles, production, etc.—all exist within close proximity, fashion production is characterized by spatial agglomeration rather than dispersal.[39] In the midtown garment district, design studios and sewing factories share the same block. Within those spaces, sewers and sample makers execute designs for high-end labels, recent design-school graduates, and large-scale retailers alike, functioning at times like an atelier (with workers handcrafting special collections) and at other times like a sweatshop.

These boundaries are further blurred in the practice of fashion design. While the designer's name (label) implies the work of an individual, fashion design—like many other forms of cultural production—is a collective endeavor. Designers sketch the original outline, but they frequently collaborate with pattern makers to translate image into garment.[40] This is the case in part because many designers do not know how to sew (though even those who do often employ a professional pattern maker). While it is understood that sewing skills certainly help in this profession, they are not considered a requirement. As one how-to book told aspiring designers: "A designer does not need to sew. Many of the biggest names in the fashion business would be lost behind a sewing machine."[41]

In this process of translation, there is much give and take between the designer and the pattern maker: though the former guides the process, the latter frequently tweaks the design—adding here, taking away there—in order to generate a usable form. Therefore, while pattern makers are technically a part of the production process—the title signifies the highest level a sewer can reach—they are crucial to the process of design. In larger firms, they play an even more central role, often generating original samples themselves, based on vague instructions to replicate a certain silhouette or even mood. In these circumstances, the pattern makers must rely on both their technical and aesthetic skills. They must, in other words, design.

As many fashion historians have noted, the history of couture is filled with these behind-the-scenes sewers who have had a hand in developing the look of a house. Couturiers have always relied on their craftsmen to carry out, and at times originate, their aesthetic visions. "Even the greatest designer of the twentieth century, Coco Chanel," notes the fashion scholar Yuniya Kawamura, "did not know much about the garment construction or textile."[42] Chanel apparently "did not enter the workrooms herself, but after she had chosen the materials, would gather her staff together to explain to them what she wanted. She needed to prove her authority but at the same time often failed to find the correct terms in which to express her requirements to her staff."[43]

Given this, the question of authorship, of who actually designed a particular garment, can be difficult to answer. But, like the auteur in films, designers are assumed to be solely responsible for their designs, in part because they rarely acknowledge the blurred boundaries of their work. This is not simply oversight. Designers have a symbolic and material interest in maintaining the purity of their white-collar professions and the belief in their individual authorship. They operate within an entrenched global division of labor, which draws clear distinctions between the material and the symbolic—between the poorly paid labor of sewing and the creative, potentially well-compensated work of design. The value of their own labor requires the maintenance of these boundaries. The protection of their creations by such structures as intellectual property laws depends on the continued faith in their identities as individual artists.[44]

In this context, Lim's and Pham's interest in seeing continuities rather than disconnections between the craft of sewing and the profession of design represents a significant departure from the norms of the industry. And yet they were not alone. Perhaps because of their comparable family experiences, many of the designers I interviewed articulated a similar respect for the craft of construction, and a disrespect for fashion, its cognate industry. To be sure, these designers were all invested in protecting their own work and identities as professionals. But they also saw that the distinctions between these forms of work were certainly not as entrenched as the spatial divisions between the front room and back room, between fashion cities and garment towns, might suggest.

Regardless of their family histories, in my interviews Asian American designers consistently referred to sewers as "craftsmen," and "experts," and as possessing "skills" surpassing their own. They repeatedly spoke about how they "learned" from these sewers, who understood their "sensibility." The milliner Eugenia Kim admitted to me, for instance, that because she started her business after taking just one class at FIT, she had to rely on the knitters and sewers for a lot of the technical details: "I didn't have a lot of experience, but they did, so at least I could count on that."

Comments like these emerged often in our conversations. In fact, if families figured prominently in these designers' origin stories, sewers played an equally prominent role in their survival narratives. When designers talked to me about their career trajectories, their narratives often followed a common dramatic arc: the surprising circumstances that landed them in the business; their bungling efforts to get their career off the ground; the struggles to make ends meet; the doubts; and eventually success (or at least lack of failure, for most were still working their way up the fashion hierarchy). The turning point in their stories often came when they stumbled upon a sewer who helped them, who taught them, and with whom they developed a close relationship.

Alpana Bawa's account of her start in the business is typical. Though she got a degree in fashion design from Parsons, she told me that she began her own line quite by chance. While working at a retail boutique as a student, Bawa became close to the owner, who agreed to help her make and sell her first collection. The owner paid for the production costs, and Bawa took a portion of the proceeds. The retailer eventually closed, but this did not discourage her from continuing. After graduation, when many of her fellow students headed off to work for large corporations, Bawa decided to strike out on her own. Friends helped to sew and contributed money; Bawa took on a day job and made all the clothes in her apartment at night. The first few years were a struggle, she admitted, but then she met "this half-Indian, half-Jamaican seamstress." According to Bawa, "she saved my life!" The seamstress was willing to take on Bawa's small order at an affordable price. It sounds simple enough, but finding a cost-effective way to produce one's collection is perhaps the biggest challenge a young designer faces. These designers are caught in a bind: they must keep their costs low because they are a new brand, but because they are a new brand and cannot trade in large volumes, their production costs are higher. In this regard, Bawa was extremely lucky indeed to find a cost-effective mode of production. But as the designer told me about this seamstress, it became clear that she "saved" Bawa indeed:

> I was doing the patterns and the cutting. And I would take it up to her on, like, 86th Street. Then I would pick them up from her and do all the hand stuff myself. But we did a lot of work together. She was there to see me through my orders, and to help me. Here was a woman who'd been sewing for twenty-plus years. And me, who had no sewing experience. How do sleeves fit into arms? What kind of hems do you use—there are a lot of different ones? What are the different kinds of buttonholes? She taught me all that basic stuff that I guess I hadn't been taught in school. She'd been probably sewing all her life, so she knew everything.

Bawa characterized her time with this woman as something of a second education. And as she spent more and more time on 86th Street, the two women became something like friends: "I used to come up there to just use her iron—she had an industrial iron, and I didn't. I was there all the time. I think she liked having me around, because she was all alone in her little place." They worked together for nearly ten years. When Bawa's company grew large enough to transfer her production to India, she still employed the seamstress occasionally for small projects. Even after their working relationship ended, "we stayed in touch for a long time. She would just call me once in a while, and we'd have a chat. It's been, like, four or five years since we've spoken. But if I put my mind to it, I bet her number will come back to me. I called her so often, I'm sure I can still remember it."

The bridal designer Selia Yang's account of her entrance into the New York fashion industry was dotted with similar tales of unlikely intimacies. Yang entered college with the intention of becoming a dentist. When she decided to switch to fashion design, she remembered her mom "crying, like someone had just died." It should not have been a surprise, given the way that Yang was always making clothing or working with her hands as a child. But though her parents recognized her proclivities, they thought she could put them to use in a different profession. "My dad would always watch me doing things with my hands," she told me, "and he said to me, 'Selia, you like to work with your hands. I have the perfect job for you. You should become a dentist.' That's how I ended up going to school for dentistry."

It was Yang's brother who encouraged her to pursue design, despite her parents' disappointment. When she graduated from college, he took out a $20,000 loan to help her start her business. Yang used the money to rent a small retail space in Manhattan's East Village and sewed the first collection herself. As the demand for her dresses grew, she took on an additional sewer, who turned out to be, as she put it, "one of those angels that walked into my life. In this business, you need talent, money, and some angels—and he was mine." She went on to explain:

> This gentleman, he had just quit Donna Karan. His mother had died, so he had to go back to his home country. And he was late getting back, so he ended up needing a job. We met and we've been working together ever since. He's an incredible sewer. He's like three men in one. He can do everything—sew, cut, alter. If I had not met him at that time, I don't know if I would be here today. There are only a few people I think like that about. [Ten years later] he still works with me. He's been going to school [studying computers] for the last five years, so he's in part time, here and there. But he's still around.

The angel for the sisters Jennifer and Sally Wang was a Chinese sewer named Richie. The Wangs told me they met Richie when he responded to their ad for a pattern maker, posted on the bulletin board at Parsons. Richie was taking classes there at night and working in the garment factories during the day. He became their pattern maker because "he was the only person willing to do it at that price. Fifty dollars a pattern. We didn't know how much a pattern was supposed to cost." His first impression on them was less than dazzling. "We couldn't believe it when we first saw him," said Jennifer, "He was this super fobby [slang for new immigrant, "fresh off the boat"] guy, who had thick glasses, a huge book bag, and could barely speak English. But he was the only one we got, and we thought we were so dead." Smiling as she recounted their days with Richie, Jennifer declared that, despite initial reservations, "it turned out kinda nice."

"He didn't really know what he was doing, because he had just started," Jennifer said. "But we would work on it together. We would go to his house at night, after he finished work, and his wife would cook dinner for us. It was *always* Chinese fish. Eventually we figured it out, we got it to work." For the Wangs, who came to New York with liberal arts degrees and no design training, the unfashionable Richie was their unlikely guide into the world of fashion.

In these narratives, constructed to reveal the "almost hadn't" and the "nearly didn't" beginnings of the young designers' professional lives, sewers were situated as the real heroes. They rescued these designers in distress and won their hearts in the bargain. Certainly designers talked about (and perhaps felt) these feelings of closeness only in retrospect. The friendships and intimacies were forged to some extent in the glow of nostalgia. But there was a certain familiarity, and even respect, in the way they spoke of these women that I could not ignore.

In this regard, these designers shared with the children of sewers an acknowledgement, if not always an admiration, of the technical knowledge that sewers possess. In narrating how their careers were made possible by sewers, the designers were also demonstrating that the craft of sewing makes the profession of design possible. The two forms of labor are interconnected and interdependent. Though the designers do not conflate their work with that of the sewers, they do recognize the level of skill involved in the latter—skills that often exceed their own. As Selia Yang put it in our interview: "Sewers, cutters—that's pure, raw talent . . . If you ask me to sew, I will. And I have always done my own patterns. But what they can do with their hands is amazing. I would not put myself in that category."

These comments diverge starkly from most understandings of sewers, including the icon of docile labor represented by transnational capitalists, the exploited worker imagined by many antisweatshop organizers, and the low-skill help described by most designers. These Asian American designers' comments are significant because they suggest a different perspective about the nature of this work, seen here not as unskilled but as experienced and expert. They suggest continuities, rather than divisions, and they argue for a different conception of labor within this industry—of what counts as skills, of what is central and what is marginal. This is not to deny that real divisions do exist, in terms of wages, opportunities, physical demands, prestige, and so forth—divisions that these designers acknowledged and in many ways accepted. But where many others see blue- and white-collars, these designers were more apt to see the shades in between.

Of course one should be wary of accepting at face value these accounts, which paint the speaker as commendably enlightened, magnanimous, and even socially responsible. These should not be read as self-evident statements of the designers' feelings, but as discursive productions that frame a collective representation. The question then becomes: Why would they talk about sewing in this way?

It is certainly possible that my interviewees crafted these narratives to burnish their image, or to simply tell me what they thought I wanted to hear. But at the same time that I struggled to determine the accuracy of these representations, I realized that my skepticism also bears some investigating. Was I suspicious of these accounts because of what these designers were saying, or because of what I believed about the nature of this work?

Social theories about U.S. labor structures generally suggest that the labor force has become polarized in the last few decades. This has been achieved through a process of "up skilling" and "down skilling." Technological innovations have enabled the downgrading of jobs that previously required moderate skills—think, for instance, of how the job of the cashier has been remade with the advent of the bar code and scanner—at the same time that it has driven the proliferation of high-skilled professions, resulting in an hourglass structure, with a preponderance of jobs at the high and low ends, but virtually none in the middle.[45]

Seen through this lens, these designers' implicit arguments about the continuities between low- and high-skills work seem somewhat sentimental. Worse, they may even seem casually dismissive of the real challenges that sewers, as supposedly low-skill workers, face. But, as the sociologists Roger Waldinger and Michael Lichter have pointed out, "while there may be some jobs for which the label of 'unskilled' means what its say, this number is small." Skill level and educational level are not equivalent, they insist, and almost all work, even jobs that demand little education, still requires "know-how of more than trivial degree."[46] The middle still holds, in other words, obscured rather than erased by the acceptance of these theories of skills polarization.

This is certainly the case within the fashion industry, which maintains a polarized labor structure that is stratified by race, class, and nationality: predominantly native white designers and retailers on the top, and predominantly ethnic immigrant sewers and manufacturers on the bottom.[47] And yet while it parcels out prestige, power, and rewards according this high-low axis, it actually operates through the blurred boundaries of knowledge, skills, and expertise. Sewing, after all, is typical of those occupations that have been down skilled but that still require tremendous knowledge. The rendering of these skills and experiences as unnecessary or superfluous is "a management strategy and motivated figuration, *not* an ontological fact or subjective experience."[48] In pointing this out, my interviewees were, in the end, only recounting the realities of their daily working lives. It is in some ways simply stating the obvious to admit that sewing is a skill, and that this skill is central to the production of fashion. The larger question here is not why these designers would talk about the work of sewing in this way, but why other designers seem so reluctant to do so.[49]

Perhaps it was the family histories of Asian American designers that heightened their awareness of these realities. It is easy to imagine that a child of a sewer might think differently about the work of sewing. Or perhaps it was their professional histories. Perhaps because these designers were forced to gain their own professional education outside of or after school, they understood differently what constitutes skills and knowledge, and where these are located. Perhaps it was the structure of their work, which resonated with other, less glamorous forms of labor and which demanded an acknowledgment of their inspirations and investments. Given this foundation, perhaps they could not help but see that design and sewing are contiguous practices, which converge, overlap, and are proximate, despite the discourses and processes that rend them apart.

CONCLUSION

The genuine desire on the part of some Asian American designers to acknowledge the centrality of garment work in their creative productions—to see the labor of assembly as essential rather than marginal to the creation of fashion, and to see the workers who perform these tasks as expert rather than unskilled—is not just an acknowledgment of the elephant in the room but an implicit critique of the process of fragmentation that continually divides manual from mental, material from immaterial. Labor historians have written about the ways that workers in the early days of industrialization understood themselves to possess technical knowledge and fought against the appropriation of such knowledge to grease the wheels of mechanization. In recent decades, those battles seem to have been entirely lost, as the technologically driven deskilling of the workforce has made such struggles seem anachronistic. The world, after all, has been divided up between skilled and unskilled in what we have come to accept as the new international division of labor.

Narrating their connections to those on the other side of the assembly line allows these designers to challenge this organization of labor. In the next chapter, I want to look more closely at the interactions between designers and sewers or manufacturers in their everyday lives. How have these different conceptions of labor shaped designers' experiences and interactions with garment workers? Have these feelings of intimacy, real and imagined, enabled them to form bonds across their myriad differences?

If nothing else, Asian Americans' presence in the fashion industry has made it apparent that the line that separates the skilled from the unskilled, the industrial from the creative, is far less than rigid—it is porous and movable at the very least to this small group. The surprising number of designers whose families have been involved in the clothing industries is certainly evidence of this—evidence that it is possible to move across the line. But, getting there has never been as easy it appears, relying as it does on the labor and investment of so many people, especially relatives and friends. The accounts gathered here are helpful reminders of this and of the fact that mobility has never been as easy or clear-cut as popular depictions of Asian Americans' effortless strides up the economic ladder may suggest.

But the different perspectives and affective relationships that Asian Americans bring to the industry can be instructive in a much broader sense. Scholars like Ethel Brooks have argued that the transnational activist movements that emerged in the last decade to protest the excesses of free trade—often called the "globalization from below"—have been weakened by their inability to generate an anti-sweatshop discourse that does not rely on narratives of workers as abject victims or models of resistance.[50] If, as Brooks notes, activists need to generate a new language of labor, one that recognizes these workers' agency as producers, then the activists would do well to start here, by rethinking what we mean by skills and where we might find knowledge.

There is much to be gained in recognizing that creative workers share some commonalities with supposedly noncreative workers. This recognition makes it possible to see interconnections, to imagine a common cause and perhaps even collective action. By showing us how the lines that divide us can move, these Asian Americans may point us in new directions, leading us to new languages and perhaps even new politics. At the very least, they can show us what is to be gained by forging intimacies.

Chapter 2

ALL IN THE FAMILY?

KIN, GIFTS, AND THE
NETWORKS OF FASHION

The shop on Elizabeth Street that used to house Wang's—one of Nolita's first clothing boutiques—was long and narrow, giving the impression more of a hallway than a store. It could accommodate no more than a rack of clothing against one wall and a register and a few shelves on another, but it was well lit and bright, fronted by a large, glass entryway. The small shop stood in stark contrast to the crowded restaurant supply and "Oriental" food stores just a block away. Wang's was located right on the edge of Chinatown, separated from it only by bustling Grand Street, and though its facade suggested otherwise, it was tied to this immigrant neighborhood in ways far more intimate than even its geographic location indicated.

For Jennifer Wang this was a good location—a crossroad of the many different peoples, cultures, and goods that inspired her creations. She liked being able to see all "the Chinese women huddled by the subway stop," she told me in an interview. She liked to watch long-time residents playing cards while shoppers just in for the afternoon stopped to ask for directions. These people all inspired her, she said, but it was the neighboring women who had the biggest impact on her work. Wang had on occasion hired some of the Chinese women who lived nearby to sew for her. She claimed that the arrangement was simple: they wanted the extra work and she needed the extra help. But how they found each other, how she described this work, and what they forged in this process of exchange was far from simple.

The women she occasionally employed often stopped by her shop to visit. Once, during an interview, we were interrupted by a woman who looked to be in her mid-50s. Wang spoke to her in Chinese, but from the gestures and expressions I could guess that the woman had come in looking for work and Wang had said there was none at the moment. "Come back later, though," the designer advised her in English. "We're starting a new season soon." The woman nodded, smiling. She looked over at me with my tape recorder and hurried out, gesturing that she did not want to keep us. She left a small bag of oranges for Jennifer.

Jennifer told me that these visits happened often. The term "visit" struck me as a euphemistic way of describing what appeared to be a fairly straightforward act of looking for work. She explained, however, that this was just part of it: these women would come to see if she needed any extra help, but they also came to bring her little treats, to chat, to see how she and her sister were doing. I looked again at the bag of oranges. As I listened, it became clear to me that these women were more than just employees. Jennifer and her sewers had formed a relationship, one characterized by an informality, even intimacy, and expressed through such things as the exchange of small gifts—of fruit and, as I came to find out, so much more.

I first discovered the existence of these informal exchanges at Wang's boutique, but they were, in various guises, present in the lives of nearly all my interviewees. Accounts like these were woven into many of my conversations with designers, emerging casually as we talked about the early days of their careers. Designers often told me that in the beginning they were "helped out," as they invariably put it, by a host of people who made their work possible. I expected these tales to center on the reporters who covered their first collection, the retailers who agreed to sell it, and other fashion insiders who typically open doors for young designers. But while those figures were no doubt important, designers talked to me less about them than about the sewers, sample makers, factory owners, and other garment workers who could not get them into the pages of *Vogue* but who were nonetheless considered central to their work.

These included, as I discussed in the previous chapter, the sewers who taught them and who "saved" them (many of whom were their own family members). It was familial ties, as I have said, that fostered in many young designers an understanding of the importance of the craft of sewing and of the production process more generally. But these workers occupied an important place in the stories designers told about themselves, even if they had not grown up with relatives in the industry. Sometimes the workers figured as heroes (as I described in chapter 1), but more often, it became clear to me, they were seen as allies who offered designers small acts of accommodations, exchange, and intimacy.

These small exchanges allowed designers and sewers to forge connections that extended beyond their roles as, essentially, employers and employees—building relationships that functioned, in their words, "like a family." This was made most obvious in the ways that designers often called these workers "aunties" and "uncles," but it was also clear in the ways that they sometimes gave up power and authority to these "elders." The invocation of these loaded terms interested me because they seemed to hide as much as they revealed about how these relationships were enacted, and for whose benefit. Why cloak what are essentially market relations in the dress of intimate relations? What did these performances enable? Why did they seem to occur only between these constituencies?

If familial and other close relationships fostered in Asian Americans a desire to imagine proximity across domains deemed distinct, the construction of a familial rhetoric helped them to forge intimacies with people who are essentially quite different. By performing a relationship of kin, designers are able to cut across (and at times paper over) these differences—of class, nationality, professional position, and so on—and construct themselves as allies and intimates. These acts of intimacy were bolstered by the practice of gift exchange, an inherently unequal and implicitly coercive process that nonetheless signals interdependency and facilitates social solidarity. In this way, gift giving and kin making allowed designers to tap into those processes and locations where social distance is minimized. It enabled them to forge what scholars would call "thick solidarity," small but deep social networks based not on abstract causes but on personal responsibility and direct commitment.

The family constructed here is a small one. Limited by sympathies that are not easily extended to those on the outside, these networks are in many ways exclusive, bounded by who was present and who could belong. In the pages that follow, I want to map the historical conditions that have brought together Asian American designers and Asian garment workers in New York City. My interest here is in exploring how, according to the designers, this obligatory economic encounter was transformed into a relationship that was in so many ways extra-economic, and how gender and ethnicity functioned to both secure intimacy and to deny it. My focus is on the designers and the ways they describe these relationships. I am less concerned with asking whether their expressions of familiarity and intimacy are indeed genuine than in considering why they were presented in the first place and what such an expression might suggest.

GARMENT TOWN

If, as many have said, fashion is a money-eating proposition for most designers, it is still big business in New York. In 2003 alone, the fashion industry brought an estimated $32 billion to the city. Indeed, the garment industry has been a crucial sector of New York's economy for over a century. Ever since the 1840s, when ready-made clothing became widely available, New York has been at the center of apparel manufacturing. In 1880, it was producing 40 percent of the nation's ready-to-wear clothing; by 1900, it was home to 50 percent of all the nation's clothing establishments. At the beginning of the twentieth century, men's and women's clothing were the two leading industries in the city.[1]

The centrality of garment production to New York's history has been well documented by scholars in urban, immigration, and labor studies.[2] The accounts of the industry's spectacular rise in the 1880s and its subsequent fall and resuscitation are extremely rich, punctuated by dramatic tales of conflict and compromise among labor, state, and capital. In what follows, I present only a brief sketch of this history. What I want to emphasize here is how shifts in the industry over the last few decades have made it possible for Asian American designers and Asian garment producers to come into contact with each other, and to forge the kinds of relationships that have played such a vital role in these designers' work.

By most accounts, New York was the unchallenged fashion capital of the United States from the 1880s until the 1960s. As a leading port city with access to both the domestic and international textile trades, relatively convenient travel to Europe, an influx of immigrant laborers, and a burgeoning cultural scene, New York was uniquely situated to attract and keep fashion buyers. However, by the 1920s its hegemony was already being tested. Menswear began moving to places like Chicago and Rochester, New York, where it could be made in larger, less expensive factories. During the Great Depression, the industry had another downturn.[3] The economic boom after the First World War had helped to buoy its flagging job rate—100,000 new jobs were generated between 1920 and 1950—but by 1960 the industry fell into a decline from which it would never fully recover.[4]

The exodus of menswear in the 1920s was in some ways the beginning of the end, for it revealed to New York's leading manufacturers an effective way to circumvent the city's relatively high labor costs. Since the 1900s, workers in the industry have fought for and won concessions in their wages and working conditions. A series of effective strikes in the early part of the twentieth century (including the so-called Uprising of the 20,000 in 1909 and Great Revolt in 1910) helped to bolster their position and drive up union membership. The infamous Triangle Shirtwaist Factory fire in 1911 brought public attention to their plight and, subsequently, a variety of factory regulations. A spike in demand after the Second World War—coupled with a labor shortage brought on by the restrictions on immigration mandated by the Immigration Act of 1924—strengthened the position of workers during the middle part of the century. All these conditions helped to drive up the cost of labor in New York's garment industry.

Menswear was the first experiment in the process of outsourcing that would eventually become standard practice in the industry. Manufacturers found that they could send these relatively simple garments, which varied little from season to season, outside of the city to be mass-produced. Advances in communication technologies and decreased costs in transportation enabled manufacturers to coordinate manufacturing and distribution activities from a distance, allowing them to still sell goods in New York without having to produce them there. After the Second World War, when consumer interest in simple and comfortable sportswear greatly increased, manufacturers found that they had even less need for the skilled labor that abounded in New York. Beginning in the 1960s, the production of sportswear and other easily mass-produced items moved first to New Jersey, Pennsylvania, and upstate New York, then to the West, Southwest, and Midwest, and soon after that to locations in Asia, Africa, and Latin America. Despite efforts by unions to halt this movement—through wage and benefits concessions and protectionist lobbying—garment production fell in all major cities across the United States in the following decades.[5] Between 1950 and 1980, New York lost about 130,000 jobs; its share of the garment industry nationwide fell from 39 percent to 13 percent.[6] These numbers have only worsened in recent years, as free-trade agreements like the General Agreement on Tariffs and Trade (GATT) and the North American Free Trade Agreement (NAFTA) have made outsourcing an industry norm.

Though New York's garment industry never fully recovered from its precipitous fall, it did not collapse altogether. The conditions that made New York a fashion center at the beginning of the twentieth century saved its garment industry from extinction at the end of the century. The city's rich cultural institutions, concentration of communication and finance capital, and abundant immigrant labor meant that it had the media infrastructure to market fashion, a local population of shoppers to consume it, and a continuing influx of immigrants to produce it.[7] As a result, designing, merchandising, supplying, advertising, and wholesaling activities remained clustered in the city, ensuring that high fashion—at least those style-sensitive garments susceptible to built-in obsolescence or shifting consumer tastes—would continue to be made there. While New York has never regained its dominance in mass production, it continues to produce many of the high-priced, stylish garments that make up the designer market. Shops making small batches of designer clothing—mostly women's wear that can be easily transported to the city's retail outlets should demand rise—have thrived in the city since the 1980s.[8]

This shift to the designer or "spot" market was a result of global exigencies, but it was also a product of local efforts. After the 1980s, as mass manufacturing increasingly moved elsewhere, the city poured its energies into remaking itself into a fashion capital. These efforts had already begun as early as the 1940s, when the Nazi occupation of Paris effectively cut off New York buyers and manufacturers from their fashion source. Having relied since its inception almost solely on the dictates of Europe, selling and reproducing its fashions, New York's fashion industry was left high and dry. It was then that industry leaders began working to improve the quality and style of their own products and to nurture local design talents. Editors, buyers, and retailers began to, in the words of one editor, "encourage our American designers to make greater and greater efforts in the field of original and daring design . . . and to buy and believe in their creation." Publications like *The New Yorker* and *The New York Times* began promoting American styles and American designers; the *Times* launched the first "Fashion of the Times" show in 1942.

Since the 1970s, in response to increased overseas competition, New York has thrown its weight behind these efforts. The city government passed measures to reduce traffic and crime in the garment district, changed the name of Seventh Avenue to Fashion Avenue, and established a special zoning amendment to preserve the district for manufacturing. New York's new identity as a fashion capital (rather than a garment town) was confirmed in the 1990s, when the city founded the Fashion Center Business Improvement District and supported the Council of Fashion Designers of America (CFDA) in establishing a New York fashion week.[9]

This shift in the industry toward design-led production was well-timed, coinciding as it did with the consumer market's greater interest in segmented, individualized, or customized goods after the Second World War.[10] Because demand for these designer clothes has been so strong in the last few decades, New York is now the second largest apparel producer in the United States, behind only Los Angeles.[11] It is now also home to the densest concentration of designers in the country (18 percent reside in Los Angeles, while 43 percent reside in New York, making it the nation's true fashion center).[12]

This make-over has not meant that garment production no longer happens in the city. While assembly is increasingly performed overseas, and some forms of production have left the city altogether (knitwear, for instance), design-linked tasks like pattern and sample making are still carried out locally.[13] In fact, the emergence of New York as a site of high-end, design-intensive production relies on the maintenance of a local workforce. The young designers who are driving this sector of the industry must have some or all of their lines produced within New York City. Unlike major couture conglomerates or mass-market firms, these designers produce only small batches of clothing, primarily for distribution to local boutiques and department stores. Few have the large orders or extended turn-around time to make outsourcing necessary or possible. Most young designers as a result rely on the local industry to ensure quality production and faster delivery.[14]

The shift to the designer market that propelled New York into a new, profitable future did not eliminate the need for garment production, but it did exacerbate the inequalities that were always endemic to this industry. First, it triggered the reemergence of the sweatshop and revived the concomitant poor wages, unsafe working conditions, and weakened labor force of the last century. Seasonal work and nonunion firms have all returned. Because the local garment industry now centers almost solely on fast-changing high fashion, it relies on a jobber-contractor system, which uses decentralized shops small enough to produce short runs quickly, and to evade union and governmental regulations. These shops require their workers to maintain an inordinate amount of personal flexibility. It is not uncommon for a worker to be unemployed for months when orders are low, and to put in an eighty-hour workweek when demand is high. Wages currently average approximately $6.50 per hour, though reports of under-paid or unpaid wages are rampant, particularly in fly-by-night nonunion shops, which appear to fill short orders and vanish before workers can collect their pay.[15] In 1998, for instance, a U.S. Department of Labor inves-tigation of New York garment shops found that only 35 percent of them met federal minimum wage and overtime standards.[16]

Second, it greatly intensified the polarization within the industry be-tween highly paid professionals (retailers, designers, marketers, and mod-els) and poorly paid laborers (contractors and sewers)—organized around divisions of age, class, nationality, and immigration status. Like the gar-ment firms of the last century, these small shops depend almost solely on immigrant labor. In fact, as many scholars have shown, apparel manufac-turing in New York and elsewhere has historically been the work of immi-grants. The historian Nancy Green has argued that the industry, "(in)fa-mous for its multiethnic labor force," can be seen as microcosm of the city's immigration history.[17] Jewish and Italian immigrants originally dom-inated the trade, but immigration restrictions and opportunities in other sectors, especially for second-generation Americans, had greatly decreased the presence of those groups by the 1940s. Between the Second World War and 1965, African Americans migrating north and Puerto Rican immi-grants filled most of the positions. After 1960, their numbers too began to decline, due in part to the increases in employment opportunities man-dated by the Civil Rights Act of 1964.[18] Asian and Latino immigrants, whose numbers swelled after the Immigration and Nationality Act of 1965 eased restrictions on immigration from Asia and Latin America, have since come to dominate the industry. As of 1998, 83.5 percent of operators, fabricators, and laborers in apparel manufacturing were Asian or Latino. At the same time that Asian and Latino immigrants became the industry's new workers, Asian men—primarily Chinese and Korean—became the new owners of its businesses. At its peak in the 1980s, there were nearly 500 Chinese-owned garment shops in New York, employing about 20,000 workers, 95 percent of whom were women. Korean-owned shops, located primarily in midtown, numbered 400 and employed 14,000 Latino work-ers at that time. These employees hailed almost exclusively from Mexico and Ecuador and were nearly evenly split between men (45 percent) and women (55 percent).[19] In recent years, the number of Asian-owned factories has dropped dramatically. As of 2001, Chinatown had lost about 50 percent of its shops, dropping its numbers down to about 246.[20] Still these factories remain the most important centers for the production of women's apparel in New York, producing about 70 percent of all clothing made in the city.[21]

These local demographics were shaped by global dynamics—migration patterns and labor histories. It is no coincidence that Chinese, Koreans, Mexicans, and Ecuadorians came to dominate the industry in New York, given the central role that those countries have played in transnational garment production. Through networks that at times spanned multiple nations, these same populations came to be "niched" into the local garment industry. Korean migrants, for instance, dominated garment work in Brazil during the 1960s; many Korean Brazilians later took up the same work in Los Angeles. If patterns of ethnic succession opened up opportunities for them to enter the industry, it was these migration networks that allowed them to continually replenish its labor force.

It is no surprise either that women became its primary workers, though this was not always the case. Despite the popular perception that this is naturally "women's work," tailors have traditionally been men. Women gradually became the principal workforce of ready-made production only when the contracting system became firmly established at the beginning of the twentieth century. Under this system of production, the myriad tasks required to make a garment became disaggregated and divided along gendered lines: men became owners, cutters, and pattern makers, while women were largely restricted to sewing.[22] This division, as Daniel Bender has shown, was reinforced by male workers, labor organizers, and social reformers, who constructed women's role in garment production as temporary or supplementary to the work of men.[23] As the clothing industry gradually became deskilled, women were slotted into its system because their gendered bodies had already rendered their labor inferior. As the industry became more mobile, Asian and other nonwhite women became more valuable, both locally and globally. Reported to be technically proficient and constitutionally docile—by factory owners, government officials, and even by some transnational activists—the women were seen as perfect subjects for this low-wage, low-skill work.

These women occupied the lowest rungs of the industry, most vulnerable to its demands. But the predominantly male immigrant contractors faced immense pressures as well, to constantly reduce profits and shorten lead time, especially as overseas manufacturers have worked to improve their own production capabilities. Profits in this industry are concentrated in the upper tier, with large manufacturers, retailers, and jobbers keeping about 88 percent of the revenue from each garment. The sociologist Yu Zhou has shown that movement into this higher end is extremely limited for these immigrants who lack the capital, experience, and language skills that it requires. Certainly there have been occasions where members of the immigrant generation have taken their place in the fashion spotlight. The label Lafayette 148, for instance, which retails at high-end department stores like Saks Fifth Avenue, was started by a Chinese factory owner who paired up with an Asian designer (formerly employed by Liz Claiborne).[24] My own research has shown that the designer Shin Choi also began as a manufacturer, first as an assistant for a Jewish owner, then overseeing the entire operation. Choi worked in manufacturing for over a decade before starting her own label.[25]

Sewers too have made some strides up the fashion ladder. In her study of garment workers in New York's Chinatown, Xiaolan Bao found that as early as 1980, women garment workers were already trying to cross this sartorial line. At that time, when working conditions and wages in Chinatown were at some of their worst, garment workers began taking courses at nearby FIT to train in sample making and other design-related techniques. Their numbers grew significantly after 1984, when the Garment Improvement Development Corporation (GIDC, a nonprofit organization serving the New York apparel industry) began its "super sewers" program, which provided financial and other support, including language classes, to help workers succeed in school. In coordination with GIDC, administrators at FIT instituted an open admissions policy to most of their programs for Chinese workers, many of whom are currently employed in midtown design firms, primarily as sample makers and pattern designers.[26]

Programs such as these have certainly benefited sewers, allowing them to have better wages and less-taxing work. But these types of opportunities remain rare for the majority of them; limited language skills and family responsibilities make schooling difficult for most. Moreover, these programs have very limited aspirations for their students, geared as they are toward giving the women new technical skills, such as cutting, to support others' design efforts. Ultimately, the programs do little to alter these sewers' place in the industry. Moreover, those instances of moving up the fashion ladder are quite unusual, far more the exception than the rule.[27] As

Zhou concluded: "The borderline between the two tiers is a well-guarded one," buttressed by barriers of class, language, cultural, social, and educational barriers.[28]

This border reflects the broader divisions between creative and manufacturing labors that, as I detailed in the previous chapter, have become entrenched in the structure of and discussions about the clothing industry. That designers have a part to play in maintaining these divisions is clear. Because young designers run small businesses, with at most several assistants, they typically oversee the entire production process—from the initial sketches to the final fabrication. Therefore, they must work directly with shop owners and their sewers. Yet this is rarely, if ever, mentioned when designers talk about their work. Instead, they tend to dwell on their inspiration and their "creative process." When asked specifically about the business of fashion, they usually focus on pricing, sales, and the financial uncertainty endemic to this line of work. The production process exists largely as a necessary but unremarkable part of their creative practice.[29] Often it is even characterized as the most difficult and least enjoyable part of the designer's job.

Yet the designer's relationship with her manufacturer is extremely important, for it determines how fast and how well her garments are made. Designers are often advised to build good relationships with their producers precisely for this reason. How this is achieved is left unclear. What is clear, however, is that this relationship is imagined as inherently conflictual, requiring active management on the part of the designer. One fashion how-to book, for instance, warned that in this business "you need to be tough and assertive . . . Business owners must deal aggressively with factory supervisors . . . who bully, intimidate, and try to rip them off."[30] On the border between fashion and its fabrication, then, the relationship between designers and producers is seen both as symbiotic and as adversarial.

WE ARE FAMILY

As young designers working in New York, Asian Americans too must rely on this predominantly Asian and Latino immigrant workforce to produce their fashionable goods. If, as I have discussed, their family histories have fostered in them a different understanding of the nature of garment work, of the locations of expertise and knowledge, they still occupy a privileged position vis-à-vis these workers. The generational divide that characterizes the clothing industry overall—with a predominantly immigrant cohort occupying the lower rungs and a predominantly native population inhabiting the upper ones—holds true for this group as well. The Asian designers who have graced the pages of *Vogue* have been primarily second-generation Asian Americans or international students who came specifically to study fashion or, armed with an overseas education, to try their luck on Seventh Avenue. They share few of the burdens of the immigrant generation— family responsibility, limited opportunities—and are distinct from them in terms of class, occupational location, citizenship status, and so on. Like all other designers, they are firmly perched on the upper rung of this bifurcated industry.

But while they share the social location of other designers, some Asian American designers have built relationships with workers that are quite unusual. There is a scene in Douglas Keeve's 2005 documentary, *Seamless* —about the competition to win the first CFDA/Vogue Fashion Fund prize— that hints at this difference. In this scene, Doo-Ri Chung is filmed arriving at a garment factory; she is the only designer in the documentary shown in this context. As she bounds in, she greets the manager in Korean. Chung seems at ease, friendly even, as she goes over her order with him. She asks him when it will be ready and he replies, to her great surprise and satisfaction, that he will have it for her the very next day.

Chung's interaction with this manager is remarkable, not the least for its contrast with that of another contestant, Alexandre Plokhov (the designer for the label Cloak), who is shown in the film having a heated argument with his contractor over a late order. This different dynamic is in part idiosyncratic—a product of each designer's personality and their individual challenges—but it is also emblematic of a larger trend. During the course of my research, I have found that the accommodation, ease, and even intimacy that Chung seems to enjoy with the factory manager is characteristic of the relationship that some Asian American designers have forged with their producers.

Unlike most, these designers engage in interactions with their Asian sewers and contractors that extend far beyond their roles of employer and employee, contractor and client. While these two generations were brought together through the domain of the market, their interactions exceeded the realm of economic exchange. Designers certainly needed the formal, paid labor of Asian immigrants, but they depended on them for much more. Many of the designers I interviewed offered remarkable accounts of having been "helped out," as Jennifer Wang put it, by these workers: sewers who donated spare fabric, owners who offered informal credit, and shop managers who fast-tracked their orders—probably at the expense of other clients. Each off-the-books act of generosity tied the two generations even closer together, creating "families"—as many dubbed their relationships—out of these often disconnected communities.

The centrality of the family in these designers' lives, then, functioned both literally and figuratively. Asian American designers are tied to the production process not just through their mothers, aunts, and uncles, but through the connections they have voluntarily forged with Asian workers in the garment industry. These relationships, like those with their real kin, were also uneven, fractured here by ethnic, gender, and class differences. Fashion designers, who were predominantly young, middle-class women, found themselves being helped along, but also held in check, by male contractors and female sewers alike. While designers negotiated their relationships with both of these producers in similar ways—at once giving up authority to them and accumulating resources from them—this "family" was also shaped by subtle differences of gender and power.

The story of the Wangs best illustrates how designers saw these dynamics. The proprietors of Wang's boutique, Jennifer and Sally Wang, were born in Korea of Chinese and Korean parents and grew up in Los Angeles's Koreatown, where their parents owned a restaurant. Jennifer and Sally were always close, and when Sally dropped out of school and "used the find-my-roots excuse to go to China," as Jennifer put it in an interview with me, Jennifer was not far behind. Traveling through the country gave the sisters the idea to start their own label. They were inspired by the everyday stylishness of Chinese women, who "with their cropped pants, little flip flops, and chic haircuts, looked like they came straight out of a Comme des Garçons ad," said Jennifer. Two years later, they relocated to New York to pursue their design dreams.

As the older sister, Jennifer moved first. Armed with a degree in political science and philosophy from the University of California, Berkeley, she found a job in advertising. When Sally arrived a year later, the two started experimenting in their studio apartment. Neither sister had any training in design, and it took them months before they could come up with four salable pieces. "We had no idea what we were doing," Jennifer admitted, but it was not long before they got some invaluable help. Soon after they started, as described in chapter 1, the Wangs placed an ad for a pattern maker on a bulletin board at Parsons. It was through this ad that they met Richie,[31] and that, though they didn't know it at the time, was their first bit of luck.

Through Richie, a pattern maker, the Wangs were introduced to "Alice and her Chinese circle." Alice, a garment worker in her fifties, coordinated a large but close-knit community of sewers who alternated between factory and home sewing, depending on the demand. "These women are always around," explained Jennifer, "and they'll do great work for you, but you have to find them." Alice and her friends produced the Wangs' first samples, despite their embarrassingly small order, because Alice considered them "Richie's girls." When they finished their first collection, Jennifer remembered "being so proud of ourselves, because we didn't go to school, or know anybody."

By "anybody," Jennifer was referring to the fashion insiders—buyers, retailers, editors, and writers—who can make or break a young designer's career. But outside of these people, she and her sister did know quite a few individuals whose help proved indispensable. She remembered the support she received, particularly in the early days, from "all these people who saw us as their kids, and wanted us to succeed." Sometimes it was small allowances, like when the sisters opened their shop in what would become the fashionable neighborhood of Nolita, and their Chinese landlord "let us take the place without a deposit because we reminded him of his daughters." More often, these "treats" were the tangible bits and pieces that made their work possible.

As I indicated earlier, the women of Alice's circle often popped by the boutique, looking for new work or simply bearing small gifts—usually some fruit or a hot lunch. But they would also show up regularly with "the little scraps that they found lying around the factories, like a bag of trimming, zippers, or buttons," said Jennifer. Shuffling through floors and bins of their workrooms, these women collected and hoarded all the bits that seemed reusable. "Whatever gets thrown away, they'll bring to us," said Jennifer. "One time we even got an old sewing machine." The Wangs never wasted these pieces: "We used whatever we had. Even now, when we can afford more, it still helps."

These treats extended well beyond the occasional bag of zippers and trimmings. Sometimes they included yards of valuable materials that had slipped through the cracks of fashion production. In slightly hushed tones, Jennifer told me:

> When we first started, we met these guys who owned a cutting room and a factory. They used to cut for all these high-end Barneys types: Isabel Toleda, Tocca, Calvin Klein, etc. And when you cut for the big designers, you always order more fabric than you need, just in case there is a problem. So, after the season is over, there would be huge stockpiles of remainder fabrics—silks, wools, cashmere. Really expensive stuff. Sam, the owner, would keep it all, and, after we got to know him he would sell it to us. He would give us the wool that Calvin Klein or Donna Karan used for $4 a yard instead of $50 a yard. It worked out for both of us. Sam would get some money, and we would get great fabric that Calvin Klein paid for.

It is not unheard of for a younger designer to use the same fabric that has appeared in a major designer's collection, a fact that they openly advertise. To do so, however, is rare, since the costs are so prohibitive. When a young designer orders the same fabric being used by a larger firm, the price difference can be as high as 50 percent, since he or she is often required to pay a surcharge for the small order, while established firms are often granted discounts for their greater volume. Under normal circumstances, then, the Wangs would not have been able to get fabric used by a firm like Calvin Klein. But, with the help of Sam (and the subsidy by Calvin Klein), they were able to craft their collections from these remainders and from the bits and pieces handed down to them by their sewers.

Selling remainders at a grossly discounted price and offering up little treats are certainly not common practices in the industry. When I asked about the prevalence of these practices, Jennifer coyly replied: "Well, it depends on who you are . . . In this business, being Asian is like a secret weapon. Sam would never have given us all that fabric if we weren't Asian girls. He really wanted to help us out. Most of the owners and sewers are Asian, and they want you to do well. You're like their daughter, and they're proud of you. Especially the ladies who sew for me—they're very maternal."

Several other designers also reported getting some "help." Gemma Kahng told me that when she first started, she "ran around all the factories" trying to find someone to produce her collection. "Luckily, I'm Korean," she said, "and a lot of the factories are owned by Korean people. So, I'd go and say 'Hi.' And they helped me. You know, they sewed my first season at . . . cost. And they never charged me like they charged other people. I still keep in touch with them. They're still upstairs from me."

Kahng's account—which constructs this exchange as easy, even natural —belies the unusual nature of this accommodation. There is a common misperception that because garment production is a low-wage industry, it is easy to find the labor to fill its needs. But many young designers have an extremely difficult time locating someone to do their production. This quest involves a tremendous amount of legwork—knocking on doors, asking for referrals—and information about production businesses is guarded as a trade secret. Moreover, manufacturers often hesitate to work with young designers because their orders are typically small and their inexperience is considered a risk. The competition for well-respected manufacturers' business is especially high. A handful of these firms produce samples for all the major labels, and getting accepted as a customer, many designers told me, requires referrals, luck, and the insider connections that are usually associated with the more glamorous side of fashion. Kahng's account is thus unusual. To find someone to produce her collection was tough, but to find someone who would do so at cost was extraordinary.

Why these exceptional accommodations? Echoing Jennifer Wang's assertion that these owners and sewers simply wanted her and her sister to "do well," Wenlan Chia gave me this explanation:

> When I first started, a lot of the factory owners would say to me, "We have confidence in you. We think you will be successful. So we want to support you." They would help me with a lot of things. I think my background was useful in that sense. Even now, . . . [if I need fabric] and there is a Chinese person and an Italian person, and they can produce the same fabric—I go to the Chinese one. Not because I think the Chinese person is better, but because I think he will help me more.

While sewers and contractors may have had a similar desire to help, they did not have equal capacity to do so. It was the contractors who could offer these concessions and allowances. Sewers could give only their own knowledge and labor, and these they could tender only occasionally (as when they took on designers' additional orders to sew at home, or when they helped out with advice about how to construct a particular garment). Yet designers always talked about these two types of workers together, even though the benefits came primarily from contractors. And, as I will demonstrate below, the extra-economic relationships they highlighted certainly involved both groups.

When I asked one interviewee, Sarah Ma, who also admitted to enjoying certain advantages in her relationships with her contractors, why she received these kinds of favors, she answered simply that she and her contractors were "on friendly terms." Though Ma was somewhat circumspect about the matter, it seemed obvious that she and other designers were getting a break because of their ethnicity, and their perceived similarities to these manufacturers and sewers. But in what ways were these designers like their daughters, as Jennifer Wang put it? In part, these connections were formed on the basis of shared language. A number of the designers I interviewed spoke Chinese or Korean (though not fluently) and thus were able to at least exchange pleasantries with their sewers and contractors. This common language certainly bolstered the sense of collective identity. In part, it was the perception that they came from similar backgrounds. After all, many of these designers grew up with parents who worked in the industry—a fact they often shared with the sewers—or in similar types of service positions. And demographically speaking, these producers were not so different from the designers' parents: most of them were first-generation, middle-aged immigrants (the average age for Chinese sewers is forty).[32] Finally, in at least some small part, there was a sense of joint purpose—a desire to see certain sartorial traditions represented in contemporary fashion. The designer Yvonne Chu speculated that the obvious "Asian influence" in her clothing might have been the reason her Chinese contractor was so willing to "help [her] get things done." "I think they like that my clothes are Asian-inspired," Chu told me. "I mean, they make clothes for everybody, but with me they get to see a little bit of their culture in their work."[33]

All these factors helped to put Asian American designers and Asian garment workers "on friendly terms," as Sarah Ma put it. However, she was quick to say that her special treatment was, in the end, not that special: "I'm sure everyone gets a break on the basis of something. I might have gotten some help because I speak Chinese and I'm comfortable around these people. But let's face it, I'd be much better off if I was white, went to the right schools, and had rich parents." Echoing those sentiments, Wenlan Chia cautioned against attributing to much significance to any advantages Asian American designers may have gained from their ethnic background. "Let's say you're an Italian designer," she told me. "When you tell buyers and editors, 'I'm from Italy. I studied at Saint Martins'—they think you are somebody. When you say, 'Oh, I'm from China,' they will say, 'Uh, I have to see your portfolio.' " To Chia and Ma, the real advantages in the industry invariably went to Euro-American fashion-school graduates.

These offhand comments point to the tremendous odds that Asian American designers, indeed most designers, face in this industry. In a business populated by children of the rich and famous (like Stella Mc-Cartney, daughter of the former Beatle Paul McCartney), celebrity designers (such as Jennifer Lopez and Jessica Simpson), and a handful of powerful couture houses that pass along designer positions like royal thrones, it is extremely difficult for a young designer without family money or industry connections to survive. Since most Asian American designers do not enjoy these kinds of advantages, and are in some ways disadvantaged because they did not formally train at fashion schools, little favors from suppliers and sewers can make a big difference.

Ma and Chia were in fact underestimating the value of their comfort with these workers. Many young designers have suffered from paying too little attention to their producers and the production process. Designers have no shortage of horror stories about manufacturers who failed to deliver orders on time, execute the designs properly, or buy the right fabric. There are stories of producers who deliberately buy too much fabric in order to keep some for themselves and, increasingly common, of those who copy a client's designs for their own lower-end production.[34] It stands to reason that by forming close relationships with their manufacturers, young designers can minimize their risk of such unscrupulous treatment. Ma and other Asian American designers' comfort with these workers kept them closely linked to the production process, making it more difficult for them to be cheated and easier for them to receive their little treats.

Through this informal practice of helping out, these immigrant workers were supporting, even if inadvertently, the creative work of the second generation. But helping out often extended to formal business issues such as pricing and scheduling. Some of the designers I spoke to noted that manufacturers were willing to accelerate their schedules in unusual ways. Yvonne Chu said that her manufacturer has "helped me out by getting things done for me fast. That's really important. If your order is delayed even a few days, you're going to lose a lot of money." Others admitted to getting the "family price"—insider discounts—on everything from patterns to production. Some, like Gemma Kahng, received not just discounts but what amounted to informal credit. In a fiercely competitive business built on social connections, corporate backing, and formal education, this support was critical. In this context, Asianness, if not exactly a "weapon," as Jennifer Wang put it, was certainly an important resource.[35]

What the Wangs and other Asian American designers lacked in professional connections, they were able to make up in these other types of connections. The networks they forged with garment producers provided them with access to knowledge, labor, informal credit, and social support—all resources that have, under other circumstances, been crucial to immigrant entrepreneurship.[36] Korean greengrocers, Chinese laundry owners, and the like have all utilized these types of resources, circulated along ethnic lines, to establish their entrepreneurial niches. The networks forged here work in very much the same way, helping Asian American designers to sustain their careers. Ethnicity in this instance also functions as a type of social capital, giving these designers an edge—though in their eyes a very limited edge—in the fashion marketplace.[37]

I have already said that the work of these designers shares much, in both structure and practice, with the immigrant businesses of their parents' generation. In this sense, it would not be inappropriate to characterize their occupation as a new form of ethnic entrepreneurship, one that similarly relies on and benefits from family and social networks. There are, however, some differences that must be noted. The ethnic networks forged here are in a sense broader, connecting Chinese sewers to not just Chinese designers but to Korean and Vietnamese as well, and to others who identify themselves, at times, as simply Asian American. While these connections were bolstered by designers' ability to perform ethnic-specific practices—speaking the national language, for instance—they were not bounded by such performances. These relationships may have been stronger between co-ethnics, but they were not limited to them.

Moreover, these networks are traveling across, rather than within, generational cohorts. The process of mutual assistance—or, more precisely, the mixing of individualistic competitive behavior with collective efforts at cooperation—that has made possible the high rate of self-employment among Asian immigrants has traditionally taken place within the first generation, for whom cooperation served as a strategy to circumvent the barriers—of language, capital, and so on—common to the newly arrived.[38]

The exchanges recorded here are a bit more voluntary, though certainly not free of constraints; built less on shared circumstances and necessities than on active identity work.[39] How and why did these actors choose to assert such a pan-ethnic network? How should we interpret these informal and sporadic instances of helping out?

A FAIR TRADE?

If interactions between Asian workers and Asian American designers sometimes went beyond the realm of economic exchange, they were often characterized in terms that hid the operations of the market altogether. As Jennifer Wang's comments about workers' desire to help an Asian American designer because "you're like their daughter, and they're proud of you" revealed, designers frequently described their relationship with producers in the language of the family. "Unlike most designers," Yvonne Chu told me, "I relate to them [garment workers] on a personal level. They're like a family to me. And they're very good to me."

Indeed, the very term "helping out," invoked to express the various accommodations and allowances designers received, is most often used to signal the assistance of friends and family—not the labor of employees. It suggests an informality that belongs outside the sphere of public commerce. It is used, for instance, by the children of ethnic entrepreneurs, who employ the phrase to frame their work in parent-owned businesses—as waitresses, cooks, cashiers, and so on—not as employment but as informal assistance.[40] Its prevalence here denotes a similar sense of intimacy, allowing what are public exchanges—between designers and producers—to be transferred into the context of the private or the domestic.

This jettisoning of the public into the domain of the private requires a well-orchestrated performance in which each party plays a defined role. In this family, designers are invariably cast as the child, a role that they did not always relish. Thuy Diep made this clear. In describing her relationship with an older Chinese pattern maker in her employ, she told me: "Because I'm Asian, and I'm young, I think there is this sort of natural mother and daughter thing that happens. She sees me as her daughter. And she definitely treated me like a daughter."

Diep went on to talk about the ways this daughter-mother dynamic played out in their working relationship. According to the designer, the older woman continually questioned and admonished about her design choices, and this eventually became a source of tension:

She was constantly telling me, "Do this, don't do that." They try to guide you. And, you know, okay, maybe sometimes they're right. But we butted heads. It's really weird. I mean, you would think that since I'm the client, they're going to listen to me. And I never want to get to that point where I have to be authoritative with her. Because I'm Asian, and I'm not saying this is only an Asian thing, but I've been taught to respect women or men older than me. So there's this gray area, where, okay, it's a business, but she's older, and I can't rudely tell her something. So it's a delicate thing.

This delicate situation got better after the first season. By then Diep had proven herself to be a capable designer and felt that she had earned the older woman's respect. "The clothes came out really great," she said. "She's thinking okay, maybe. She's starting to see that I know what I'm doing." The stories Diep told about this relationship sounded, indeed, very familial —a child being guided and reprimanded by her parent, working to earn her approval. With a mixture of frustration and amusement, she told me about even being scolded for being too skinny. "You laugh," she said, "but if you're in it, it's not funny."

Diep was actually quite sanguine about it all. But as her comments hinted, these constructed families, like most families, were not free of conflicts. A few interviewees, like the women's wear designer Margie Tsai, believed these relationships to be more of a burden than a blessing. "Sometimes they take advantage of it," she complained to me. Once, when a few of her pieces were two weeks late, she said the contractor was "not at all apologetic . . . He called and acted like I shouldn't care because we are family. Just because I speak to him in Chinese and ask him about his kids he thinks of me as a little sister. I don't think he would have been late like that with a regular customer. It's that family thing. They really try to take advantage of it." Tsai resolved that in the future she would refrain from speaking to contractors in Chinese so as to avoid any possible personal connections.

Jen Kao also spoke about these frustrations. Kao, who had shown only a few collections when I first spoke to her, was already annoyed with what she saw as the ethnic expectations within the industry. She too had determined that her ethnicity and her gender could become something of a hindrance: "I think being Asian in this business can help in some ways, but it can also be a huge disadvantage. People think that you're going to be polite and nice—that you're not going to freak out and yell at them for every little mistake. And it's true. I'm definitely by nature not that type of person. So it's really difficult for me sometimes, because they think they can step on me." Wayne Lee added: "I get a lot of [being told what to do] too. Sometimes they even reprimand me. And I'm thinking: I'm the one giving you the job. You don't need to tell me how to handle things. But it's okay, they mean well. It's just sometimes they're giving advice that's not needed. And so in the end it gets a little annoying." Even Jennifer Wang, who harbored no such resentments, had to laughingly admit that her "family duties" could "get a little out of hand." "We used to have to go to Sam's [the contractor's] house to visit his mom," she remembered. "We took care of his kids. I was always thinking to myself: Other designers don't have to do this."

Certainly this type of familial relationship was not shared by all. Some of the designers I interviewed felt no personal ties to the men and women who labored for them. Such ties appeared far more commonly among women, suggesting that these relationships were perhaps more easily foisted on or accepted by female designers. It is important to note as well that designers seemed more resentful of the admonitions and reprimands given to them by male contractors than by female sewers. They described relations with these men at times in very paternalistic terms—as the above comments reveal. This subtle difference suggests a gendered dynamic in which these men—by virtue of their gender and, to a certain extent, their occupation—were seen as having more social power, and thus perhaps as more threatening than the female sewers. I noticed these tensions far less when designers spoke about female sewers; their "inappropriate" comments and behavior were more often excused or simply laughed away. Though designers saw both sewers and contractors as "family," relationships with their "uncles" could produce fears about "being taken advantage of" or being "stepped on" that did not exist with their "aunties." Gender, then, served to both enable and minimize these ethnic networks.

In my observations, the exchanges between designers and their manufacturers were generally friendly: warm greetings, exchanges of casual conversations, joking manners. But in the two separate instances when I accompanied a female designer to a factory, I heard each interviewee express a worry that the contractor did not fully understand her instructions, despite repeatedly telling her "no problem." I wondered if this was just his way of dismissing her, and if he would have treated male clients with equal carelessness. I also wondered whether such expressions of intimacy were really attempts to manage these women, who may have been seen as more pliable, more likely to accept male authority. Then I wondered, conversely, whether the women were simply using their gender—their performance of the daughter's role, willing to acquiesce and needing assistance—to ensure that they would get some extra help.[41]

It is certainly possible that this intimate relationship was no more than a management strategy, used by both parties to their own advantage. As the comments above suggest, if designers consistently benefited from the help of producers, the latter enjoyed some advantages as well. Occasionally, these benefits took material forms. Wang and other designers reported that they often "helped out" sewers by allowing them to work at home or, in some cases, in the designer's studio, where they could avoid the pressures of the factory. "A lot these women are older, and I worry about their health—those factories are so high stress," Sarah Ma told me. By allowing sewers to work elsewhere, the designers were able to circumvent the factory system and pass along some benefits in terms of work schedule and especially pay.[42] "If I'm going to spend, say, $7 on a shirt," Ma explained, "I'd rather give it straight to them than to some guy who will only pay them $1 a shirt. I mean, they're the ones doing the work."

Even in their dealings with contractors and factory owners, designers like Kelima K. expressed a desire to help out. These designers were all aware of the challenges that small manufacturers faced—physically demanding work, long hours, financial uncertainty. In recent years, those challenges have been exacerbated by increased pressures from overseas production and the rising cost of rents in the garment district, which have resulted in manufacturers' being pushed out of Manhattan, seeing their profits shrink even further, or going out of business. According to a report by the Center for Urban Future, by 1998 fashion industry employees no longer constituted a majority of the employees in the fashion district.[43]

I remember speaking at length to Kelima K. about this. It was an issue of great concern to her, as it is for many designers in New York who fear the loss, both material and cultural, from the shrinking of the district.[44] A bridal designer who grew up in California, Kelima had studied international relations and worked in the public sector before becoming a designer. During our conversations, she seemed quite knowledgeable about the global labor issues surrounding fashion production, and the challenges facing the local garment workforce in particular. But to her this was not an abstract problem. Like Sarah Ma, she described feeling "very comfortable" with her manufacturers and sensed "a level of connection" with them. She spoke at length about the need to find a better, more "ethical" solution to these challenges. It was this sensibility that encouraged her to do small things like ordering from her manufacturer more buttons than she actually needed. "I was thinking 'Oh, let's help him out,'" she explained to me, and then added, with a laugh, "but it's not like our button order is actually going to help him all that much."

Kelima was right—a bag of buttons and a few extra dollars are not likely to fix the problems of the industry. In offering these types of accommodations, young designers were doing less to alter the material conditions of these workers' lives than simply articulating some sense of responsibility to them, a necessary admission but not in itself a solution. For their part, producers were not likely to see these small gestures—or the friendly relationships of which they were an expression—as adequate relief from the demands of their work.

In the few instances when I was able to observe their interactions first-hand, I saw the limitations of these relationships clearly. The sewers who dropped by my interviewees' shops seemed genuinely pleased to see their handiwork hanging in the windows. I saw one smile as she fingered a dress, letting it slip gently through her hands. They did not appear shocked or offended by the prices marked on the garments, as I had thought they might be. Indeed, they seemed to understand perfectly well how the system worked, and if they were angry about how little they were paid to create these expensive items, they did not show it. Curious about their thoughts, I spoke with a Vietnamese sewer during her visit to a shop.[45] When I asked what she thought about working with Asian American designers, she quickly replied that she greatly enjoyed it, and that they were "nice girls." The response seemed rote, and not altogether frank. When I pushed her further, the woman answered that while she would "rather help out these girls" "it's still hard work, whoever you do it for."

The sewer's comment reveals that while the construction of a family diminishes the distance between producers and designers, the differences remain. The fictive kinship structure cannot erase the economic gulf that lies between first-generation immigrants and the "children" who profit from their difficult labor. In fact, it can even obscure these inequalities. These two groups occupy not only different but sometimes antagonistic socioeconomic positions, where designers' gains often require workers' losses. After all, the designers' profit margins depend directly on keeping production costs (and workers' wages) down. Their accommodations depend on pliant workers who can, for instance, work faster and stay longer to fast-track an order. The familial narratives produced here function, in effect, to minimize crucial differences. Reimagining the differences as interpersonal dynamics reinterprets workers' economic necessities as no more than familial sacrifice.

Moreover, such relationships seemed to end there, at the point of helping out. There was no indication from my interviewees that such collaborations could or would translate into other forms of solidarity—collective organizing, for instance—or other forms of tangible benefits—such as healthcare, child care, and pension plans. Moreover, there was no sign that these designers felt similarly obligated to the sizable number of Latino sewers. Ultimately, the kinds of accommodations these designers have offered are acts of volunteerism that circumvent rather than confront the conditions of garment work. This informal system of mutual assistance does little to affect change within the industry as a whole and can actually prevent broader collective struggles to do so by providing individual solutions to structural problems.

As such, this type of community-building effort can potentially gloss over important points of difference and uneven power relations. In fact, we have seen these types of familial narratives and networks enacted elsewhere in the garment industry, to similar effect. Within global processing zones like the maquiladora, the discourse of the family, as Melissa Wright has shown, has helped to secure a young, female labor force by rearticulating women's entrance into the workplace as the entrance into a new family—with the owners as the "fathers" and the workers as the supposedly protected "daughters."[46] In the United States, familial networks have long served as an important site of labor recruitment. According to the sociologist Roger Waldinger, the majority of all new workers in New York City are introduced to the industry by family members.[47] This is particularly true of Asian workers and business owners in the apparel industry, and the familial and ethnic networks that led them to their occupations have also served as an effective source of their workplace discipline.

In her fascinating book about immigrants in New York's garment industry, Margaret Chin noted that none of the garment shop owners in her study got into the industry without the aid of friends and relatives who gave financial help, tips about how to start, and leads to get contracts. In Chinese shops, almost all new workers are brought in by co-ethnic friends and family. In fact, the owners have come to rely on sewers to replenish the workforce by bringing in family members and training them on the job (acting as their sponsor in the shop). In return, the owners offer these recruiters such favors as smaller bundle work that they can do faster, thus making more money. This sets up a paternalistic system of personal debt and obligation—the new employee to the old employee, the old employee to the boss—that, as Chin found, actually reinforces status quo wages and work structures. By contrast, Korean shops, which do not run on similar ethnic referrals,[48] have much higher wages, since they are based on hourly rates rather than on piece rates. Moreover, workers in Chinese shops, Chin found, were less willing to complain about their bosses, even though many felt they were being "taken advantage of" by their Chinese employers.[49] It is thus obvious that the informal accommodations set up by some de- signers and sewers may produce a similar structure of debt and obligation that does not, in the end, benefit the workers.

In this sense, the sociologist Jin-Kyung Yoo may have been right to insist that the establishment of networks like those found in the apparel industry "should be considered an economic activity rather than ethnic solidarity."[50] But while it is clear that the material gains from these relationships were enjoyed almost solely by designers, it is not accurate to say that, as a result, the production system was left entirely intact. As the comments above reveal, the interactions between these constituencies, while productive and beneficial, were also at times tense, strained by designers' sense that they were not being treated like most clients. Many complained that they were too often questioned and even reprimanded, and that they were expected not to protest or dispute what they were told.[51] They argued that they were being held to different standards, but in truth they were being asked to operate within a different social order. By entering this "family," willingly or reluctantly, designers were also entering a set of obligations that weak- ened their ability to function as independent entrepreneurs—to be the ones who pay the bills and make the rules. They submitted themselves to a social order wherein economic, educational, and social advantages did not always result in unfettered authority.

By putting workers in the role of "elders"—to be heeded and endured— this performance of a family gave them a certain moral authority. This moral authority did not supplant the economic and social authority of the designers, who still had the final word, but it did offer the workers a certain amount of license, influence, and even power that cannot be thought of as meaningless. In essence, this constructed family disrupted—inverted, even—the traditional relationship of the employer to employee, the buyer to supplier. The ostensible employer was being managed in some ways by her employee—contrary to what many, including the designers themselves, might have expected.[52] Clearly, this is not a relationship of equals, but it is one that allows for a certain amount of give and take and for the occasional relinquishing rather than accumulation of power. Thus, while the intergenerational networks forged here might be seen, following Yoo, as an economic activity, it is not solely an economic activity, distinct from expressions of responsibility, interconnectivity, and perhaps even solidarity. We can see this more clearly when we examine the language that designers use to characterize these acts of exchange and consider why they have translated them into the idiom of kinship.

THE GIFT OF FASHION

According to my interviewees, the various acts of generosity and accommodation they received were, simply enough, "just a gift." I believe them, but I also know that a gift is never just a gift. A gift, as anthropologists and sociologists dating back to Marcel Mauss have said, is a complex social practice that gives expression to all kinds of institutions and social relationships. According to Mauss's seminal study, *The Gift*, in what he called archaic or primitive societies, gifts functioned to build solidarity by binding the giver and receiver together in a process of obligation and reciprocity. In Mauss's formulation, gifts are never free; though theoretically given voluntarily, they always come with an expectation of return. Their primary function is to foster social relationships and to instantiate a system of exchange and interdependency.[53] Gift giving is thus a pretense of disinterestedness and generosity that conceals the self-interest at its heart.[54]

Mauss's claims about the norms of reciprocity have been challenged and revised by other scholars, who suggest that surely not all gift givers receive, or expect to receive, something in return. Some scholars have insisted that different forms of coercions and sanctions govern different forms of gift giving: a charitable donation, for instance, carries a different set of obligations than, say, a dinner invitation.[55] Others have pointed out that reciprocity is not the only motive for gift giving; altruism and spontaneity must sometimes play a part.[56] But most studies of gifts in modern societies still posit that the purpose of the gift is to cement useful social relations or to exercise power.[57]

In offering their little gifts, were the garment workers simply exercising their self-interested expectations of reciprocity? Did their gifts come with strings attached? Perhaps these workers knew that they could get something in return: a better relationship with the designers, which could result in wage and workplace accommodations, or in a more loyal or acquiescent customer. Perhaps they understood all too well how debt and obligation worked and deliberately positioned themselves on the receiving end of such transactions. Perhaps it was they who held the upper hand all along, manipulating their younger partners into granting accommodations they would not have otherwise offered.

It is entirely possible, and in many ways satisfying, to read this relationship as one governed purely by rational self-interest. Such an interpretation makes sense and allows us to locate power in more than one site. While I do not rule this out, my sense is that there is more at work here. There may be no pure gifts, but gifts nonetheless resist rational delineation. They are disinterested, not necessarily in the sense that there is no expectation of return, but in the sense that what is given and what is received is not always equal, nor expected to be so.[58] While gifts depend on an economic system, or presuppose an economic structure, they cannot be reduced to economic concepts of losses and gains alone.[59]

Governed not by a logic of necessity, but by what David Cheal calls "moral economies"—"small worlds of personal relationships" that consist of "normative obligations to provide assistance to others"—gift giving lies beyond the realm of simple economic exchange.[60] Gifts may function in a primarily utilitarian manner, but they do so through a system of relationships that is intrinsically social.[61] Considered in this way, it is possible to see the process of helping out and the performance of family in the apparel industry as more than solely expedient—more than can be explained by the logic of market forces alone, by an assessment of the wins and losses of self-interested constituencies that characterize most discussions of the garment trade. What those types of discussions cannot capture is the moral dimension at the heart of these relationships. As the sociologist Aafke Komter has explained, there is an essential, if implicit, assumption underlying the process of gift giving: the mutual recognition of the identity of the giver and the recipient. While participants in this relationship may not go so far as to feel a "normative obligation to provide assistance," as Cheal put it, they must at the very least recognize each other as social actors who are in various ways interdependent.[62] Without this recognition, there can be no reciprocity.

This seems a fairly obvious observation, but when we recall Angela McRobbie's comment about the curious refusal of the designers she studied to acknowledge their connections to their sewers, we begin to see why Asian American designers have been able to forge relationships with Asian garment workers when other designers have not.[63] A common language, backgrounds, and so forth certainly helped, but as is evidenced by countless instances of intra-ethnic conflict seen all over the world, they do not in and of themselves enable community building. What holds these groups together is this fundamental recognition of each other as actors capable of entering into more than just market relations. In order to exchange these gifts, designers and workers had to be able to recognize each other as having more than just utilitarian value. Designers had to be able to see their producers as not just docile labor, exploited workers, or low-skill help. Without this recognition, they could not give and take as they do. They are reproducing the structure of debt and obligation, but here they deploy it to signal not just an expectation of return, but also a relationship of empathy and interdependence.

This was made clear, paradoxically, in the way that my interviewees described their formal, economic relationships with their manufacturers. Here is Thuy Diep, relating the differences she discerned between working with an Asian and a non-Asian producer:

> If I deal with another vendor, they have certain prices for certain services —no questions asked. I've worked with German people before, and they're very upfront. You know how much something will cost, and then they send you a bill. With a Korean vendor, it's like a guessing game. I'll give them an order and ask them how much. But they'll say, 'Oh it's generally this,' and when they're done they'll say, 'So how much can you give me for this?' And I'm thinking, shouldn't you be telling me how much you want? But they'll say, 'You tell us,' and then I give a number and then we go back and forth. The whole business dealing is so indirect. With them it's about the relationship. It's not about the money. It's about, really, loyalty, trust. They have to trust you, and honor is very important to them.

This account, which can be read as a stereotypical rendering of Asians' inscrutability and perhaps even their inability to master the conventions of Western capitalism, provides a good example of how even the most fundamentally economic exchanges can become more than economic. What this "back and forth" actually does is create a social, perhaps even empathetic, relationship. It is a performance that forces the designer to articulate the value of the manufacturer's labor, and the latter to access the former's economic constraints—what she is able to give. The priorities here become not just economic but also social. Though the function of this exchange is unchanged, the practice of it alters the employer-employee relationship in important ways, fostering connections that belong more to a gift economy than to a market economy.

This is not to suggest that these relationships then exist outside of the market. On the contrary, their very purpose is to enable and facilitate Asian American designers' ability to participate *in* the market. The contribution of uncompensated time, energy, imagination, and affect on the part of workers (and, to a lesser extent, designers) leads ultimately to the creation of economic value. In this sense, the relationship is not so different from the high-tech gift economy in which, as Tiziana Terranova has written, the contributions of "free labor"—"chat, real-life stories, mailing lists, news-letters, and so on"—while not given to meet economic needs, nonetheless are "part of a process of economic experimentation with the creation of monetary value out of knowledge/culture/affect."[64] Gift economies can thus be seen not as a resistance to capitalism, but as an important force in its reproduction; interpersonal relationships can likewise become central to economic relationships rather than ancillary to them.

But I want to emphasize too the importance of the social connections that these informal exchanges enable. The lesson Diep learned was reiter-ated by many of my interviewees, including Gemma Kahng, Calvin Tran, and Kelima K., who all claimed that, as Tran put it, "in the factory world it's all about loyalty and respect." They all contended that both parties need to feel that they can trust each other, and that this is the key to a successful business relationship. Kelima went so far as to say that what was needed from both parties was a commitment to "ethical behavior."

What did all this talk of trust, loyalty, respect, commitment, and respon-sibility amount to? Many of my interviewees, especially those who had been in business for a while, were indeed quite loyal to their manufac-turers. Many had stayed with the same one for nearly a decade. Others, however, told me that they kept their eyes open for "better options," or for different manufacturers who could fulfill their various needs. There was, in other words, a limit to their loyalty. Still, there was a sense that it was never just business between the designers and the manufacturers and sewers, though some of my subjects might have preferred it to be that way. Like most designers, my interviewees often shied away from any discussion of politics, which they saw as either beyond their purview as "just a designer" or as secondary to their practical economic concerns. But unlike most designers, they often spoke about obligation and responsibility—about their sense of "debt" to garment workers, their families, their "Asian upbringing," etc.—defying the typical image of an independent entrepreneur.

This recognition of interdependence sometimes translated into meaningful material exchanges, as when designers proffered their own little gifts—an extra order or special consideration for a late one. Or when they formed (limited) partnerships with their sewers, bringing them into the marketplace and helping to ameliorate some of the more taxing aspects of their labor. Rather than reproducing the status quo, this informal helping out did affect the structure of the production system.

However, in my estimation, the real worth of these exchanges lies in their bonding value. Ultimately, what designers and workers have done here is to carve out a small space where they can emphasize responsibility, loyalty, and respect—vague concepts that have far more symbolic than material value. The construction of a familial narrative helps them to do precisely this. It enables people who are essentially quite different and disconnected to imagine mutual interdependency. It allows them to forge what Marshall Sahlins would call a "generalized reciprocity," in which the expectation of return is implicit but indefinite, where giving is just as (or more) likely to arise from pleasure and spontaneity as from calculation and self-interest.[65] The language of kinship here is not meant to invoke blood and nationality, but to tap into those locations where social distance is minimized.

In creating "families" out of such disparate communities, designers cannot solve the problem of social difference, but they have brought into much closer proximity constituents traditionally seen as quite distant. Through this imagined intimacy, they can form a "thick solidarity," based on personal responsibility and direct commitment rather than abstract causes. The networks built here demand personal accountability, for these are "mothers," "sisters," "uncles," and "aunties," not abstract workers. The networks are thus by nature small and selective. After all, sympathies that exist in the family are only reluctantly, if at all, given to those outside— as the designers' lack of solidarity with Latino sewers makes evident.[66] Voluntary and makeshift, this fictive kinship structure cannot ultimately transform the garment industry. But, in its recognition of mutual responsibility and interdependence, it does represent a remarkable departure from a labor system that, as Carl Proper has shown, is based on "organized irresponsibility."[67]

What I hope to have shown here, then, is not that emotional ties are nondisciplining, or that they do not serve economic ends, but that they can also contribute to an "extramarket morality," as the political theorist Wendy Brown might call it. In her critique of the political rationality of neoliberalism, Brown has argued that neoliberalism, "while foregrounding the market, is not only or even primarily focused on the economy." It involves "the extension of market rationality to every sphere" of life, so that all judgments become reduced to a cost-benefit calculus and an instrumental rationality.[68] By undercutting the need for an extra-market morality, the political logic of neoliberalism reduces the body politic to a group of individual entrepreneurs and consumers.

In this context of a greatly diminished social and political sphere, it is important, I think, to emphasize the social connections fostered here. Born of market relationships, these networks nonetheless reprioritize the social and, crucially, reassert the relevance of moral authority within a context where power is traditionally aligned with economic and social authority. Such subtle shifts require not an acknowledgment of sameness or equivalence, but an admission of interconnectedness. It requires that actors see themselves not only as individuals but as members of a social body—however small or transitory—who bear both liberties and burdens and who can see each other if not as kin, then at least as allies.

CONCLUSION

I remember once waiting as one of my interviewees dropped off a sample for a contractor. She told me it would take only a few seconds, but the exchange took a full thirty-five minutes. From where I sat, I could see that they were chatting, but not about the sample; she did not proffer it for some time. When she left, she was carrying some sort of a trinket. She explained that the contractor had gotten it on a recent visit to China, to the same province where her family had come from. He thought she would like it. She said that it was sweet of him, that her parents would be thrilled, and that she would keep the trinket in her studio. It was a small offering, but I could tell by the look on her face that for her it truly was a gift.

To think of these exchanges, these instances of give and take, these moments of helping out, as a gift is to see how the bits left over or left behind, and the accommodations large and small, are significant above and beyond their use value. There is certainly material worth to the relationships that designers and workers have forged with each other. But in many ways the relationships are not rational, for they do not hew to rules of equivalence, calculations of losses and gains, or the logic of necessity. It would be difficult to argue that workers get enough in return for their support, or that designers absolutely need this extra help. The value of the gift lies instead in the social bonds it fosters.

Seeing their relationship in this way helps to explain an anomaly in the fashion industry, but perhaps more important, it sheds new light on the broader question of social solidarity within Asian America. In fashion, the privileging of ethnic connections—of a perceived common culture—between designers and producers can recreate some of the central problems of ethnic coalition building that have plagued Asian America.[69] These efforts at community building can, as many scholars have demonstrated, often mask the inequalities of power within the community, disguising the divisions and competition that can exist among people of different social positions.

While the relationships discussed here are certainly not equal, they cannot be dismissed as simply naive or, worse, exploitative. If Asian American designers were able and willing to cooperate with manufacturers in this way only because they were Asian, they were not doing so out of some essentialized understanding of their culture. The Asian American designers I spoke to often did see themselves as different from their non-Asian colleagues and pointed to many reasons for this: having had parents who worked in the industry, not having been trained at fashion institutes, feeling pressure from parents who wanted them to do something more "practical," feeling the stigma of having to literally wear their ethnicities on their sleeves,[70] and so on. This difference, however, was not marked as a racial difference, since many felt uncomfortable labeling themselves in those terms, at least in speaking to me.[71] Even in such matters as their ability to speak Chinese or Korean, these designers never referred to it as an innate ability emerging from their ethnic background—presumably because none of them were fluent—but as a learned skill.

If Asian American designers see themselves as a distinct group at all, it is only in their relationship with their producers—in the ways they see sewers differently (as skilled rather than unskilled) and in the ways they are treated differently by them—as daughters or sisters, rather than as abstract clients. This community is generated actively (through the traffic of material resources) and provisionally (in those moments of exchange). It is worth noting that Asian American designers do not see themselves as necessarily linked to other Asian American designers, who are, in theory, their equals. In fact, they often resent being lumped together solely on the basis of their ethnic identity. It is only in thinking and performing their identities as these workers' "children" that they regard themselves as part of a collectivity. This performance entailed the cultivation of perceived commonalities —of language, background, and purpose. But this intimacy exists because of and not in spite of their different occupational locations. It is only because they occupy these different positions that they can form this productive relationship. In the end, it is the differences that hold this group together; this family works by strategically deploying its members' diverse resources.

Recognizing this helps to shed new light on some of the central questions within the field of Asian American studies: What holds this fragile coalition together? How can we even talk about unity (cultural, political, and otherwise) among a population as diverse as this one? Scholars have hypothesized that at different times and among different constituencies it has been shared histories of struggle, political utility, cultural similarities, and willful performance that have bound people together. To these explanatory models we have to add the insights gathered here. Social differences can be less of a barrier to collectivity than social distance. Connections can happen when we can see each other as intimates, and when we can extend to each other something like a gift. Perhaps what holds Asian Americans together, then, are the small, voluntary acts of unequal exchange, which broadcast the mutual interdependence of giver and receiver and foster in each something like a commitment.

Part II

Chapter 3

THE CULTURAL ECONOMY OF ASIAN CHIC

In 1673, the French paper *Le Mercure* reported that a new style of coat—a manteau—painted with exotic flowers and imported from China had become all the rage in Paris. Fashionable women wore the coats everywhere, despite their relatively casual style, and begged for them from shops throughout the city. They were first introduced by a merchant named Gaultier, a fabric importer, and as the demand for these "Chinese coats" escalated, *Le Mercure* urged readers to buy theirs only from Gaultier, where they could be assured of the object's authenticity. Imitations of these popular garments were already circulating, and readers were warned against these lesser quality items, whose flowers were reportedly printed rather than painted onto the fabric. In the decades following, clothes made from Chinese fabric became so popular that the court of Louis XIV, which saw the material as a threat to both the French textile industry and French profits, made the sale of Oriental imports illegal and ordered local textile manufacturers "to imitate and thereby eliminate" foreign fabrics.[1]

Impassioned as they were, the tastes of these seventeenth-century Parisians were hardly idiosyncratic. Textiles and apparel were among the first and most prominent items to be exchanged between the East and West, but Oriental goods of various kinds—porcelains and fans, shawls and screens, objets d'art large and small—were very popular at the time and became increasingly so with the expansion of European trade and colonialism, and the rise of the importation and reproduction industries.[2] The manteau craze was just one moment in this larger history, but it was a crucial moment for the student of fashion. As the scholar Joan DeJean has pointed out, the manteau gave France's nascent couture industry not just a new form, but a new mode of dress: casual wear.[3] Moreover, it allowed couturiers—a new class of artisans formed by the 1675 couturiers' trade guild, who were barred from designing formal dresses for aristocratic women—to build an empire based on the production of casual clothing for the nonaristocratic and, in so doing, to usher in modern fashion.[4]

That a "Chinese coat" could inspire such a sartorial and social transformation gives some indication of the central role that the East has played in the formation of Western fashion. As both a material and symbolic resource, it was always there, in the fabric of the manteau and in the imagination of the couturiers. The prevalence of these exotic influences has certainly ebbed and flowed throughout fashion's history, but they were a persistent presence. At the end of the twentieth century they returned to prominence, as so-called Asian-inspired fashion began appearing in runway collections and on mass-market racks alike, and as magazines, museums, galleries, and publishers all struggled to make sense of their most recent revival.[5] Emerging in the United States alongside an expansion of the popular interest in all things Asian—from yoga and feng shui to Hong Kong cinema and Japanese anime—this revival seemed to confirm what commentators at the time were saying: we were witnessing the "Asianization of America."[6]

At the same time that chinoiserie-clad models were filling the pages of fashion magazines, Asian students were filing into classes at Parsons and FIT, and young designers were setting up downtown boutiques and midtown showrooms. While some had already gained prominence by the 1990s—Anna Sui, Yeohlee Teng, Vera Wang, Gemma Kahng among them—it was really from the mid-1990s to the mid-2000s, the decade of Asian chic, that Asian American designers began to emerge as a force in the industry. This rare convergence—between the taste for Asian chic and the prevalence of Asian American designers—provides a unique opportunity to consider how this symbolic context shaped the material conditions of possibility for young Asian American designers.

In arguing that these two phenomena are linked, I do not mean to suggest that the work of Asian American designers should be understood in relation to the problematic of Asian chic alone. These designers are, after all, influenced and constrained by the same forces that affect everyone in the industry. By asking questions about their relationship to this moment, when the signs of Asianness were so visible, my intention is not to suggest that they should be defined by these discourses. I mean, instead, to make clear how the sartorial imagination produced Asianness as a fashionable commodity and how Asian American designers were, as a result, able to access Asianness as a resource, in George Yúdice's terms, to be utilized for instrumental ends.[7] Though neither of these phenomena caused the other, they certainly put pressure on each other. To the extent that Asian American designers participated in these style trends, they were both helped and hindered by fashion's interests in the East; when they resisted, ideas about Asianness nonetheless informed their work, though often in quite surprising ways.

Since the ideas about Asianness that were generated, challenged, and transformed during this time inevitably framed the ways Asian Americans were understood, within fashion and beyond, in this chapter I want, first, to consider the contours of those productions. What did Asian chic look like during this period? The anthropologists Carla Jones and Ann Marie Leshkowich have characterized Asian chic as "the utopian and euphoric embrace of elements of particular Asian traditions that have now come to stand in for an undifferentiated Asia."[8] But which elements did this include, and, more importantly, why were they embraced?

Following this, I want to reflect on what the obsession with the elements, icons, and styles of this undifferentiated Asia might say about American culture at this time. Many scholars have argued that in the United States, such periodic embraces of the East—of goods from Asia; of American films, literature, and performances about Asia; of missionary accounts and world's fairs that served as a documentation of life in Asia—have fulfilled different purposes at different times.[9] In some moments, these practices of consumption worked to shore up Americans' sense of difference from, and superiority to, these othered cultures. At other times, though, the practices engendered in Americans a spirit of affiliation, a sympathetic connection to a culture they were struggling to understand. Christina Klein has shown, for instance, that during the cold war, when America was attempting to forge an identity as both a global nation and a nonimperialist nation, middle-brow cultural productions about Asia—from Reader's Digest to The King and I—helped to foster in Americans an intellectual and emotional relationship with the very countries that the United States was attempting to form political relationships.[10] This cosmopolitan sensibility allowed Americans to be both sympathetic to these nations and supportive of the expansion of U.S. power over them. In this sense, consumption of Asianness has historically been quite fraught, expressing at once affiliation and subjugation. What operations of domination and desire, distance and intimacy, were at work in the U.S. revival of Asianness during these last two decades?

This most recent embrace of Asianness has been no less ambivalent than its predecessors. As I will show, though Asian chic was ostensibly an expression of appreciation for Asian sartorial traditions, the production of Asianness in these sites actually worked to reinforce its inferior position within the dominant cultural hierarchy. This has been achieved in part through what Arjun Appadurai has called a "cultural economy of distance," in which exotic goods are posited as desirable and valuable because they exist at a cultural remove.[11] Consumption of these goods, far from suggesting an intimacy with the cultures from which they purportedly emerged, demands a certain amount of distance: it is precisely because they are geographically and culturally distant that consumers have the cultural capital to see the value of these exotic objects and the economic capital to purchase them.

In this context, then, the production of fashion as a symbolic good relies on a similar logic of distance that has structured its material production. Yet, I argue, the resurgence of Asian chic during this period should not be read simply as a reiteration of Americans' cultural power, of their historically privileged position on the high-low, north-south divide. It should also be seen as an expression of a certain anxiety about their status in an increasingly globalized world. At a time when politicians and pundits continually worried about U.S. economic losses and Asia's attendant gains, Americans were repeatedly reminded not of their distinctions from the East but of their connection to it. If Asian chic could help to symbolically shore up their sense of distance from and superiority to Asia, the discourse of global competition served as a reminder that such detachments could not be maintained, and such victories could not be ensured. As designers began to outsource not just their manufacturing but their inspirations to Asia, these centuries-old images and discourses were put into the service of new cultural needs. They were used to alleviate the anxiety of global competition by offering consumers a way to be both untainted by modernity and at its cutting edge, both beneficiaries of globalization and untouched by its forces.

Seen in this light, Asian chic can be understood as a symbolic resolution to the dilemma of global interconnectedness, which has enriched American consumers with a world of goods but has also opened them up to a world of competition. In the face of such inescapable intimacy, it provided a means to reassert distance and distinction, even as such efforts were belied by Americans' everyday lives. Both a diagnosis of and a cure for this cultural anxiety, it structured Asia always as a place out there, an ideal to be revered or reviled.

In this chapter, I trace the shifting strategies of representation that have been used to articulate this rhetoric of distance. These representations, I argue, set the context for Asian Americans' engagement with the signs of Asianness. To be sure, Asian American designers certainly contributed to these constructions as well. Yet, as subsequent chapters will reveal, their work failed to hew entirely to such a logic of distance. In various ways, these designers struggled to forge connections to Asia (and beyond), materially and symbolically, and to assert the types of transnational intimacies precluded by Asian chic. Employing what I have called an aesthetic of intimacy, they fashioned a diasporic imagination that challenged the operations of the fashion market even as it was driven by it.

FASHION'S EXOTICS

It is something of an understatement to say that Western designers have been greatly inspired by the East. The history of fashion is littered with collections decorated in Eastern motifs, constructed with its fabrics, or borrowing from its forms. The work of Paul Poiret (the so-called King of Fashion), for instance, was infused with such Oriental styles and imagery. At the beginning of the twentieth century, Poiret established himself as a fashion innovator by banishing the corset and offering women such innovations as the *jupe culotte* (1909), a variation on the harem pant, and the hobble skirt (1911), a long, narrow column with a tight band around the knees to constrict women's movement to something resembling a geisha's gait. He went on to contribute to Western fashion the kimono shape, the turban, and other elements drawn from his vision of the Orient.

Following on the heels of Poiret, designers like Madeleine Vionnet, considered one of the twentieth century's greatest couturiers, was inspired by the kimono to reinvent the way clothes were constructed, with minimal cutting and draping. Jeanne Lanvin also took cues from the East, creating dresses with large, flowing sleeves in the manner of the kimono. Charles Worth and Coco Chanel were both fond of using chrysanthemum prints and other exotic fabrics.[12] The list goes on. These influences waned during the Second World War—when European designers began to hark back to the nineteenth-century forms that represented to them the golden age of European culture—but reappeared during the 1960s, with the rise of youth culture and the emergence of street styles.[13] Yves Saint Laurent, for instance, launched a chinoiserie collection in 1974 that turned fashion's attention back East. In fashion, as in other forms of cultural production, Asia has been a long-standing, if episodic, part of the European imagination.

Such visions of the Orient were transplanted to the American context by U.S. businesses eager to sell the latest European looks. In the early twentieth century, well-known merchants like the Gimbel brothers, R. H. Macy, and John Wannamaker all imported gowns from the leading European couture houses each season. These merchants made much of their relationship with designers like Poiret, staging elaborate in-store fashion shows to present his latest creations, while customers stood in line for hours just to catch a glimpse.[14] Though it is not accurate to claim that fashion's Orientalism was imported entirely from Europe—American designers like Elizabeth Hawes and Bonnie Cashin were also borrowing motifs and techniques from the East in the 1930s—it is safe to say that European designers were its most active and persuasive proponents.

Indeed, the influence of Poiret and other European couturiers on the U.S. fashion landscape cannot be overstated. By the 1890s, American socialites were travelling annually to Paris to see the collections and order their wardrobes. Reporters for *Vogue* and *Harper's Bazaar* were stationed there, ready to send back the latest sketches. Department stores were setting up buying offices in Europe so that they could advertise the latest looks, "direct from Paris." Parisian designers so dominated the American scene that U.S. dressmakers often adopted French names and used French labels in order to boost sales. Though various efforts were waged to fight Parisian hegemony and to encourage the support of "American Fashions for American Women," as one reform campaign was called, U.S. fashion mavens refused to give up their place in what they saw, according to Kristin Hoganson, as an international "imagined community of dress."[15] Until the decades following the Second World War, U.S. fashion took all its cues from Paris.

Thanks to the efforts of fashion retailers, manufacturers, and journalists and of local and state governments, those circumstances have changed. New York is now also a center of fashion, hosting its own fashion week and boasting a cadre of internationally recognized designers. Yet, while the U.S. fashion industry has greatly expanded since the war, and no one city—not even Paris—can dictate fashions by itself, European designers are still very much in vogue. Like Poiret before them, these designers still court U.S. consumers and, as evidenced by the dominant presence of Chanel and Prada on Fifth Avenue and in the pages of the U.S. *Vogue,* the fashionable continue to heed their calls. U.S. fashion magazines still faithfully report the latest trends from Paris and Milan and the shows in these cities remain a must-see for any critic worth his or her weight. Though each of these fashion cities has its particular history and structures and reflects its unique cultural and social milieus, they all intermingle, at least for the "imagined community of dress." It is possible to think of them together, as a collective force in fashion, sharing trends, styles, and visions—of the Orient and much more.

The zeal with which Asian chic returned to the United States in the 1990s was certainly spurred on as much by developments in European fashion as it was by those in the United States, and in many ways this return inspired the same passions and perils that could be seen in 1670s Paris. Like those Parisians, U.S. consumers were thrilled at their cultural adventures into the East. But they were far less happy about the economic and political ramifications of the shifting balance in cultural trade, and some called for government intervention that, at times, sounded not so different from the French king's dictates. The reemergence of Asian chic—called by any other name—always carries with it these earlier historical precedents and associations. Yet this discursive formation also continually intersects with new, historically specific material practices and, as a result, changes its nature as it expands its connections. How was it shaped by the material practices of this new context, which were framed in large part by the cultural, political, and economic shifts wrought, or at least intensified, by the forces of globalization? How were these expressed by the images, ideas, meanings, and metaphors generated during this time?

In order to address these questions, I turned to the pages of popular fashion magazines, where discourses of Asianness were circulated far more systematically than in any single designer's collection or event. The trend reports, fashion advice, designer profiles, and advertising campaigns that the magazines contained all helped to shape a visual vernacular of Asianness. During the 1990s, narratives of Asian chic could be found in all types of magazines—from fashion to home furnishing, from lifestyle to literary. But in order to mark the changes and continuities in these representations, I focused in particular on three publications—*Vogue*, *Harper's Bazaar*, and *Elle*—all blue-chip U.S. fashion magazines, each with a slightly different focus and audience.[16] I looked at the issues from 1990 to 2005, a total of 529 issues.[17] Taking such a longitudinal approach allowed me to look back to the beginning of the decade in which Asian chic thrived and up to the time after September 11, 2001, when the foreign and exotic became less politically acceptable. Here I was taking note of the prevalence of images of Asian chic, their shift in meaning over time, and the ideas about Asianness that they assembled. How did these publications construct knowledge about Asia and, more precisely, its significance in Americans' daily lives?

It is difficult to talk about fashion's representation without referring to Roland Barthes, whose *Fashion System* offered seminal insights into the reading of the fashion magazine. Barthes understood clothing to have three forms: technological ("the real garment," or the material object), image (the photograph of the garment), and written (the description of the garment). Though each of these forms refers to the same reality, they are distinct entities. The image and written clothing that appeared in the fashion magazine were, for Barthes, entirely different from the "real garment," since each relied on a different structure of signification. The former he considered to be translations of the latter.[18]

In drawing clear distinctions between real and image clothing, Barthes was offering an implicit critique of photographic truth—an insight that has become a cornerstone of much scholarship in visual studies. But, for me, the usefulness of this semiotic formulation lies less in what it can teach us about reading fashion's image than in what it might suggest about the production of fashion itself. Acknowledging that clothing has distinct forms makes it possible to see how magazines are themselves manufacturers of fashion: they produce image and written clothing. These garments, which enable and articulate fashion's symbolic value, are more easily and widely consumed than the real thing. As we know, magazines engage in acts of translation and interpretation; Barthes helps us to see that in doing so, they are also generating objects of consumption, a fashion commodity that coexists with but also exceeds the material object.

It is this fashion commodity that actually frames how consumers see Asian chic. After all, these ideas are not for the most part formulated through observations of "the real garment," to which few have access. Nor are they always self-evident to the designers or their customers, who often do not intentionally participate, or fail to see that they participate, in constructing discourses about Asianness. Editors, marketers, and advertisers serve as the cultural intermediaries whose acts of presentation and representation construct the value of fashion as a symbolic good.[19] Recall that it was *Le Mercure* and not Gaultier that set the standards of authenticity and desirability for the "Chinese coat." Then as now, it is these intermediaries who offer up the most articulate and comprehensive visions of Asian chic. The Asian-inspired fashions they have to offer—manufactured through words and pictures—are, far more than the real thing, the objects that can convey most clearly how to see Asia—what it looks like and why it is desirable.

NATURAL AFFINITIES

If fashion magazines were the most articulate about these matters, they still struggled at first to find the right words. Between 1990 and 2005, there was not one year in which so-called Asian influences—or elements that could in retrospect be categorized as such—failed to find their way into a fashion spread, article, editorial, or advertisement.[20] In the spring and fall of 1994, the fall of 1997, the spring of 1998, the fall of 2003, and the spring of 2004—the peak years, as calculated simply by the number of times that elements of Asian chic appeared in fashion spreads, editorials, advertisements, and so on—Asian influences could be found in nearly every issue.[21] But the content of the term "Asian"—and its cognates such as "exotic," "ethnic," "Oriental," and "Eastern"—shifted within the course of the decade and a half. These changes reflected not just a different understanding of the East, but a different conception of the West's relationship to it.

At the beginning of the 1990s, the terms "exotic," "ethnic," and "Eastern" were quite supple, elastic enough to refer to vast geographies—from North Africa to the Middle East, from East Asia to South Asia—and ethnicities including Native American and African as well as Asian. A 1991 *Vogue* note on Yves Saint Laurent, for instance, described the designer's assortment of "long scarves" and "harem trousers" as a "fantasy of . . . the Orient." The accompanying images showed clothes embellished by beading most commonly associated with Africa and models donning head wear reminiscent of the Moroccan fez, and the prints were revealed to be "YSL's own drawings" from his 1980 vacation to Marrakesh.[22] That same year, *Vogue*'s piece on "the lure of the East" in home décor cast "Indo-Persian

Orient express "Betty Catroux and Loulou de La Falaise Klossowski are always my inspirations," observes **Yves Saint Laurent,** "though for different reasons." He says Catroux represents "rigor and the discipline of fine tailoring"—the kind of style that showed up in graphic navy-and-white sailor looks and pea coats in the first half of his collection. He calls Klossowski "*féerique,* the fantasy of exotic dreams, the Orient"—which made up the second part of the collection. To heighten the point, YSL drew inspiration from "the deep erotic romance of Léon Bakst" (his odalisque for the ballet *Scheherazade,* RIGHT). Models drifted down the catwalk swathed in long scarves and in harem trousers made of Bakst-like prints that were actually YSL's own drawings he made while on vacation in Marrakesh in 1980.

Material girl Madonna (OPPOSITE PAGE, center, at the MTV Awards rehearsals) is the Andy Warhol of fashion's young rat pack. Not only did she sit in the front row of **Jean Paul Gaultier**'s last show in Paris, but she had Gaultier prance onstage during her Blond Ambition tour. "I was hyperemotional that night when I walked onstage in Bercy and the crowd cheered me," Gaultier says. "When Madonna then thanked me for being her designer, I was shaking at the knees." The singer, he says, was an inspiration because of her intelligence, energy, and vitality. To Deee-Lite's "Power of Love," Gaultier showed fuchsia silk walking suits with matching Marie Antoinette wigs in a brilliant synthesis of underground irreverence and humor. "Life must be lived in the pink at all times," Gaultier jokes. "Even dreams should be thought of as a wonderful life filled with color."

Figure 1 Yves Saint Laurent's "fantasy" of the Orient, *Vogue,* January 1991.

throne-style sofas," "antique kilims," "Turkish pillows," and "Japanese screens" all as elements of "the East." The article instructed readers to add a "hint of exoticism" to their homes by inserting decorative elements culled from anywhere in North Africa, Turkey, Iran, southern Spain, and the Middle East.[23]

In these accounts, the East was drawn from an older Orientalist imagination, one in which a vast range of cultural and geographic locations could be collapsed into an undifferentiated non-West. The specifics were unimportant; it was the sense of difference that mattered. At the beginning of the decade, Egypt could be labeled "an exotic backdrop," as could Russia. Floral prints could be "ethnic," as could gold trims, African textiles, and obis.[24] Such lack of distinctions meant that a spread on "Indian-oriented" clothing could include both a Nehru jacket from the subcontinent and a fringed top commonly associated with Native American dress (the latter, indeed, could later be found in a layout on fashion's "tribal influences").[25] The East existed, for the most part, as a set of differences, the contours of which were relatively fluid.[26]

By the mid-1990s, however, as the interest in Asian chic grew, the Western sartorial imagination became increasingly focused on China, Japan, and India, though such distinctions were often collapsed as well. In 1994, European couturiers like John Galliano, Jean Paul Gaultier, Yves Saint Laurent, and Martine Sitbon, as well as American designers like Ralph Lauren, turned out collections filled with silk dresses in kimono shapes, tunics with intricate embroidery, and wool coats with mandarin collars. These collections, which drew clearly on sartorial forms associated with South and East Asia, made their cultural references explicit. Editors, quick to spot a trend, responded with a slew of headlines about these forays into the East: "Passage to India" and "Eastern Exposure" (*Harper's Bazaar*), "Orient Express" (*Vogue* and *Elle*), and "Indian Summer" (*Vogue*) are just a few from that year.

But while magazines could not ignore the prominence of the East, they (and their readers) were circumspect about how to treat this fascination with other cultures. The use of Eastern elements and styles in these collections was hardly new—Yves Saint Laurent's 1974 chinoiserie collection was a recent forebear—but they now occurred in a new historical context. In the United States, this context included a tremendous increase in immigration from Asia—as a result of a series of legislative changes, beginning with the Immigration and Nationality Act of 1965—and an expansion of the political rhetoric of multiculturalism, as a result of the demands made by the civil rights movement. Where previously images of Asianness traveled in the absence of a significant Asian population, in the 1990s they coexisted with an Asian presence—an increasingly politicized presence that was acutely felt in urban centers and fashion cities. In this post–civil rights moment, when discourses of multiculturalism were flourishing, cultural sensitivity was a widely held if ultimately politically empty sentiment. Was it permissible at this time to speak of a particular ethnic look without appearing to participate in ethnic chauvinism?

In light of these material conditions, audiences were at first reticent about fashion's move eastward. Responses to the use of Asian elements at first suggested a certain anxiety, or at least apprehension, about their propriety. When Ralph Lauren debuted his Mao-inspired navy suits in a runway show with models wearing "rice paddy" hats, for instance, *The New*

Figure 2 From the collection of Jean Paul Gaultier, "cultural marauder," *Harper's Bazaar*, January 1994.

York Times deemed it "inappropriate," tantamount to an ethnic joke.[27] This response led one writer to denounce the U.S. fashion industry, unlike its European counterpart, as one "confined by the boundaries of political correctness."[28] These comments suggest that at least initially there was some uneasiness and confusion about how to interpret signs of Asianness.

Amidst this confusion, fashion magazines—especially the advertisers who filled their pages—took up the task of cultural intermediary, helping consumers to decipher this new sartorial world. It was they who helped to frame fashion's return to Asian chic in the 1990s as more cultural appreciation than cultural exploitation. The magazines did so primarily by presenting the rampant use of Asian elements as an expression of designers' cosmopolitan interests and, ultimately, their cultural knowledge. Writing about Gaultier's collection, for instance, *Harper's Bazaar* defended the self-described "cultural marauder" with the comforting claim that "his appropriation of other cultures is never irreverent; it is completely sincere, executed with an almost anthropological precision." The accompanying images show models wearing Gaultier's creations but adorned with head-dresses, nose piercings, and elaborate jewelry to suggest a native look.[29]

The reference to anthropology here was not accidental, for readers were encouraged to think of these designers as something like ethnographers and their creations as something like cultural artifacts. This was especially clear in the advertisements from the time. In 1994, when Gaultier, Kenar, Ralph Lauren, and Chopard Casmir (a fragrance brand) launched campaigns to introduce their Asian-themed collections, the ads all situated these goods within their supposed "native" context. With the exception of Ralph Lauren, who styled his models with "authentic" accessories—the aforementioned rice paddy hats—the ads all pictured Asian-inspired items in ambiguous exotic locales. In doing so, they removed the clothes from their social context and remade these Western sartorial inventions into approximations of local dress, not so different from the "native costumes" worn by the people who shared the fashion model's frame. Kenar's ad, for instance, featured a white woman wearing a tunic, standing bare-legged in a sea of anonymous Asian children. In the series of photos that comprise the ad, she is framed in more or less the same manner—at the center, surrounded by an authenticating backdrop. In one she stands against a large tree, bordered by lush tropical scenery; in another, she is in an open-air market. The precise location of this exotic place is unclear, but viewers' suspicions are confirmed when in the final page the model is pictured wearing a cheongsam, holding a fan, and standing next to a portrait of the Asian icon Bruce Lee.[30]

Chopard's campaign, which also sent its heroine to an exotic locale, went even further in gesturing toward this anthropological mode. The ad featured the model India Hicks and was structured to resemble a series of personal photographs taken from her trip abroad. Juxtaposed alongside posed photos of Hicks are snapshots of local fauna, architecture, and arti-facts that are reminiscent of the random pictures a tourist might take. "A would-be travel photographer," the text read, "India Hicks has filled dozens of photo albums with visual reminders of her journeys, including a much-beloved trip to the magical country that shares her name."[31]

The use of native landscape and people in these ads, conveyed through the medium and metaphor of photography, gives the impression of first-hand knowledge, of experiential immersion. Drawing on a quasi-naturalist aesthetic, they bear more than a passing resemblance to the colonial photo-

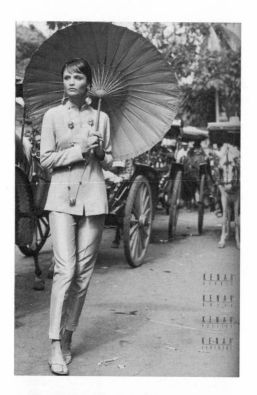

Figures 3.1 and 3.2 Advertisement for Kenar, *Vogue*, March 1994.

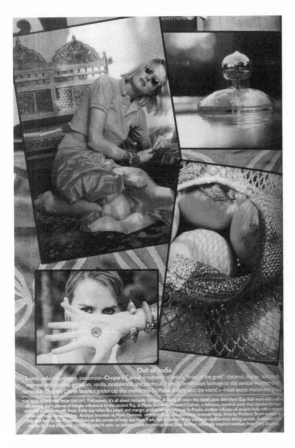

Figure 4 Advertisement for Chopard, *Vogue*, May 1994.

graphs of the past. Those images, which similarly placed Western subjects in foreign settings and alongside natives, were meant to serve as documentations of life in the colonies.[32] Presented as artifacts brought back from an adventure abroad, these ads too exposed mysterious, unknown lands in their naked truth, thrilling consumers with their details and intimate knowledge.

Of course, these fashionable productions were always more fanciful than real, as Richard Martin and Harold Koda's long history of fashion's Orientalism makes plain.[33] But it is important to note that as fanciful as the invention of Asianness was in this early part of the decade, its chief metaphors were of realism, naturalism, and authenticity. These productions sought to present fashion's ideologically charged images as objective reality. There are some striking formal similarities between these advertisements and the Orientalist paintings of the nineteenth-century realists.

These include the visual absence of other Western presence; the nostalgic and idealized setting that is both lush and decaying; and, most crucially, the centrality of the Western female figure. Models in these ads form the center around which the natives circulate, and their moral and economic authority is established—in the classic Orientalist mode described by the art historian Linda Nochlin—through the juxtaposition of their lightness and the darkness of the people and landscape surrounding them.[34]

These strategies of representation worked ultimately to reestablish the dominance of the Western consumer, largely by reminding them of their social and economic distance from the people and places depicted. While these images encouraged a sense of proximity—of having been there—they also reinforced a "cultural economy of distance."[35] The exotic setting interpolates the readers (and potential buyers) as cosmopolitan elites, whose temporary appearance at these sites as explorers and thrill seekers is made possible only by the cultural and economic capital they accrued by having come from elsewhere. Thus, the consumption of these advertised goods could both give them safe passage to the East and reaffirm their superior positions in the West.

In this context, while Asian chic was marketed as an appreciation of and desire for knowledge about the East, it worked to construct Asia's peoples and places as distant from and inferior to the West. Such representations endured throughout the years I examine. But the aesthetic of realism that dominated depictions of Asian chic during the early part of the decade ceased to captivate designers and their cultural intermediaries by its end. This shift in strategies of representation was not, as I will detail below, just an indication of changing fashions, but a reflection of a different imagination of America's relationship to Asia and the world at large.

THE DESIGNER AND THE REAL: OUTSOURCING INSPIRATION

By 1997, Asian chic was in full swing, and the cheongsam was the hit of the year. The actress Nicole Kidman wore a pea-green version from Christian Dior to the Oscars and won rave reviews for it. Prada's "updated" (essentially, shortened) cheongsam was the star of countless fashion spreads. Chanel, Christian Lacroix, Christian Dior, MaxMara, Fendi, Dolce and Gabbana, Ellen Tracy, Liz Claiborne, Bisou Bisou, Donna Karan, Nicole Miller, Etro, and Gucci, among others, presented collections with various Asian-influenced flourishes—a frog closure here, a splash of embroidery there. Advertising campaigns from stores like Neiman Marcus posed models as calendar girls, awash in rosy hues, hair held up by chopsticks, wearing mandarin-collared dresses and carrying paper umbrellas. Early that year, *Vogue* predicted that there would be "a major Asian influence" in fashion; the following year it confirmed that "chinoiserie" had indeed been one of the "7 musts of '97."[36]

By the end of the decade, Asian chic had become the lingua franca of fashion. In one indication of its entrenchment in the fashion vocabulary, various consumer goods companies began to use the language of Asian chic even when they were not advertising Asian-inspired items. For instance, an ad for hair gel by Salon Selectives showed a woman in a cheong-sam, carrying chopsticks, standing in what appears to be a Chinese restaurant.[37] A promotion for Reebok showed an image of a cowboy wearing sneakers with the caption "Western classic" next to one of a geisha, titled "Eastern classic."[38] An ad for Virginia Slims showed a geisha enjoying that brand of cigarette.[39] Perhaps the most striking of these was the ad for Ebel watches featuring the entertainer Madonna, her hands hennaed and extended to show her watch.[40] From 1996 to 2000, there were ten campaigns by major consumer-goods companies using such imagery in *Vogue*, *Harper's Bazaar*, and *Elle* alone. Though none of these companies was selling any specifically Asian-influenced item, they used the idiom of Asian chic to present their products as similarly stylish and desirable.

A mere three years after Ralph Lauren was chastised for making an ethnic joke, Asian chic was being celebrated without justifications or apologies. In fact, in a speedy about-face, fashion magazines completely abandoned the discourse of authenticity that had sought to rationalize acts of Western sartorial borrowing. The magazines no longer sought to assert some indexical relationship between designer creations and their professed cultural source. Quite to the contrary, these publications fully embraced the designers' interpretations of Asian themes and motifs as value-adding, creative acts. When Western designers culled ideas from Eastern sources they were, according to *Vogue*, "transforming [the] fashion," "reinterpret[ing] chinoiserie in a manner more cutting edge than costume."[41]

Concomitant with this shift, fashion spreads during this period began distinguishing between "designer versions" of Asian chic and "the real thing," or supposedly authentic clothing from Asia. A piece in *Harper's Bazaar* on "chinoiserie-chic," for instance, advised readers that if they could not afford Jean Paul Gaultier's jacket and pants at $1,200, they should head to Chinatown stores like Pearl River Mart, where they could find a similar—

and purportedly more authentic—outfit for a mere $35.[42] These "real things" were more often than not made in Chinatown, of course. But the boundaries being drawn between "the designer" and "the real" were not, in fact, about establishing notions of cultural origins or authenticity. Rather, they were being employed to establish economic value, the financial worth of the Western designers' so-called creative input.

In distinguishing between Western "interpretations" and Eastern "costume," magazines like these were, first, drawing the line between what counted as fashion and what was merely dress, clothing, garments, or a variety of other words that have been used to describe non-Western attire. At a time when Asia, with the exception of Japan, was still considered to have no fashion, the incorporation of these ethnic touches constituted not an appropriation of Eastern dress, but the elevation of it—the transformation of stagnant traditions into objects of modern life. An editorial in *Elle* made this distinction clear: "While the [Asian-inspired floral motifs] take a leaf from traditional chinoiserie, the bold ways they are designed and worn are clearly modern."[43]

More importantly, this lauding of the Western designer's ability to turn the raw materials of Eastern sartorial traditions into the stuff of style was an important way of establishing fashion's value. By highlighting the work of design—through the use of such terms as "reinterpretation" and "transformation"—these publications were helping to highlight the designer's value-adding function, a function that was not always immediately apparent. To most readers, the Prada cheongsam probably looks remarkably like "the real thing." Comments like these, by a New York socialite gushing about Prada's 1997 collection, helped to establish the crucial difference: "I've always admired the cheongsam but . . . I think Prada did a special thing. I love the dress and the reaction I get wearing it."[44]

These distinctions helped to rationalize the tremendous difference in price. (That the real always cost considerably less than the designer's version is a clear indication of their relative place in this fashion hierarchy.)[45] But more important, they helped to reestablish the sanctity of the global apparel value chain. As Richard Appelbaum and others have explained, in this value chain, the designer and the retailer (located primarily in the West) are positioned at the very top because they participate in what are considered the higher-value functions. Designers are considered to contribute to the production process their knowledge of consumer markets and, to a larger extent, their innate creativity; their value lies in their creative input.[46]

If the designer is the creative genius, then his or her creation must be seen as original and unique. But fashion is by nature notoriously unoriginal. Designers recycle styles, forms, and images; they admit to (or are exposed as) being inspired by, even borrowing from, other sources. These are accepted norms. When, for instance, the Balenciaga designer Nicholas Ghesquiere was revealed by *The Smoking Gun* to have copied almost exactly a vest created three decades earlier by the artist and designer Kaisik Wong, the fashion press defended Ghesquiere by claiming that all designers draw inspiration from elsewhere.

This reinforcement of the designer's autonomous role belies the fact that fashion is created by a process of assemblage, both materially (garments are put together in pieces across continents) and symbolically (designs are inspired by various far-flung sources). Moreover, it denies the possibility that these other sources amount to a type of creative input. But to be inspired by Asia is also to extract value from its culture. In the rampant cultural borrowing that characterized Asian chic, Asia served as more than just inspiration; it was a resource that Western designers could utilize for their own economic ends. In much the same way that Hollywood's remakes of Asian film, like *The Grudge* and *The Ring*, can be considered a form of outsourcing, Western designers' remaking of Asian styles can be thought of as a form of cultural subcontracting.[47]

This cultural outsourcing threatened to radically destabilize the Euro-American fashion industries. With their manufacturing all but lost to places like Asia, these industries had to hold onto their dominance in the realm of cultural production. They had to reassert the idea of their designers as individual creative geniuses; without this mythology, they could not hold onto their elite place at the top of the apparel value chain. The discourses produced by fashion magazines at this time sought to shore up these claims precisely because they were under threat. In the face of such rampant unoriginality, the magazines strove to reestablish the designer as genius precisely because that identity was in crisis. Doing so also required that they continually reassert Asia's place in the high-low fashion divide, resulting in the creation of a particular economy of Asian chic wherein, defying the much-cited Benjaminian dictate, the copy would always be valued above the original, the aura not lost but enhanced by its reproduction.[48]

Such faith in the magic of the Western designer's touch marked an important shift in the practice of Asian chic. The earlier concerns—however misguided or disingenuous—about cultural knowledge had dissipated, giving way to the sense that the West might in fact know Asia better than it knew itself. This was reflected in the strategies of representation. By the spring of 2001, when fashion magazines announced, yet again, that designers were "turning to Asia," the quasi-naturalist motifs that characterized Asian chic at the beginning of the 1990s had all but disappeared.[49] Instead, designers sent out incredible, fantastic renderings of the East. Emanuel Ungaro's fashion show that year, reported *Vogue* with enthusiasm, "resembled a spectacular Indian wedding party in a Bollywood musical." Not to be outdone, Jean Paul Gaultier's show featured a lacquered runway and hanging lanterns, and gowns named "Shanghai Express" and "Fu Manchu," shown by models moving to the tune of David Bowie's "China Girl."[50]

Like other Orientalists before them, fashion's cultural workers were empowered to create, imagine, and authorize knowledge about Asia. Their theatrical productions, culled from Hollywood films, Bollywood musicals, and a hodgepodge of other references, constructed the people and place as lively spectacle. But if the East was indeed being transformed by these designers' imagination, it was an imagination that did not wander far. When freed to dream and invent, they seemed only to return to long-held ideas about an exotic and erotic Orient.

At the beginning of the twenty-first century, the Asian-inspired clothes that inundated fashion were almost invariably "updated" or "reinterpreted" in the same way: as sexualized objects made tighter and shorter than their "inspirations."[51] In 2003, Roberto Cavalli reworked the cheongsam into a minidress and Tom Ford, a designer for Gucci, remade the kimono into sexy lingerie. (Gucci's collection of 2003, in fact, was shown with models going down the runway in little more than printed silk kimonos and lacy underwear.)[52] The idea was to make it "very sensual," "very sexy," said Ford. Or, as Cavalli put it: "I was inspired by Asia; the bold colors and the cheongsam. But I corseted mine to reveal all the beautiful curves of a woman's body."[53] In eroticizing these garments, designers transformed them from objects of everyday life into the stuff of fantasy.

Not surprisingly, these sexualized treatments of Asianness proved to be extremely popular. The market for these goods was quite strong, so robust that it was able to withstand even the most radical of political changes. In 2001, the events of September 11 set into motion a series of political, economic, and cultural shifts that altered many Americans' perception of difference, foreignness, and global interconnectedness. But in the fashion industry, these changes hardly registered. Discussions following September 11 in these quarters were centered on shoppers' somber mood and their need, in these times of terror, for more practical and comfortable clothing.[54] The United States was beginning its war with Iraq, suspicions of terrorists were spreading to include all "Muslim-looking" people (including South Asians), and China's and India's dominance in global production was fomenting anti-Asian sentiments, but there seemed to be no decrease in the sartorial appetite for Asian chic. In one indication of this, the cover of *Vogue*'s October 2001 issue showed a model wearing a cheongsam-inspired design by Christian Dior.

The taste for the exotic, in fact, only grew after 2001. In those years, it spread far beyond the confines of clothing into all corners of fashion. Magazines at this time were instructing readers not just on when to wear Asian-influenced clothing, but how to cook Asian food, where to find the best Asian restaurants, how to throw Asian-themed parties, and so on. Countless pages were dedicated to these details. During this time, signs of Asianness were creeping into all corners of American life. It seemed, indeed, to many that we were witnessing, as the historian Warren Cohen called it, the dawning of the "Asian American century."[55]

In 2003 Asian chic reached its peak, only to fall from prominence soon after. The runway reports from spring 2003 all noted "heavy Asian-influences" (*Harper's Bazaar*), "an Asian vibe" (*Vogue*), and "opulent, Asian-influences" (*Elle*).[56] Just as in 1997–98, a wide range of designers had once again incorporated Asian elements into their collections, whether as an accessory (*Elle* reported on a spate of Asian-influenced handbags by Chanel, Ungaro, Dior, Valentino, Gaultier, and others) or an entire ensemble.

The kimono was particularly prominent. Worn on the runway "over barely-there underpinnings and slinky dresses," as *Harper's Bazaar* reported, it alluded to the erotic spirit that the also prominent mini-cheongsam embodied. And, as had been established during the 1990s, these "updates" were once again framed as enhancement, "breathing new life into one of fashion's favorite fetishes—chinoiserie—[and] putting a fresh spin on the centuries-old look."[57] These types of influences, which "surfaced on nearly every runway this spring," said the magazine, were certainly made visible in the fashion companies' ads. In 2003, seventeen major brands ran advertising campaigns that featured a cheongsam or kimono.[58]

After such a spectacular showing, fashion predictably turned to something new. As early as August 2003, *Harper's Bazaar* was telling its readers to put away all that Asian chic. "Too exotic for this season," it advised, but added: "don't sell it on eBay; it always comes back in style."[59] The magazine was a bit premature. In 2004, Tom Ford created another collection for Gucci based on chinoiserie. In 2005, Prada's collection was reportedly inspired by Chinese films, prompting several magazines to run spreads paying homage to that year's hit, *Memoirs of a Geisha*. At the same time, boho chic (based on bohemian and hippie images) was also declared all the rage, and once again tunics from India took center stage. But Asian fever soon broke, and after 2005 fashion had more or less moved on (though committed enthusiasts like John Galliano and Mathew Williamson have not).

During the decade and a half when Asian chic thrived, the discourses surrounding it shifted, from a demand for cultural authenticity to praise for outrageous invention, from naturalist imagery to sexualized imagery. Neither version really had much to do with Asia, of course. Like other Orientalists before them, Western designers and their cultural intermediaries were, as Edward Said would say, inventing Asia in ways that said more about them than the continent itself. But to stop our analysis there would be to miss out on a better understanding of the social function of these representations.

Over two decades ago, the sociologist Pierre Bourdieu called fashion a form of magic, a belief system based on "collective misrecognitions."[60] Bourdieu was referring to the way that value was invested in haute couture —the way that clothing could be transformed into fashion, objects of worth far beyond their use—but his insights certainly apply to other acts of conjuring, including the production of Asianness witnessed here. In highlighting fashion's artifice, however, Bourdieu was not excusing its excesses, as many fashion writers have done.[61] He was instead attempting to reveal the ways in which these misrecognitions are produced by various social actors. If fashion deals in misrecognitions, they are collective misrecognitions; if it traffics in fantasies, they are collective fantasies. What, then, were the social conditions that contributed to this extended fascination with the East? What does this shift in modes of representation tell us about the function of Asia in the American imagination?

The absorption of Asianness into the vocabulary of international fashion—as enhancements and adornments, as touches of ethnicity and splashes of color—did little ultimately to disrupt the fashion divide. Ostensibly an appreciation of Asian culture, Asian chic was in many ways actually a demonstration of Western cultural power. By situating Western "interpretations" as superior to Eastern "originals," cultural intermediaries helped to reestablish the authority of the Western subject and the value of their creativity. In doing so, they reaffirmed the West as the true source of fashion—inspiration from elsewhere notwithstanding—authorized to set trends for the rest of the world.

Signs of Asianness in this context were, moreover, retained primarily as novelty, familiar enough to be consumable, but distinctive enough to still be desirable. Just as in other forms of popular culture—we see this in the Western taste for Bollywood films, for instance—these productions reproduced Asianness as inherently different, but as permissibly so.[62] The sartorial exotic can be seen, then, as an attempt to reshape Asianness into an acceptable form of cultural consumption, domesticated and made commercially viable even when it was politically suspect.

Considered in this way, Asian chic's emergence during the 1990s, a time when many Americans felt a dread of immigrants and their effects on American culture (sometimes called the browning or yellowing of America), and its endurance after September 11 becomes less surprising. But if this reading succeeds in showing how Asianness gets depoliticized, it leaves unanswered the question of why this particular form of foreignness was so desirable. Why did it gain such traction at this particular time? As if in response to this very question, the designer Romeo Gigli told *Vogue* in the mid-1990s—at the start of Asian chic—that "we take from the East what we need in the West." "The last time the East had a big vogue here was in the sixties," the designer said, "and that was our most positive moment for freedom and happiness in this century. Now we need that serenity and sensuality again, as an escape from our driven society."[63] Gigli's characterization of the 1960s as a moment of "freedom and happiness" is certainly debatable, but his comments are important less for what they say about that decade than for their views about the East. His use of the word "need" highlights the aspect of desire; the East in this enunciation expresses not just what is consumable, but what cravings these goods are intended to satisfy. Gigli's comments articulate not just the confidence of one whose reach is limitless, but also the longing of one whose hungers are yet unmet.

Gigli's view of the "serenity and sensuality" of the East as an antidote to the soulless modernity of the West typifies much thinking and writing about Asia. The East has, after all, historically been reviled as premodern, even antimodern. Since at least the 1960s, however, Asia's assumed position outside of the march of progress has become the very source of its appeal. Configured as the premodern, the authentic, and the ethnic, it has been viewed as a cure for the ills of modernity, "the salve," as Mathew Frye Jacobson puts it, for the homogenizing forces of commodification, bureaucratization, suburbanization, and "those postindustrial discontents that 1950s observers like David Riesman and William Whyte had spelled out in *The Lonely Crowd* and *The Organization Man*."[64]

Aiding and abetting these constructions during the 1990s were such Asian gurus as Deepak Chopra, who preached a version of new-age Orientalism that constructed India and Indians as inherently spiritual and apolitical. Chopra's *Seven Spiritual Laws of Success*, a *New York Times* bestseller in 1996, urged readers to eschew material desires, free themselves from anger, and establish a sense of well-being and peace—all so that they may ultimately find their "wealth consciousness," or state of natural affluence.[65] Chopra and his kind have found a wide-ranging audience, from businessmen exhausted by the competitive marketplace to urbanites burned out by the fast-paced modern life. For everyone needing a little less stress, Indians and their simple lifestyle became, with Chopra's help, the chicken soup for their ailing souls.

Within fashion, Asia became seen as a particularly powerful tonic for the industry's afflictions. In the last few decades, as the clothing business has become increasingly dominated by mass-market chains like H&M and Gap and consolidated luxury empires like LVMH (Louis Vuitton Moët Hennessy), the competition for consumer dollars has intensified. Younger designers were daunted by these conditions, which pitted their small operations against the massive production capabilities of larger firms. But even established designers felt the pinch. Those working in major companies or with backers felt compelled to meet retail quotas or risk losing their jobs. Many in the industry felt that the time had gone—if it ever had existed—when fashion was more than just business, when it could be fun, frivolity, and fantasy. In this context, Asia provided not just sensuality and serenity, but a return to a mythologized past, mourned as irrevocably lost.

Designers who invoked exotic influences—*Madama Butterfly*, cherry blossoms, dragons, orchids, lotuses, and so on—were understood to be doing so in great part to revive the no-nonsense, market-driven business of fashion with a dash of fantasy. Writing about the fall 2007 Christian Dior collection, for instance, the critic Kate Betts commended John Galliano by noting:

> The designer, who seemed to have been languishing lately under directives to create saleable clothes, let his wacky imagination soar again—this time from the couture ateliers of Paris all the way to the cherry-blossom-filled gardens of Kyoto . . . With it, he thumbed his nose at relevance and the drive to get designers to inveigle their clothes onto the red carpet or to compete with high-frequency deliveries at H&M. From the moment the first model stepped gingerly under a bow of blossoms in a fuchsia kimono jacket to the last sigh of a corseted bride swathed in a tulle origami cloud, the message was clear: Dream on.[66]

Whether or not this was actually Galliano's intention, the result is the same. Asianness is posited in these discourses as the absence of, and the antidote to, the demands of modernity.

Certainly the pressures associated with this "driven society" were felt far beyond the confines of the fashion industry. At the beginning of the twenty-first century, Americans faced uncertain times. Globalization in its many guises, a boat once understood to be driven by the United States, was now no longer under its sole command. Jobs were being leached abroad in a fever of outsourcing that affected both blue- and white-collar workers. Politicians, scholars, and editorialists were constantly urging Americans to "stay competitive" and offering instructions on how to do so—what kind of education they needed, what policies could increase or decrease competitiveness, and so on.[67] In the same vein, President George W. Bush announced in 2006 the American Competitiveness Initiative, which would commit $136 billion over ten years to increase investments in research and development "to encourage American innovation and strengthen our nation's ability to compete in the global economy."[68] "If you're living in Midland, Texas or living in Montgomery County, Maryland," the president said in support of the initiative, "it's important to understand if our children don't have those skills sets needed to compete with a child from India, or a child from China, the new jobs will be going there."[69]

Statements like these put a face to the name of global competition. As

Americans saw their fortunes shift in the last two decades, they were encouraged to connect these losses to the gains of Asia, particularly economically powerful centers like China and India. Various polls in the last decade have shown that a majority of Americans fear China's economic power. A poll conducted by CNN in November 2009, for instance, showed that 71 percent of Americans considered China an economic threat; two-thirds saw the country as "a source of unfair competition for U.S. companies."[70] In contrast, only 51 percent of those polled in the same survey considered China to be a military threat.[71]

In this context, the increased intimacy with Asia and other parts of the non-West that globalization made possible served as a reminder not of the West's distinctions from the East, but its connections to it. Unlike previous periods—the cold war, for instance, when Americans were still struggling to forge ties with Asia—those ties were now inescapable. The events of September 11 made this interconnectedness even clearer. The U.S. borders were revealed to be as porous as they were long, and the sense of security that many Americans had felt as citizens of a world power was being eroded by the fear they felt in the new time of terror.

The fact of proximity and interconnection was, in this sense, not a reassuring reality. And for those who found it difficult to stay competitive, the desire for the good life was matched only by the difficulties of achieving it. The use of Asia in the sartorial imagination spoke to these larger concerns. Valerie Steele and others were right to argue that Asian chic was a product of globalization.[72] But globalization aided its resurgence not just by making the delivery of Eastern goods and images easier but also by contributing to the destabilization of the West. Americans who had both benefited and suffered from globalization knew well that it was here to stay, calls to revoke the NAFTA (North American Free Trade Agreement) notwithstanding. What Americans wanted to know was, if they could not wish globalization away, how were they going to live with its demands.

To this fraught question, Asia provided a particularly malleable answer, for it offered a vision of life that was simultaneously untainted by the forces of modernity and on its cutting edge. If Asia could be seen as a place of mysticism and sensuality, and thus as authentically premodern, it could at the same time be seen as a site of hypermodernity. Countless reports about development in South and East Asia have touted the region as a model of production and accumulation. In the popular media, stories about India's and China's massive production capabilities constantly circulate. (Incredulous accounts of China's apparently lightning-fast and monumentally scaled developments for the Olympics provide just one example.) The wealth generated by these countries' economies has also become a topic of much interest. Reports of the burgeoning Asian middle class and its consumer power have captivated corporations (including luxury fashion firms), which have poured into the gleaming new cities of Asia in recent years.

In this sense, Asia could mark both the march of progress and its antithesis, both an escape from modernity and a beneficiary of modernity's largesse. The narratives about Asia found in the pages of fashion magazines expressed these contradictions clearly. Whether shrouded in naturalism or cloaked in sexuality, Asian chic during this decade and a half fluctuated between the poles of the sartorial rich and the sartorial poor. On the one hand, the incorporation of Asian elements and styles could be used to signal the height of luxury and opulence. On the other hand, they could be employed to indicate a lack of luxury—simplicity, if not spirituality—even in this domain of extravagance. These changing ideals reflected the competing desires—expressed not just in fashion but in the films, novels, and other cultural forms of the time—to achieve bourgeois success and to escape from its demands.

To cite a few examples: When couturiers like Christian Dior reworked kimonos in silk, satin, and velvet, and embroidered them with genuine gold thread, *Harper's Bazaar* in its March 1998 issue hailed the result "opulence at its most extreme." When Yves Saint Laurent and Christian Lacroix "looked to the East," they did so by blending, according to *Elle*, "sumptuous fabrics in regal colors."[73] If the aristocratic elite in Europe once coveted the silks and brocades of ancient Cathay precisely because they evoked a rarefied opulence, Western consumers in the 1990s were asked to make the same association.[74]

Uses of Asian elements in this vein were almost certain to be described as "luxurious," "lavish," "opulent," or "extravagant." *Elle*'s 1996 spread on garments "with an Eastern influence," for instance, described these objects as "utterly delectable" and "so exquisite" that "they come off best without any extra adornment."[75] As if to give visual evidence for these claims, the spread featured an image of a woman dressed in a "sari-inspired . . . embroidered and gold-lace-encrusted black chiffon gown." She is wearing a shawl, looking down at her dress and fingering the material in a reverent manner, as if it were encrusted with gold rather than lace. Standing alone against a dark background, she brings to mind a Renaissance portrait—an elegant lady shrouded in finery.

But if Asian chic could serve as the apotheosis of bourgeois lavishness, it could at the same time signify a bohemian simplicity. At the end of the 1990s in particular, when the so-called bohemian look was in vogue, countless spreads on the "Haute Hippie" showed readers "updated" tunics, sari prints, and hand-embroidered tops—all pieces that were, at other times, de rigueur for the ethnic look. A *Vogue* spread from 1999 made these connections explicit. Set in India, it showed the model Maggie Rizer wearing "elegantly free-spirited pieces," including "gypsy-print skirts and brightly colored embroidered tops." The accompanying text read: "To arrive there [in Rajasthan] is to arrive at the very heart of this season's bohemian spirit."[76]

The return of the hippie, or at least her "free-spirited" style of dressing, was presented in the pages of fashion magazines as a return to the Nehru jackets, beaded tunics, and so on that the bohemians of the 1960s and 70s had made a part of their signature style. (Asian chic was certainly integral to that generation's fashion as well.) For the contemporary shopper, "a splash of beads on a sandal, or a colorful Indian print" was all it took to become a "nouveau boho," said *Elle*.[77] A quick trip to "the Indian bangle shop" would do the job too, said *Vogue*.[78] As in other displays of antimodernism, here too the ethnic or the exotic stood in for an authentic and traditional life, one being washed away by the demands of the modern world.

A return to those styles was thus imagined as return to a particular lost ethos. One writer, a self-professed "hip hippie," described her enthusiasm for the boho look as a yearning for a "time of great freedom of expression, a time when eccentricity was applauded and creativity nurtured—and best of all, encouraged."[79] Cast in this nostalgic light, that time and those styles became the embodiment of a refusal to conform to the demands of the modern world. In contrast to the emphasis on luxury and opulence, the discourse surrounding this version of Asian chic stressed instead freedom (in the face of conformity) and simplicity (in the face of accumulation).

To be sure in the fashion world, where "rich bohemian" and "luxe bohemian" are common terms, these were hardly contradictory impulses. They were, in fact, just two sides of the same fashionable coin, both of which strove to encourage consumption even as they espoused freedom from it. Fashionable bohemians are hardly class warriors who actually reject traditional patterns of wealth accumulation and distribution. They resemble

Figure 5 "The Lush Life," *Elle*, October 1996.

much more closely the "bourgeois bohemians" of David Brooks's formulation, who reconcile their class privilege with their professed commitment to an authentic life through the consumption of "utilitarian" luxuries (like shade-grown coffee and Viking stoves).[80] Or the New Age spiritualists like Chopra's followers, who eschew material desires so that they can fill their life with riches.

Even so, this continual flux between the sartorial rich and poor is telling —at least about the kinds of social desires that designers and their cultural intermediaries were responding to and generating. The fluctuation between the opulent and the impoverished expressed, I argue, the ambivalence that many Americans felt about the demands of modernity. Asia, as articulated through Asian chic, gave them a particularly useful fantasy of dominance and dissent. Positioned as both modernity and its opposite, signs of Asianness allowed Americans to fulfill their desire to stay competitive in the global economy and also to retreat from its call. In a way, this is not so different from how Asians have been constructed in the United States, as model minorities who are robotically driven and successful, but who are also silent, noble, and accepting when success does not come their way. It is because of their capacity to bear the weight of this contradiction that Asia and Asians have been seen, as Vijay Prashad has told us, as the "solution," rather than the "problem" of the twenty-first century.[81]

Such representations of Asianness in Western fashion can be read as a sign both of Americans' confidence and, paradoxically, of their lack of confidence. At the same time that representations of Asian chic worked to shore up the authority of the Western subject and to reinforce his or her place in the cultural hierarchy, it also worked to express anxieties about the shifting terrain of global culture. If Asian chic is simply difference made permissible, it was a disconcerting difference: these representations served as a reminder not just of what Americans could have—potentially all the world has to offer—but also of what they still yearned for.

Here I am reminded of James Clifford's insights about the practice of collecting. Clifford points out that while the collector is ostensibly in the position of power—having the ability to choose, gather, and assemble—the objects too have their capacity for influence. If we return these objects to their lost status as fetishes, "not specimens of a deviant or exotic 'fetishism' but *our own* fetishes," we begin to see how they have "the power to fixate rather than simply the capacity to edify or inform." As a cultural form that can be profoundly intimate and can serve as an expression of our most private thoughts and an object of our dearest fascinations, clothing holds this same power. It can also encourage deep passions and intense yearnings. If these fashionable objects—real, image, and written clothing all—are viewed not as cultural signs or icons that are easily classifiable and consumable, but as disconcerting sources, they may actually have the power to disrupt Orientalist fantasies of control and authority. These objects could instead serve, as Clifford puts it, to "remind us of our *lack* of self-possession, of the artifices we employ to gather the world around us."[82]

ASIAN AMERICANS AND THE ECONOMY OF ASIAN CHIC

Certainly these anxieties about global competitiveness have not ceased; indeed, they have only escalated with the recent economic downturn. But the taste for Asian chic has subsided (though it has not altogether disappeared), having perhaps momentarily lost its usefulness as an ideal. (Trend reports for spring 2010 indicate, though, that it is returning.) Yet if it was, for a time, an expression of vague cultural anxieties, Western interest in Asian chic had very tangible material effects. This can be seen in the ways that it altered the fashion landscape in Asia itself. When the cheongsam entered international fashion, for instance, the trend stimulated a new market for the garment among young consumers in China. The number of cheongsam boutiques grew, and young brides began to wear them as a part of their wedding ceremonies again.[83]

The embrace of these styles, which had become increasingly rare in Asians' everyday lives, opened up some opportunities for local designers to insert themselves into international fashion. Asian designers found that they were able to capitalize on this trend by producing their own version of Asian chic for both local and foreign markets. But participation in this arena often required that they reproduce Western fashion's Orientalizing gestures. As Leshkowich and Jones have written, Asian designers and consumers who aligned themselves with this international trend often gained their cosmopolitan cachet by marking the local population as different— economically, ethnically, and geographically. Further, they often reinforced the tendency in international fashion to see Asia as traditional and time-less by playing up notions of femininity and traditional values in their own work.[84]

The cultural economy of Asian chic certainly shaped the experiences of Asian American designers as well. Those who entered the industry during this decade found themselves in the position of being both hailed as cultural authorities (who possessed knowledge about Asia) and damned as ethnic representatives (who could only represent their own culture). Thus while they may have shared the interests, anxieties, and longings that animated American desire for these goods, their ethnic identities made their relationship to these goods and images far more fraught.

In this economy, it was the editors, marketers, large fashion houses, and other industry insiders who formulated the parameters of Asianness, even as they purported only to observe it. To be sure, Asian American designers found their place, too. Those who were willing to wear their ethnicities on their sleeves found they could extract value from their culture, and some exploited that culture for their own economic benefit. But while Asian designers were given, or took, a certain amount of power because of their assumed cultural knowledge, it was the industry insiders who demarcated the lines between East and West, and who oversaw the terms of Asia's presentation.

This was made most obvious by the precarious position that Asian American designers found themselves vis-à-vis the fashion market. The designer Vivienne Tam provides a good example. Tam is perhaps best known for her self-professed "dedication to innovation and exotic imagery."[85] Her clothes have drawn on a range of Chinese images and styles, which are reworked in slim silhouettes and body-conscious materials. Dresses with mandarin collars and butterfly clips fabricated in silk and embroidered with dragons and lotuses are staples of her collections. These clothes make visible and manifest the idea of the East as opulent, colorful, erotic, and intriguing. To enhance this understanding, she displays them in boutiques designed to look like ancient emporiums, complete with elaborately carved shelves, porcelains, lacquers, and massive, sprawling dragons. Tam became a top designer during the 1990s in great part because she understood how to exploit the taste for Asian chic. In fact, she became one of the preeminent authorities on the subject. During this decade she was called upon to comment on its various incarnations and even wrote a book on Asian style.[86]

But while Tam drew on the same styles and motifs that made shoppers swoon for Prada and Yves Saint Laurent, her creations were often cast in a different light, as the natural expression of her ethnic identity rather than the feat of creativity and imagination attributed to Euro-American designers. Tam's work was often interpreted by fashion writers through the lens of her personal history. Writers often referred to the motifs or elements she employed as a product of her upbringing in China, an association that she partly encouraged. They were particularly fond of emphasizing her parents' Confucian beliefs, as exemplified by their decision to take only their son with them when they fled Communism and relocated to Hong Kong, leaving their daughter behind in China. These narratives continually linked Tam's work to her identity and ultimately posited her not as the creator of culture but the embodiment of it. One writer commented, for instance, that "style is spiritual to Tam."[87]

The tendency in fashion commentary to treat non-Western designers in this manner is common. A particularly egregious example is one editor's comment about the work of Rei Kawakubo, Comme des Garçons' radically deconstructionist and aesthetically elusive designer: "It's ethnic [sic], that's all. It's the *National Geographic* school of design."[88] Such treatment had an important effect on the evaluation of Asian American designers' work.

These essentializing narratives contributed to the understanding of their creations as more "real" than "designer." If such perceptions gave their products a certain aura of authenticity, it also positioned their designs as less valuable than the fantastical renderings of Gucci and Yves Saint Laurent. Asian American designers participating in Asian chic were never able to command the same price as those fashion houses, in part because of their position in the industry but in part because their goods were treated less as cultural creations than cultural artifacts.

Moreover, when the market shifted and Asia was no longer deemed fashionable, those who had mined it for inspiration—whether to exploit a trend or to express their aesthetic preferences—found themselves once again on the margins of fashion. Young Asian American designers who were first covered by magazines when Asian chic flourished, lost their in-style status when it ebbed. Alpana Bawa, who once saw her brightly colored, embroidered designs in the pages of *Vogue* and a host of other publications, explained the bind to me in this way: "The whole ethnic thing helped in some ways, but it mostly hurt me. When 'ethnic' went out of fashion—you know, *Vogue* didn't call me anymore. None of those magazines called."

Asian Americans, in this sense, fit awkwardly into the economy of Asian chic. Though some were able to benefit from this market, at least for a while, they never drove the trend, controlled its command metaphors, or profited largely from it. Asian Americans were never at the center of this development, though they were certainly affected by it. After all, Asian chic was not fundamentally a demonstration of an appreciation for Asia or its peoples, despite designers' and advertisers' claims. It was, as I hope I have demonstrated, a discursive production that strove to maintain a distance between East and West in the face of their growing intimacy.

Asian Americans certainly contributed to this construction of Asian chic, as the next chapter will reveal. Yet while some engaged in acts of exoticization, many contested the belief that Asian influences could be made manifest through the simple inclusion of a motif, color, element, or style alone. Moreover, while these designers were complicit in the production of Asian chic, they were not resigned to its logic of distance. Instead, they struggled to forge connections to Asia, materially and symbolically, and to enact an aesthetic of intimacy that these productions precluded.

Even when Asian American designers imaged Asianness in spectacular ways, these signs could, at times, be used to invoke more than just a set of essential differences. In the next chapter, I examine these designers' use of exotic imagery, focusing in particular on the work of Vivienne Tam. Tam's use of Mao's image in her 1995 collection—a collaboration with Zhang Hongtu, a Chinese artist living in New York—enabled her both to cash in on this cultural icon and to reveal the continuing importance of Mao for Chinese in the diaspora. In doing so, her work demonstrated that signs of Asianness—offered by the image and written fashions of the popular magazine—could be presented differently, made and marked by structures of intimacy.

Chapter 4

"MATERIAL MAO"

FASHIONING HISTORIES
OUT OF ICONS

In 1997, as an inexperienced and struggling designer, Han Feng showed a collection that would wow critics and launch her into the fashion spotlight. Feng, who had been working in fashion since 1985 (first as a clerk at Bloomingdale's) had started producing her own clothes just three years earlier, when the pleated silk scarves she made in her apartment sold out unexpectedly. But she managed to dazzle audiences with a collection that seemed to perfectly express the mood of the moment. Composed of loose, brightly colored pants and matching tops, sewn in silk, velvet, and other luxurious fabrics, it invoked the Chinese-born designer's cultural roots in an appropriately modern manner. Tunics were updated in sleek cuts; dresses were sewn in fabrics both opulent and wearable. To pull together the look, Feng sent her models down the runway made up as colorful coolies, complete with coolie hats and queues. Waiters at the event served tea, and the clothes were announced with the strike of a gong.[1]

Feng's liberal incorporation of so-called Eastern colors, elements, and motifs into her work (and its presentation) won her many fans during her now decade-long career. The marriage of East and West—as she has often called her style—evident in her first collection garnered her much acclaim in the fashion world and beyond. Feng became recognized as an expert on Asian culture and was able to parlay this expertise into opportunities in other cultural realms. In 1998, she was commissioned by the John F. Kennedy Center for the Performing Arts, in Washington, D.C., to create costumes for the East-meets-West themed production of David Maddox's "Gandhara: East West Passages." Feng was later tapped to design the costumes for Anthony Minghella's *Madama Butterfly*, a co-production of the English National Opera and New York's Metropolian Opera in 2006. It was clearly Feng's touch with exotic imagery that enabled her expansion into these other performative realms. As Minghella—perhaps best known as the director of such films as *The English Patient* and *Cold Mountain*—raved to *Women's Wear Daily*: "Han Feng is a firecracker . . . She has that special gift of taste and flair and fearlessness which mixes together strange foods, strange fabrics, strange colors, and alchemy happens."[2]

This flair for the "strange" is a characteristic that Feng has worked hard to cultivate. During the 1990s, she could often be seen on television and in magazines instructing viewers on how to throw Asian-themed parties and where to find the best Asian food. Describing herself on her Web site as "one of the few figures capable of bridging contemporary Chinese style and culture with a global perspective," Feng was (and still is) more than just a designer.[3] She continues to offer her expert knowledge to the entertainment world, most recently as a costume consultant for *The Karate Kid* remake starring Jackie Chan and Jaden Smith.

During the heyday of Asian chic, designers like Feng could—by virtue of their ethnic identities, both claimed and imposed—assume the mantle of guide and guru, able to unlock Asia's many secrets in fashion and beyond. Many took up these roles with zeal. These designers spurred on the appetite for Asianness by offering the industry an Asia filled with romance and nostalgia, glamour and spectacle, and by embracing its strategies of representation and its logic of distance. There is ample evidence to suggest that Asian Americans can at times be as Orientalist as any other designer. Yet if we stop our analysis there—at critiquing their complicity in these regimes of representation—we would discover very little about what else these exotic creations might have enabled their designers to say.

Because these creations reference hypervisible signs of Asianness, we may be tempted to assume that they clearly convey their meanings. Yet, as Anne Cheng has so convincingly demonstrated, there is a trick to seeing the readily seen. In her analysis of Josephine Baker, Cheng encourages readers to think about Baker beyond the duality of complicity and subversion. Against interpretations that commonly present Baker—despite the sometimes pandering and primitivist tendencies of her performances—as an agent struggling to contend with and subvert the racialized and gendered norms of her time, Cheng argues for a reading that would see the performances themselves as a crisis of visuality. Although they offered viewers a smorgasbord of seemingly recognizable racialized and gendered tropes, these performances were not easy to read. Audiences often registered confusion about them, in part because despite such dramatic visibility, the "truth" of Baker's primitivism was at times difficult to see. Rather than reveal the transparency of the surface, Baker's performances actually demonstrate, as Cheng puts it, "the difficulty of looking at the visible."[4]

Following Cheng, I want to suggest that we face similar difficulties in looking at the exoticizing work of some Asian American designers. Although they too reflect very recognizable racialized tropes, these images can also be sites of visual confusion. In what follows, I want to examine the exotic productions manufactured by Asian American designers, in particular the work of Vivienne Tam, in order to highlight the range of other utterances that can be articulated through these tropes. Focusing on Tam's Mao collection, I reveal the transnational intimacies that can exist at those sites of visibility (and of visual confusion) and locate in these intimacies the grounds for historical memory. At a time when Asian images and icons travelled freely, unmoored from their historical and social context, Tam's collection—produced in collaboration with the artist Zhang Hongtu—reaffirmed the importance of history, here posited neither as time or place, but as a set of questions to be continually repeated.

HISTORIES AND ICONS

Han Feng was certainly not the only Asian designer during the 1990s to participate in and benefit from the production of Asian chic. By 2003, at the height of Asian chic, the market for Asianness had become so voracious that it pulled in even those Asian designers who had previously eschewed such influences. A year earlier, Vogue reported that Anna Sui, known in the industry for her punk-inspired clothes, had been "all over South Asia and the Far East in search of sartorial inspiration."[5] A month later, it announced that come spring, the designer Andrew Gn would also be "going East." "It's a funny thing," he told Vogue, "a lot of Asian designers begin their collections with a dragon or Buddha or a peony, and I did everything else first."[6]

It is unclear why Sui and Gn capitulated to the trend after having avoided it for so long. But what is clear is that because Asian designers were re-warded for invoking their culture in their work—witness Han Feng's rapid ascendance—some were quite willing to convert culture into economics. The Indian designer Anand Jon was perhaps the most outlandish in this regard. Born in India, Jon studied fashion in the United States and became a hit in New York at the beginning of the twenty-first century for his collection of reworked saris and embroidered dresses. Throughout his ca-reer, Jon styled not just his clothes but himself as the perfect fusion of East and West. On his website, the designer told readers that he has "deep involvement in the Yogic disciplines." He writes, "I meditate every night and when I wake up, I check my e-mail."[7] Jon sold his brand of spiritual snake oil wherever he could. In a *Vogue* article on "Zen style," for instance, he was quoted spouting such aphorisms as "you can never be really spiri-tual unless you live in the mud." He told the same writer, whose palm he offered to read, that wearing his brightly colored skirts decorated with *yantras* could produce a "calming effect."[8]

Had he been trained in a different trade, Jon would have given gurus like Deepak Chopra a run for their money. As was the case with Chopra, Jon's strategic self-exoticization—the handiwork of a "postcolonial exotic," to borrow a term from the critic Graham Huggan—won him numerous awards and made him one of the most successful Indians in the world, according to *Newsweek*'s 2004 "Power and Influence" list.[9] (In a reversal of fortunes, Jon was convicted of sexual assault in 2008.)[10] But while he might be faulted for reinforcing popular Orientalist assumptions, Jon's work was part of a market already capitalizing on, as Huggan puts it, "the widespread circulation of ideas about otherness and on the worldwide trafficking of culturally 'othered' artifacts and goods."[11] Jon's brand of exoticism was, in that sense, both a symptom of and a response to the ongoing spiraling process of commodification, in fashion and the culture at large.

Though Jon was particularly bold at exploiting this market, he could be seen as a fellow traveler to many of the designers I spoke with. In my interviews, I found few things provoked such a passionate response as the topic of Asian chic. With some exceptions (like the designer Yvonne Chu, who admitted to being drawn to the bright colors, the silks, and the intricate embroidery that typifies Asian chic because it reflected her cultural back-ground), most of my interviewees vehemently denounced the use of such motifs. But they were also quite aware that there was cultural, symbolic, and economic value in their assumed or prescribed relationship to Asia.

This knowledge, irrespective of their own aesthetic interests, led many to "do something ethnic," as one designer put it, even as they understood it might reinforce the understanding of their work as "only ethnic."

"Doing something ethnic" involved a range of visual techniques that responded to marketplace visions of Asianness—that is, ideas about Asianness that are widely recognizable and thus may have more exchange value than personal or communal resonance. At times this entailed the explicit incorporation of what fashion journalists and large design houses understood to be traditional signifiers of Asia—from dragons, lotus, and bamboo to slash necklines, and shantung silk—into some (though never all) of their clothing. The inclusion of just a few elements could yield big results for these small designers. Since magazine editors were constantly searching for new fodder for their endless "East meets West" spreads, a well-placed dragon here and there could land designers in the pages of *Vogue* or *Harper's Bazaar*. When the appetite for Asian chic peaked, editors flooded to these designers and hailed many of them as important forces in fashion.

At other times, this use of Asian elements was less direct, as when designers incorporated them into their boutiques—reproducing Asian chic not in the clothes but in their presentation. In this case, the boutiques spoke what the clothes and the designers would not say. Margie Tsai, for instance, told me that she was not at all interested in incorporating Asian motifs in her clothing—that she made modern clothes for the modern woman. Tsai's knit dresses and skirts, done in black and neutral tones and absent of any obvious signifiers of Asianness, were, however, displayed in a boutique that made it impossible to ignore its relationship to the East. The small shop was filled with blue-and-white porcelain, bamboo plants, and Chinese reproduction furnishings; its sign bore Tsai's name in the Roman alphabet and Chinese characters. Such discrete references could also be found in Jussara Lee's boutique, which once had a *hanbo* over the door.[12] Similarly, Alpana Bawa's shop was once called "The Style Swami." Even as these designers' clothes steered clear of Asian signifiers, they were presented in a context that called forth an exotic experience.

Doing something ethnic certainly involved designers' aligning themselves with marketplace visions of Asianness. But at times it also involved the introduction of ideas and images that resonated beyond the market and into the domain of politics, history, and memory, rendering the surface a bit less apparent. When and how does history get made in this context? In one sense, fashion is always historical. It constantly quotes from the past,

Figure 6 Margie Tsai's Boutique, on New York's Prince Street.

making the new by recycling the old. Designers are often lauded by buyers, critics, and scholars for their ability to reach back in time, whether by borrowing the styles of a past era, reviving the look of a decade, or recycling the materials of vintage clothes. There is, as the fashion theorist Ulrich Lehman has noted, a "transhistorical character" to fashion: "it always appears as the most immediate present, affecting the future with its constant changes, yet it always quotes from the past."[13]

But what precisely does this reconstructed past look like? What can fashion reveal about history? Consider again for a moment Han Feng's 1997 collection. What set it apart from the other works of Asian chic at the time was Feng's unusual and in some ways daring invocation of the coolie, perhaps one of the most lasting anti-Chinese images in U.S. history. The coolie entered popular visual culture at the beginning of the nineteenth century, when it helped to frame debates about the so-called Heathen Chinese and to legitimize the movement for Chinese exclusion from America. Films, political cartoons, and other forms of popular culture have kept these images alive, allowing them to reappear again, for instance, in 1997 (in a *National Review* cover which portrayed President Bill Clinton as a coolie for having accepted campaign money from so-called Asian sources) and in 2002 (when the clothing retailer Abercombie and Fitch briefly attempted to sell T-shirts that coupled the coolie image with slogans like "Wong Brothers Laundry Service—Two Wongs Can Make It White"). While the meanings of these images have certainly changed over time, their significance—as markers of alterity and difference, as elements to be contained or simply consumed—have not diminished. By citing this image, Feng resurrected the specter of that history.

Yet Feng's collection revealed that history can quickly become style. While she referenced the coolie at a particularly charged moment (in the same year as the *National Review* cover), she also showed that the racism and exclusion that had made this image particularly potent could be transcended in the present.[14] Posed as playful actors in an orchestrated performance, Feng's updated coolies invoked neither the conditions of marginalization marked by this image nor the struggles waged by their historical referents. Rather, they served only to make the narrative of an opulent and exotic East more plausible. By juxtaposing them with mythological figures (dragons) and abstract symbols, the show jettisoned them into a time long, long ago and a land far, far away. While Feng's collection incorporated particular histories and peoples, it neatly transformed them into vague symbols of the East, not so different from the dragons and lotuses appearing everywhere that year. The effect of these historical or mythological figures was not to produce categorical confusions—between what is represented and what can be seen, between East and West, between history and myth—but to authenticate those very categories.

Given the complexities of this practice, how do fashion designers develop their rapport with the past? How is it forged in the realm of the hypervisible? How does this work for Asian Americans in particular, whose histories are often shaped by the various continuities and discontinuities engendered by processes of migration? What does history look like in this cultural medium?

If it is true that, as Ulrich Lehman puts it, fashion can be the "perfect vehicle for fusing novel aesthetics with an underlying recourse to the past," very few designers have been able to capture this possibility.[15] Yet in 1995 Vivienne Tam, a postcolonial exotic par excellence, introduced a collection that seemed to do just that. Tam fortuitously began her career in New York at a time when all of fashion seemed enamored with signs of Asia. Like many of her contemporaries, she freely incorporated Asian motifs into her work. Indeed, Tam has been working to make her name synonymous with Asian chic since she launched her first collection in 1994. For the last decade, her success has cast a long shadow over other Asian designers. During the mid-1990s, Tam, more than perhaps any other Asian designer, fueled the collective appetite for Asian chic by giving consumers a vision of China freed from political complexity, social unrest, and economical turmoil—one indelibly stamped with the romantic image, though hardly the reality, of 1940s Shanghai. The marketing of Tam's book, *China Chic*, a hefty primer on Chinese style, made this very clear. Bound in bright red vinyl to invoke Mao's "Little Red Book," it was filled with gorgeous reproductions of cheongsam-wearing calendar girls, revolutionary knickknacks, stills from the film *The World of Suzie Wong*, and the like. According to Tam, the book takes its readers on a (head-spinning) tour of "Eastern style meeting Western style."[16]

It is easy to see how these articulations of China can be absorbed into a fashion world already enamored of the exotic. Tam's clothes do not normally challenge what her audiences think they already know about China. In fact, the clothes are appealing precisely because they keep a safe imaginative distance from China. Like other works of Asian chic, they reference a beautiful place somewhere out there, a romantic China to which cosmopolitan consumers can travel without leaving the comforts of the fashion boutique.

Yet amid these fantastical renderings, Tam also brought to the fashion world one of the most fascinating images in Chinese political history. As noted earlier, in 1995 she collaborated with Zhang Hongtu to create a collection of shirts and dresses bearing the altered image of Chairman Mao. By employing this image, Tam participated in the robust debate within China about Mao and his legacy, forging transnational intimacies that are normally precluded by the discourses of Asian chic. Moreover, by extending the debate into the sartorial realm and its gendered structures, she also used fashion's rapport with the past to demonstrate continuing importance of this figure for Chinese in the diaspora.

MAO AND THE ECONOMY OF INTIMACY

In the lexicon of Asian images, few are as prominent or as widespread as the image of Mao Zedong. During his term as chairman of the Communist Party of China (1943–76), images of Mao appeared on stamps, currency, and schoolbooks, in public spaces and private homes. These images proliferated during the late 1960s, at the height of the Cultural Revolution, when they were used to shore up support for Mao's most ambitious reforms. At a time when advancing age and flawed reform initiatives like the Great Leap Forward (1958) had tarnished his revolutionary sheen, Mao's pervasive images worked to emphasize his authority and to generate the spirit of affiliation that his movement to "revolutionize daily life" demanded.[17] In those years, Mao inundated the everyday. His "Little Red Books" were mass-produced, his big-character posters were plastered throughout the country, and his portraits graced the walls of millions of homes.

Mao's likeness appeared most ubiquitously on Chinese citizens themselves, who showed their commitment to their nation and to the revolution by donning one of the several billion Mao badges churned out in a variety of materials and in over 10,000 different designs. Badges appeared as early as the late 1940s, handmade by students out of toothpaste containers, but they were not widely available until the Cultural Revolution. At this time, everyone was allowed to produce and consume the badges. Permits were no longer required, as they had been before the Cultural Revolution, and production was no longer centralized. Each badge bore the face of Mao, in a pose from his youth, middle age, or final years. The badges were typically of two colors—appropriate colors included red, blue, yellow, green, and white—and were frequently stamped with Chinese characters expressing good wishes for the Chairman.[18]

During the Cultural Revolution, demand for these badges was so high that manufacturers constantly struggled to keep up. Production infamously ate up the country's supply of aluminum, prompting Mao himself to declare: "Give me back my airplanes. It would be far more useful to make airplanes to protect the nation out of the metal being expended in the production of Mao badges."[19] In 1969, the Chinese Communist Party halted badge production; only three factories were allowed to continue to manufacture the badges, in very limited quantities. At the end of the Cultural Revolution, citizens were ordered to recycle the estimated 2–4 billion badges.[20]

Badges, as Melissa Schrift makes clear in her *Biography of a Chairman Mao Badge*, were never merely decoration. Rather, they were an outward manifestation of the loyalty and devotion their wearers were supposed to feel within. In large part it was this desire to make visible one's political and affective allegiance that drove production to such heights. Citizens eagerly displayed multiple badges at once, and the objects were a source of great desire and fascination. Badges were traded based on certain hierarchies— of size, quality, and uniqueness—but, as Schrift notes, accumulation was never a goal in and of itself. Badge exchanges rarely involved money, and it was socially unacceptable to frame the transaction as buying and selling. The image of the Chairman was, after all, not for sale. Instead, consumers spoke of "inviting" or "requesting" a badge. These words, as the political scientist Michael Dutton argues, reconnected "the act of acquisition to an economy of intimacy and sacrifice that lies beyond the logic of money and market."[21]

It was this play at intimacy, says Dutton, that fostered the sacred commitment to Mao. It was only because citizens could feel and demonstrate their personal allegiance—participate in this economy of intimacy—that they could engender the political intensity, unachievable through politics alone, that made the Cultural Revolution possible. Wearers themselves testified to these ecstatic feelings. One woman, for instance, remarked that when she pinned a badge onto her chest she was sure that she "could feel Chairman Mao's radiance burning into" her.[22]

Call it devotion, enchantment, or zealotry, the affective relationship forged in the crucible of Mao's image had a lasting effect on the Chinese people. After his death on September 9, 1976, many in the Party hoped that the deceased Chairman would be safely relegated to the ranks of other elder revolutionaries, whose contributions to China were unmistakable but whose actions were better left unexamined. But while the party struggled to deal with Mao's mixed political legacy, a Mao craze (*maore*, literally "Mao heat") took off without their control. Starting in the late 1980s, at about the same time that the tenth anniversary of Mao's death was being quietly noted by the party, Mao was making his first appearance as a consumerist icon. Fashionable young artists began showing up at exhibitions wearing Mao suits and Mao badges. Entrepreneurial villagers began organizing tours of places Mao supposedly lived in, slept in, or visited. Soon after, Mao's writings were reissued, as were the badges, and Mao-themed restaurants, musicals, operas, and millions of cigarette lighters, T-shirts, yo-yos, and alarm clocks bearing his likeness flooded the country. As one indication of the magnitude of this resurgent interest, between 1980 and 1991, the number of official Mao portraits printed rose from 370,000 to 50 million.[23]

If, as Michael Dutton has argued, the Cultural Revolution was a "movement that pronounced the word *materialism* while simultaneously whispering in tongues the word *sublime*," this new Mao cult was unabashedly commercial.[24] During the early 1990s, Mao was packaged to be sold, and to sell. Massive billboards bearing his face and words were used to market everything from interior decorating products to tours of the Great Wall—until that use was officially banned in 1994.[25] Entrepreneurs lured tourists into their over-priced establishments by hanging up signs announcing: "Chairman Mao slept here." Interest in Mao badges resurged, though in a new tenor. No longer couched in the politically correct language of barters and gifts, these were openly bought and sold in a competitive market guided by so-called badge experts and institutions like the Mao Badge Collection and Research Society. Falling in the midst of the reform age, the

Mao craze bore the stamp of the nation's new mercantilist interests and the consumerist fervor of its youth culture. Many of the Mao products were bought by young people who, born after his death, saw in his image not the violence and upheaval of the Cultural Revolution, but a reflection of their own rebelliousness and idealism.[26]

As has often been said, the figure of Mao Zedong—his images, words, and life—became a floating signifier in this period, invested with a range of meanings: nostalgia for a simpler past, a critique of the present political regime, a satire of political culture more generally, an expression of consumer fantasy and desire, and so on.[27] Even as the party attempted to harness this popular energy for its own interests—claiming that the Mao craze was an expression of the people's deep admiration for the party and its values—they could not control it.[28] It was never easy to tell whether Mao was being adored or undermined.

As Mao's image inundated commercial culture, it also pervaded Chinese avant-garde (or experimental) art.[29] Post–Cultural Revolution artists, particularly those associated with the "cynical realism" or "political pop" styles, repeatedly deconstructed Mao's iconic images.[30] Some, such as Yu Youhan in *Imam and Whitney* (1991), juxtaposed Mao with figures of Western popular culture—in this case the singer Whitney Houston, linking together these two international superstars. Others, such as Wang Jingsong in *Taking a Picture in Front of Tiananmen* (1992) parodied famous monumental works, in this case Sun Zixi's *In Front of Tiananmen*, considered a masterpiece of socialist realism. In a reversal of proportions, Wang conspicuously obscures Mao's portrait and enlarges instead images of foreign cigarettes, providing a commentary on the relative importance of socialism and capitalism under Deng Xiaoping's "socialist market" reforms.[31] Still others, such as Feng Mengbo, placed the Chairman in new environments. In his series of meticulously reproduced video games, *Game Over: Long March* (1993–94), Feng had the Chairman and members of his Red Guard fight with the Ninja Turtles, following plotlines taken from Cultural Revolution operas. "Once these heroes were fighting revolutions," Feng explained; "now they are only caught in a game."[32]

These artistic appropriations of Mao were overwhelmingly satirical. Like many contemporary Chinese artists, the artists working in these styles attempted to critique ideology and ideological commitment. But working largely after the protests at Tiananmen, when the "utopian enthusiasm so typical of new art in the 1980s met its nemesis in the gun barrels at

Tiananmen," as one writer put it, they moved away from the iconoclastic tendencies of the 1980s and turned to sarcasm and satire.[33] Cynical realists used their formal training to create realistic images to mock authority, in the tradition, some have suggested, of Sots (or Soviet socialist) art. Political pop artists employed "double kitsch"—which deconstructed political visual culture and fused its images with various sources, most often commercial —to wink knowingly at the parallels between propaganda and advertising.[34]

Inspired in part by Western pop art, these works echoed Andy Warhol's 1970s Mao portraits, which rewrote the Communist icon in the idiom of capitalist advertising. Employing the same process he used to create paintings of Marilyn Monroe, Elvis Presley, Jacqueline Kennedy, Campbell's soup cans, and Brillo boxes, Warhol recontextualized Mao as just another of his beloved celebrities. After all, Mao's ubiquity made him one of the most famous men alive. While the repetition of Mao's image—nearly two thousand of Warhol's Mao paintings were produced in different sizes— were undoubtedly a nod to its ubiquitous presence in China, the painter recast the Chairman in an irreverent, ironic, and markedly non-devotional tone.

Like Warhol's paintings, Chinese works using Mao sold extremely well; this style of modern Chinese art is by far the best known in the West. Provocative shows such as the 1989 China Avant-Garde Exhibition in Beijing (in which Wang Guangyi's *Mao Zedong No. 1* caused a stir and ushered in the era of political pop) and the 1993 China's New Art: Post–1989 Exhibition at Hong Kong's Hanart T Z Gallery (in which works dealing with materialism and consumerism were highlighted) brought unprecedented international attention to this style of Chinese art. Works by artists such as Fang Lijun and Wang Guangyi have sold extremely well in the international art market—fetching prices as high as $20,000, which, though relatively low by Western standards, was quite extraordinary for Chinese art at the time. (This situation has changed, and Chinese art now commands top rate dollars as its value continues to escalate.) These "pop masters," as they have been called, have become millionaires and have joined the ranks of the nouveaux riches in their country.[35] As a result, many artists have felt compelled to rework these styles again and again. (Students at Chinese art institutions are reportedly required to learn them because they can be marketed internationally.)[36] In this way, a movement that began as a critique of the creeping forces of consumerism in China became itself increasingly commercialized, and the transformation of Mao from political symbol to commercial icon expanded from low culture to high, from cheap tin badges to million-dollar artworks.

Still, though Mao was newly cloaked in commercial garb, he never lost his heavenly habit. During this time, taxi drivers hung Mao's picture from their rearview mirrors in the belief that he could prevent car accidents. Villagers placed his portrait, combined with the words "may this attract wealth," in prominent places in their homes in the hopes of bringing prosperity. In death as in life, Mao maintained his ability to enchant. This was particularly true for those Chinese citizens who had lived through the Cultural Revolution. For this generation of artists and writers, Mao's image still held deep emotional significance. Writers often invoked ghostly metaphors to describe his lingering presence and saw the current Mao revival as proof of his powerful hold on the Chinese people.[37] Artists eschewed nostalgia and irony and responded with work like Xing Danwen's *Born with the Cultural Revolution* (1995), a series of photographs of people born during that time, which expressed their memories and autobiographies.

Many who lived through the Cultural Revolution understood that Mao demanded faith of a very personal nature. Their works addressed not just Mao the powerful political figure, whose tumultuous regime they had endured, but Mao the image that penetrated their daily lives, asserting its presence in their most intimate realms.[38] They responded with similarly intimate representations. In doing so, they revealed that even as Mao became marketing gold, he never ceased to be China's makeshift god, and that even as he became a global icon, he never ceased to be a personal idol.[39]

The artist Zhang Hongtu, who collaborated with Vivienne Tam on her Mao collection, belongs to this older generation of artists. Born in China in 1943, he was just six years old when the Communist Party came to power. His father was a leading scholar of Arabic who was a member of the Chinese Islamic Association and the chief editor of the government magazine *Chinese Muslim*. During the Cultural Revolution, the father was denounced as a rightist. As a result, Zhang was disqualified from joining the Red Guard, the ultrapatriotic teen militia, and—perhaps most painful—from painting portraits of Mao when all revolutionary artists were engaged in the task. (The honor was denied to those considered unreliable or in the political opposition.) Zhang threw himself into the revolution nonetheless. He left his hometown of Beijing and traveled throughout China, joining workers in the countryside. "At the beginning of the Cultural Revolution, like everyone of my generation, I completely trusted in Mao," he recalled.[40]

And, like many of his generation, Zhang became disillusioned by the political infighting, poverty, and brutality that made up a large part of the everyday reality of Mao's vision.

Zhang's travels through the countryside failed to provide him with the political conversion he had hoped for, but it did impress upon him the power of Mao and his image. Zhang recalled once seeing a student brutally beaten when it was discovered that he had been sitting on a newspaper that bore a photo of Mao. In this moment, the links between authority and imagery were made very clear to him.[41] As a child of the Cultural Revolution, he understood well the affective, psychic, and profoundly intimate dimension of this political icon. His deconstructions of Mao's image were as result never taken lightly.

Vivienne Tam came of age after the Cultural Revolution, outside of mainland China (in Hong Kong and then New York). For her, Mao was less a psychic burden than a cultural curiosity; Tam has in fact blithely announced that had she been present during the Cultural Revolution, she would have been a member of the Red Guard.[42] The generational differences are in many ways apparent in their work. Tam's designs are unabashedly commercial; political concerns are normally absent from her work. In creating this collection, Tam admitted that she wanted to "loosen up Zhang's political art with a bit of fashion."[43] In doing so, she also closed the (at times barely perceptible) gaps between art and commerce, high and low culture, and the sacred and the profane that were already being challenged in the visual culture of China after 1989. Did Tam simply commercialize Zhang's art? If so, why, at a time when the Chinese were still in the throes of their Mao craze, did her use of Mao's image in her designs cause such a controversy?

GODS AND MEN

By the middle of the 1990s, popular enthusiasm for the Chairman began to wane, partly as a consequence of the Chinese government's attempts to harness this energy for its own nationalist agendas. At a time when inflation, corruption, and egregious nepotism was breeding widespread skepticism about the effectiveness of the party's leadership, Mao was being promoted as the father of the party, army, and state in order to shore up the party's authority.[44] In 1994, when Tam approached factories in Hong Kong to manufacture the collection she collaborated on with Zhang, Mao heat was beginning to cool, but Mao's image was still very much a part of

Chinese visual culture. So it seems rather strange that dozens of people refused her order. Tam recalled approaching "almost every factory in the territory" before one accepted. "The first time the factory did the black-and-white Mao woven samples," Tam recalled, "a computer glitch made the sample number come up as 4 6 1997—then all the lights went out. In Chinese culture, reading numbers is a form of divination. Four and six were read as 4 June—the date of the 1989 Tiananmen incident when the Chinese army moved against student demonstrators—and 1997 was of course the year of Hong Kong's return to China. The whole thing was so unnerving that the staff had to go home early."[45] The factory changed the number of the sample.

When the collection was completed, the clothes were delivered wrapped in brown paper bags to disguise their contents. Shops in Taiwan wouldn't carry them, and some shops in the United States refused to put them in their windows. One U.S. magazine canceled a photo shoot for fear of backlash, and some parents in Hong Kong forbade their children to wear the T-shirts. Given the seemingly endless proliferation of Mao paraphernalia at the time, why did these garments—and not beeping Mao cigarette lighters and alarm clocks—create such a stir?[46]

The answer lies partly in the particular ways that Zhang carefully reconstructed images of Mao. After becoming disillusioned with the Cultural Revolution, Zhang had left the countryside and returned to Beijing to study painting at the Central Academy of Arts and Crafts. He received his B.A. in 1969 and married shortly afterward. As an artist in Beijing, he was constantly reminded of the ways in which art and politics were so closely fused in China. Art as a tool of propaganda certainly hit its apotheosis during the Cultural Revolution, but artists in modern China have until very recently always been considered a part of the state bureaucracy. In 1949, Premier Zhou Enlai, whose policies promoted the spread of so-called people's art, formalized the understanding of artists as government workers, employed to serve the interests of the party. Under his leadership, the All-China Art Workers Association, the Chinese Artists Association, and the Central Academy of Fine Arts were formed, based on the Soviet models and teaching virtually nothing else but Soviet realism, in order to remind aspiring artists that their true role was to serve the people.[47]

After Deng Xiaoping's 1978 reforms, these institutions became increasingly tolerant of foreign influences, allowing artists to participate in developments in Euro-American art history and to personally profit from their work. The changes allowed a host of new artistic styles and movements to emerge and made it possible for artists to work individually or in small groups, refusing any single identity or social role.[48] To be sure, the party has never fully stopped monitoring artists. It has continued to suppress various voices in the official art bureaucracies, shut down presentations like the China Avant-Garde Exhibition in 1989, and banned exhibits not vetted by authorities after Tiananmen. But, for both political and economic reasons, the context for art production and reception has been greatly liberalized in mainland China.

When Zhang left China in 1982 to study at the Art Students League in New York, he had not yet witnessed these developments. He arrived in New York with plans to focus only on his art and to distance it from any taint of politics. But the 1989 Tiananmen Square protests changed all this: "Before 1989 I had imagined that I could escape China and politics into my own artistic creations. As I watched those demonstrations on television, however, I found myself feeling Chinese . . . My whole attitude began to change, and I no longer felt that I want to isolate myself."[49] Zhang joined the demonstrations in New York against the Chinese government and auctioned his artworks to raise money for the Chinese student protesters. Tiananmen, he said, forced him to finally reconcile himself with his political history and, ultimately, his relationship to Mao, whose portrait still hung prominently at Tiananmen.

For Zhang, to "feel Chinese" was to feel the hold that Mao continued to exert over Chinese people everywhere. "I realized that even though I had left China more than five years before, psychologically I couldn't eliminate Mao's image from my mind," Zhang has said.[50] For the next decade, he incorporated Mao's image in a variety of media into his art practice. *Quaker Oats Mao* (1987), completed before the Tiananmen protests, was his first effort. In this work, Zhang painted a proletarian cap on the familiar Quaker, suggesting a family resemblance between these two icons. It is easy to see the "double kitsch" effect here, and scholars like Wu Hung have suggested that in this piece Zhang may have created the first work of Chinese political pop.[51] But Zhang has refused to claim such an association. The "only relationship between my work and theirs is that we are using the same image," he has said.[52] While he shares with other mainland Chinese artists the practice of isolating and demystifying sacred political symbols, there is an intensely personal tenor to his treatment of Mao that sets it apart from

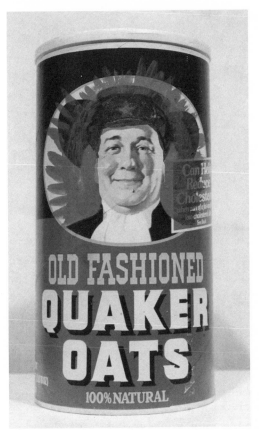

Figure 7 *Quaker Oats Mao*, from the Long Live Chairman Mao series, Zhang Hongtu. Acrylic on Quaker Oats box, 9.7×5 in., 1987.

much of political pop. And this difference may have been part of the reason why so many people were uncomfortable with Tam's collaborative creation.

Like many other Chinese of his generation, Zhang had personally experienced the political indoctrination of the Cultural Revolution, achieved, as many scholars have noted, partly through the technologies of repetition and duplication—through the production of countless copies of a limited number of text and images, including Mao's portrait. Artists were particularly vulnerable to this tactic, since they were required to paint those images again and again. Zhang's work alludes to this history. In *Last Banquet* (1989), he reworked Leonardo da Vinci's *Last Supper*, with Mao playing the roles of Christ and all twelve disciples. Christ Mao is depicted speaking into a microphone, while Judas Mao, who is holding a "Little Red Book," is reaching for a hammer as rice spills out of his bowl. In the background lies

Figure 8 *Last Banquet*, Zhang Hongtu. Laser prints, pages from the "Little Red Book" and acrylic on canvas, 60×180 in., 1989.

the Great Wall. Religious symbolism and political symbolism here become intertwined.[53] In this farcical scene, Mao's face is meticulously rendered again and again, each of the thirteen slightly different from the others. The expression of shock, horror, and surprise on the faces of the disciples as Mao announces that one among them will betray him adds to the charade, given that here it is Mao who betrays himself. The repetition of image reinforces the notion that Mao is indeed everywhere; he is every man. But it also raises the possibility that perhaps there is no real Mao, that he was always a kind of creation, more symbol than man. Either way, it highlights the fact that the different manifestations of Mao's portraits—as badges, posters, paintings, and so on—served only to reinforce the same purpose. The painting sets the context for understanding how political power gets invested, and why the demystification of images can serve to undermine that power.

In *Chairmen Mao*, a twelve-unit photo collage series (1989), Zhang begins to deconstruct Mao's image in earnest. Referencing the Mao badges, which were produced in sets like these, the *Chairmen* series refused the authority of those official representations by playing with and reconstructing them. Mao's face becomes distorted, like a television signal too weak to be properly received, rendering its images upside down, doubled, and blurred. References to the student democracy movement abound. In one of the images, Mao is depicted wearing a headband inscribed with the words "serve the people" and standing in front of a crowd of student demonstrators. In another, his face is cut out and the remaining space contains the face of Wu'er Kaixi, a leader of the student movement. In yet another, Mao is seen leering suspiciously at the statue called the Goddess of Democracy, with a speech bubble saying "Women!"

Figure 9 *Chairmen Mao*, Zhang Hongtu. Twelve units; photo collage and acrylic on paper, 8 1/2×11 in. each, 1989.

The surface humor evident here, which bears a family resemblance to the tradition of political cartooning, is different from the knowing satire of most works of political pop. Zhang's renderings suggest the strong, if at times hazy and incomplete, presence of Mao both in the events of the democracy movement and in the future of China. The paintings are not ironically dismissive—positing that Mao no longer has a part to play in the world of consumerism and materialism that he publicly denounced—but neither are they a call to remember the truth of the Cultural Revolution. Instead, they insist on a "presence of mind." "Presence of mind" as Walter Benjamin has defined it, "is an abstract of the future, and precise aware-ness of the present moment more decisive than foreknowledge of the most distant events."[54] In these collages, Mao's presence is hazy. His glance toward the Goddess, filled with suspicion and desire, hints at a future flirtation with democracy, but the results of this flirtation cannot be known.

In his work, Zhang calls for a precise awareness of Mao's continuing role in constructing the possibilities for China, political and otherwise.

While political pop and cynical realism mainly satirized a bygone political culture, Zhang is primarily interested in the present, in how it is informed and shaped by the past.[55] In his art he neither forgets history nor mocks it, but rather struggles to find his own place in it. This was made most explicit in the Material Mao series (1991–95), sculptures he created by cutting Mao's famous silhouette into blocks of different material, including corn, rice, soy sauce, fur, brick, stone, and iron. The materials—basic and necessary—highlight Mao's indelible stamp on everyday life. These cut-outs are an attempt to literally empty ideology by removing Mao's image. But Zhang cannot successfully excise this history; the negative images only remind viewers of Mao's enduring presence. At times, as in *Mesh Mao* (1993), they depict the Chairman as a ghostly specter in ways that recall the writing of Liu Xiaobo and other dissidents.[56]

At a time when China was entering the Mao craze—whether out of nostalgia for Mao or as a satire on him—Zhang's work, like that of dissidents outside of China, urged a critical consideration of Mao's legacy not just for the nation but for Zhang himself. While these works took on issues of national import, they also drew on and expressed the artist's most personal impulses. Zhang admitted: "When I first cut up a photo of Mao's face to make a collage, I felt as if I were sinning. Such feelings have made me realize how my work is really an effort to break the psychological authority that Mao as an image continues to hold over all Chinese. For me, working on Mao became a form of exorcism."[57] In other words, Zhang focused on these images not just because they spoke to China's political history, but because they spoke to his own.

Many commentators have called the strategies of political pop a form of postmodern pastiche.[58] For Zhang and other artists of his generation, however, revolutionary imagery is central to their work and does not exist as simply a set of symbols from which they freely choose. "You have to understand how powerful his image is for my generation. During the Cultural Revolution, in my teens, he was like a god," Zhang explained.[59] When asked to compare his work to that of Andy Warhol, who also used portraits of Mao, Zhang responded: "Warhol just took the image of Mao as another mass icon, like Marilyn Monroe. But for Chinese artists, Mao is a political figure . . . Mao is still controversial. Today, even if his deeds are criticized, the government still uses his ideology, image, and flag. I believe that any

Figure 10 *Stone Mao*, from the Material Mao series, Zhang Hongtu. Stone, 25.5×25 in., 1992.

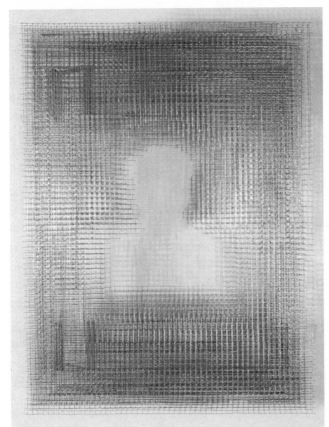

Figure 11 *Mesh Mao*, from the Material Mao series, Zhang Hongtu. Wire mesh, 36x27.5× 8.5 in., 1992.

use of Mao's image which makes him less godlike is a form of criticism. And it's necessary."[60]

These comments point not just to the differing historical contexts that shape Zhang's use of these images, but also to the differing affective relationships. Mao's image inspires in him not just awe and authority, but shame and guilt. He is not the only artist to have expressed the emotional dimension of these images. In the 1980s and 1990s, Li Shan's paintings focused almost exclusively on two portraits of Mao, a younger image from the 1930s and an older image, the one famously hung on the Tiananmen Gate during the Cultural Revolution. In his Rouge series (1994), Li faithfully reproduced these images, preserving their black-and-white photographic qualities. The portraits are transformed, however, through a process of "rouge-ization." Li tints the Chairman's face a light fuchsia, a color commonly found in New Year's prints and popular pageants in China.[61] The result is a feminized Mao: blushing and smiling, the Chairman is imbued with markers of feminine desirability, transforming him from political icon to object of sexual desire.

Works like Li's foreground the emotional content of this political image and expose the commonly felt but rarely expressed romantic feelings that many attached to Mao. Accounts from the Cultural Revolution reveal that he was loved far more than just a national leader.[62] Thanks in part to rumors of his extraordinary sexual appetite and to hush-hush tales of his romantic escapades, Mao was often seen as a romantic hero. One girl confessed: "He was, on the one hand, the radiant sun in the sky, giving life to everything on earth. This Mao I loved as millions of Chinese did at the time . . . But behind this Mao there was another: a secret, sweetheart hero of a fifteen-year-old girl . . . This Mao, to me, was not the radiant sun but a vulnerable man, a tragic hero."[63] Mao's political potency was in many ways tied to this sense of his physical potency. Even as he aged, there was much effort to show in official propaganda that he "glowed with health and vigor" and that he enjoyed a "ruddy complexion."[64]

Zhang's own work referenced Mao's attractive virility. In his multimedia installations *Front Door* (1995) and *Red Door* (1995), Zhang presented two doors for the audience to examine. With the first, a prerecorded knocking entices viewers to look through the door's peephole. But, rather than seeing the person knocking, the viewer discovers that it is she who is being watched, as Mao's eye peers back through the hole. In the second door, the audience is now the seeing subject, but what she sees in the crack is still

Figure 12 *Front Door*, Zhang Hongtu. Mixed media installation with audiotape, 84×32 in., 1995.

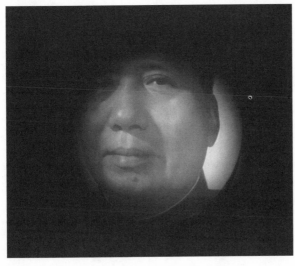

Figure 12a. *Front Door* detail, peephole, Zhang Hongtu.

Mao. Projected behind the door is a video of Mao dancing with a woman, and later, smoking with a group of women, one of whom is lighting his cigarette. The installations link Mao's political power (his all-seeing ability, which positions everyone else as the object of his gaze) and his sexual power, which is on display for all to see—and perhaps even to voyeuristically enjoy.[65]

Zhang's treatment of Mao consistently exposes the connections between national culture, collective memory, personal histories, and intimate desires. He reveals the complexities of Mao's image, and the complexities of Chinese responses to it. He exposes the role of all citizens, including himself, in contributing to Mao's authority by investing their own hopes, fantasies, and desires in this visual icon. The art historian Gao Minglu has argued that though political pop artists address the ideological content of revolutionary imagery, they do not wholly oppose it, contrary to what is often assumed. Most of these artists are in fact ambivalent about the Cultural Revolution and Maoist ideology, often glorifying the persuasiveness and aesthetic uniqueness of propagandist art.[66] Zhang's works do not exalt Maoist ideology; his creations are clearly critical of it. But they do highlight that sense of ambivalence, making visible an affective relationship that is often hidden in works of political pop. It is obvious that his struggle to "exorcise" Mao is framed in large part by his previous worship of Mao, and Zhang's works, particularly the sculptures, reveal that this exorcism can never be complete. Mao's imprint is indeed everywhere—in the earth, on the political stage, and in the bedroom. Perhaps above all else, Zhang wants to make this apparent.

DISLOYAL DISPLAYS

Though Zhang addresses very serious concerns, his collages and sculptures are not without humor. His "acupunctural art," for instance, reworks the traditional acupuncture chart by fitting it with Mao's corpulent body. The carefully graphed pressure points teach users to press on Mao's left forehead to release "class struggle," his right cheek for "revolutions," his left foot for "democracy," and so on. In these works, we grasp the psychic importance of Mao for the artist, but we also sense the humor and playfulness. Perhaps it was this playfulness that first drew Vivienne Tam to the artist. In 1994, she invited Zhang to collaborate with her on a collection that would feature images of Mao adapted from Zhang's artwork. Together they created eight different images, including "Mao So Young" (Mao with

群众是真正的英雄，而我们自己则往往是幼稚可笑的

"THE MASSES ARE THE REAL HEROS, WHILE WE OURSELVES ARE OFTEN CHILDISH AND IGNORANT."

Figure 13 *Chairmen Mao*, Zhang Hongtu. Photocollage and acrylic on paper, 8×11 in., 1989.

pigtails), "Ow Mao" (being stung by a bee), "Psycho Mao" (with psychedelic glasses), "Holy Mao" (with a clerical collar), "Miss Mao" (with lipstick), and "Nice Day Mao" (Mao as a yellow smiley face). When Zhang painted Mao with pigtails, Tam added a Peter Pan collar and gingham dress; when he put a bee on Mao's nose, she added stripes and colors to the background. Tam added a clerical collar to Mao's official portrait, Zhang smeared lipstick on the Chairman's face, and so on. As Tam put it, "Zhang's art was political, but I thought I could loosen it up a bit with fashion, to represent the new openness of China. This would show its humor and warmth, and the growing freedom of its people from Mao's image."[67]

Tam played with both the images themselves and the garments upon which they were imprinted. She created a fabric pattern by repeating these images in a series of four in the manner of a checkerboard—to allude, she said, to Mao's changing nature, and his positive and negative effects on Chinese culture.[68] Done in both black and white and in color, this pattern

Figure 14 "Fashion Mao," collaboration with Vivienne Tam, Zhang Hongtu, 1994.

became the collection's signature trademark. Tam cut dresses and tops in a sheer, slightly meshy fabric bearing this imprint, which flew off the shelves and ended up in museums. (These were without a doubt the most photographed pieces in the collection.) Though cut in a fairly conservative silhouette—with long sleeves, a crew neck, and a hemline that reached the ankle—the fabric hugged the body revealingly. On her models, these dresses took on an ultrafeminine and even eroticized cast.

Tam used these images to have fun with the garment's forms. She cleverly created a "collar" on a T-shirt by aligning Mao's neck with the neck of the shirt—nodding to the interplay between form and function (or lack thereof). She screened the black-and-white checkerboard on heavy silk and wool fabrics, and cut formal suits and coats out of them. In doing so, she created a dissonance not only between the formal style and the comical print but between the Eastern icon and the Western sartorial staple.

By far the most popular items in this collection were the tops Tam created by imprinting a simple cotton T-shirt with individual images of Mao. Each of the eight designs got its own shirt, backed by decorative patterns and enhanced by several hundred sequins. Mao's already outrageous visage was made even more so by these embellishments; in a certain light, his face seemed to actually twinkle. Sold for nearly a hundred dollars each, these pieces revealed most clearly the excesses of fashion, which could elevate a humble T-shirt to the ranks of couture. Those who could not afford the original, however, found that they could buy knockoffs for as low as a few dollars. Through these different chains of production, the images that Tam and Zhang created—in all their visual and material excess—were endlessly reproduced.

As is evident in these T-shirts, Tam's designs took Zhang's subtle wit to an extreme. In these images, Mao is overtly comical, recalling cartoon drawings in some cases (particularly in "Nice Day Mao"). Zhang's more elaborate brushwork has been pared down into simple lines, his complex texture rendered flat, and his more overtly politicized imagery remorselessly excised. These pieces play up political pop's parodic tendencies. Here, they seem to speak less the language of Dadaism than that of commercial product design. The sense of gravity that accompanied Zhang's paper collages, even in their humor, is now also largely gone. What remains is fun, cute, whimsical Mao.

When the collection debuted in November 1994, the reaction was mixed. Savvy commentators instantly drew connections to pop art, and the Metropolitan Museum of Art, the FIT Museum, the Victoria and Albert Museum, the Andy Warhol Museum, and others snatched up pieces for their permanent collections. Most U.S. buyers, however, failed to recognize the image—though, as Tam recalled, they "liked the humor of sticking this middle-aged Chinese guy in a pop fashion setting. 'Is that your father?' they'd ask. 'Who is this May-yo anyway?'"[69] The dramatic visibility of this icon failed to ensure any easy recognition or coherent reading.

Even for customers in Hong Kong, who had no trouble recognizing Mao's portrait, there was no less confusion about the collection's cultural meaning. Some people expressed outrage at Tam's use of the symbol. The designer reported that salespeople in her Hong Kong stores were harassed when she put the collection in store windows, and that young people told her they had to sneak out of the house when they wore the shirts.[70] Most Hong Kong residents, however, were unsure about how to respond to these hip, irreverent, and extremely expensive garments. One journalist who had received a promotional T-shirt in the mail expressed the dilemma thus: "A lot of the older generation in Hong Kong, I thought . . . came here precisely so that they wouldn't have to deal with Mao, pig-tailed or otherwise. I would hardly wear a t-shirt with Hitler blazoned across it in Europe, and I wasn't sure that it was morally right to parade an equivalent expensive joke around Hong Kong. Or indeed anywhere."[71] The journalist acknowledged that there was plenty of cheap Mao memorabilia available in Hong Kong but felt that these garments were somehow different—not least because they were far more costly. Unlike Mao cigarette lighters, which simply imprinted Mao's hallowed image onto objects of low culture, these garments transformed the image. The icon of political excess was remade into a symbol of commercial excess. All of this left the journalist, and certainly many Hong Kongers, wondering: "Is Mao funny?"[72]

The collection ultimately proved to be a hit, even in Hong Kong, and Tam became a certified fashion star. The designs appeared in countless fashion spreads, thousands of garments were sold, and—in a clear indication of their commercial value—millions of knockoffs circulated in the markets of Hong Kong and New York's Chinatown. In the end, these designs found a far larger audience than any of Zhang's previous work had. The commercial success of this collection has led most critics to assume that Tam's contribution was simply to depoliticize Zhang's images, making them palatable for a mass audience. But when Tam loosened up Zhang's political art, she also extended his critique in unexpected ways.

If Zhang's work attempted to expose the ways that the presentation of Mao as authoritative and charismatic leader relied in large part on the presentation of him as a masculine, paternal, and powerful figure, then this collection undermined that image even more powerfully. Tam was able to feminize Mao and make explicit the sexual undertones that Zhang's work gestured to. She achieved this by altering the images themselves and by screening them onto her visibly feminine dresses, with their body-conscious cuts and materials. She also accomplished this by inserting these garments into the gendered circuits of fashion, in which women are hailed as the normative consumers and in which ideas about femininity and sexuality are constantly asserted and reworked. Bear in mind that Tam designs only women's wear and that this collection traveled in the same circuit, on the same models, and in the same boutiques as her updated cheongsams. By presenting these garments in her catalogs and on her runways on shapely, and at times eroticized women, she situated these images squarely within a feminine context, enacting what amounted to a more radical form of "rouge-ization." Mao in these garments is absolutely and spectacularly unmasculine.

Moreover, in investing Zhang's images with "a bit of fashion," Tam was doing more than just popularizing them. Clothing as a cultural medium can communicate both the intensely intimate and the markedly public. Draped on our bodies and often used to express our identities, clothes are objects of our most intimate fascination. Yet they can also serve as the most public expression of our selves. "A part of the strangeness of dress," the scholar Elizabeth Wilson has said, "is that it links the biological body to the social being, and public to private."[73] In this linkage—this suturing of self to other—"clothing marks an unclear boundary ambiguously," making it difficult to distinguish between the individual and the collective, the profoundly intimate and the intensely public.[74] In this regard, clothing serves as the perfect medium for the types of personal struggles and public critiques that Zhang's art sought to enact. At the heart of Zhang's work lies a clear understanding that each individual, himself included, had a role to play in the collective drama that was the Cultural Revolution. The boundaries between state power and self-regulation, between personal devotion and public fealty, Zhang's art suggests, were and still are unclear. The medium of dress helps to drive home that sense of ambiguity even further.

The Cultural Revolution was a radical program that required the continual expression of individual loyalty, manifested in such outward signs as the display of Mao's photo, the memorization of his words, the wearing of his badges, the donning of Mao jackets, and so on. There was, in other words, an assumed relationship between public signs and private feelings.[75] In its delicate balance of public and private, clothing serves as the perfect vehicle for these impulses. But in Tam's hands, clothes can give voice to a range of imaginings. If items such as Mao badges were meant to serve as a public expression of private feelings of devotion, Tam's garments could allow for the public expression of entirely different feelings—loss, frustration, humor, hope, joy, and so on.

As a form that requires bodily presence, clothing does more than simply project an image; they shape those images. As bodies move through space, they make and remake images imprinted on the garments. "That was the thing that really hit me when I first saw the fashion show," Zhang recalled when seeing his images on Tam's dresses. "People who looked at the collection had different reactions to the images depending on where they were from and the bodies that wore them."[76] Scholars have written about the consumption of clothing as an inherently open-ended process, one in which wearers perform and attach different meanings to these material objects based on their social contexts.[77] Certainly the significance of Mao's image also varies according to the context and viewer. But Zhang's comments reveal the ways that bodies can enact—or generate—meaning at the point of aesthetic production. Fashion, as Ann Hollander observed decades ago, is a "form of visual art, a creation of images with the visible self as its medium."[78] Mao's image on these garments is not static, frozen, and framed like other works of art. It serves as prop, backdrop, and stage for the wearer's own performance. It shifts and changes with bodies and contexts. These images, in other words, are made and remade not just by Zhang and Tam, but by all who wear the garments.

Moreover, unlike most of Zhang's creations, these garments traveled outside the realm of avant-garde art into the sphere of popular culture, mixing together the sacred, political, and commercial. Unlike tourist T-shirts, which simply repeated Mao's likeness, these pieces remade it. And unlike avant-garde art, which straddled art and commerce but which nonetheless eschewed the masses, these pieces embraced them. To say that the clothes are more effective simply because they are more popular would be naive. After all, the costs of these garments—T-shirts for almost $100, and dresses and suits for over $1,000—meant that they were never truly mass objects. But the collection did extend the questions posed by Zhang and other Chinese artists into the realm of material culture, where they could be repeated for a wider audience.

Repetition serves an important function in this context. So effectively used as a mode of indoctrination during the Cultural Revolution, the technology of repetition here gets reinvented. The Mao collection repeats, but with a difference. We might think of it, per Judith Butler, as a disloyal or disidentifying repetition, one that allows for a reframing of the constitutive and the excluded.[79] The images are the same, but they are also constantly changing. These garments present history as a problematic to be continually addressed, not as a footprint to the future. As such, for all their flatness and cartoonish style, they worked not to undercut Zhang's critical impulse but to extend his reach.

Zhang seemed to have recognized the critical potential of this. The following year, inspired perhaps by this foray into fashion, he designed a series of T-shirts to commemorate Hong Kong's return to Chinese rule in 1997. The series, called Hong Kong 1997, similarly employs iconic images in new ways. In a fairly radical departure from his realist painting style, Zhang engaged more forcefully with commercial design. In "Hong Kong 1997"—also the name of one of the designs—the artist juxtaposed the Great Wall and Hong Kong's skyline, with the wall positioned prominently behind, as if looming over the city. The closeness of the Great Wall to Hong Kong's cityscape suggests both intimacy and distance, both similarity and difference—they may appear to belong together (both are monumental in scale), but there is dissonance in the juxtaposition. How will these two entities really fit together in the "one country, two systems" plan, the design seems to ask? In "Good Luck, Year of the Ox," Zhang paints the Chinese and British flags side by side over the face of an ox. In "Welcome!" he places an ox's head over a female body wearing a westernized *qipao*. The ox and the flag hint at the difficult internal history of Hong Kong. Enveloped by both Chinese and British flags, the ox shows its hybrid influence (this mixture is literally embodied in the ox-human hybrid in "Welcome!") as if to ask what exactly its own history is, and how will this history change once Hong Kong's political affiliations change.[80]

Like the Mao collection, Zhang's Hong Kong T-shirts similarly present history as a set of questions that bear repeating. But these shirts examine an icon from a cognitive remove, whereas Tam and Zhang's Mao collection is composed of very intimate portraits, drawn from the collective memories of Chinese still affected by Mao's legacy. The use of Mao here doesn't just rescript him as a celebrity—on a par with Marilyn Monroe and Elvis Presley, as Warhol's art might—but instead evokes the particular legacies of Chinese political history, even or especially for those who have emigrated elsewhere. Here we do not see Mao as a mass icon, as a reflection of what we know of him from a distance. We see instead an intimate figure who still haunts the imagination of immigrants like Zhang—that continues to excite deep emotions in them.

Mao in this collection may be emptied of ideology, but he remains filled with meaning—not that the viewer or wearer of these garments will necessarily invoke or read them in the same way. For many, Tam's Mao fashions are probably not so different from Che Guevara T-shirts, vague kitsch symbols of revolutionary spirit. For these consumers, revolutionary figures like Mao are attractive because they represent an ethos of defiance and rebelliousness that signals the cool and the hip.[81] For others, wearing Mao fashions may indicate a sense of national pride, a way of claiming an ethnic identity, since there's nothing that inscribes an in-group more than an in joke. For still others, these clothes may simply represent the newest and latest in fashion, the most recent must-have items. But what is certain here is that Tam's use of Mao was more than a simple case of cultural tourism. Rather than offering her audiences only another recognizable visual trope, her creation actually reminded them, as Cheng said, of the "difficulty of looking at the visible," and of the possibility of fashioning histories out of icons.

Traveling in the global marketplace, these images—like all images—are open to a range of performances and interpretations. Tam recognizes this. Though she sees it as her mission to "translate Chinese elements into fashion," she also knows that she must make the translation for more than just Chinese consumers.[82] As she often tells the fashion press, her clothes are "for everyone." For most of Tam's customers, the history that is being invoked here will not be readily available. But for those who "get it," who share in the "popular preconscious," as Victor Burgin might call it, of those who lived through the Cultural Revolution, ideas about power, authority, commitment, desire, and so on linger in the field of meaning evoked by Mao's image.[83] One student from mainland China who came to Zhang's studio, for instance, claimed that he "saw" his piece—that he could see Mao's image where Zhang had cut out only a hole.[84] For this constituency, these objects of luxury, frivolity, and commerce can communicate very intimately a sense of collective history, and a psychic release from it.

The collaboration between Tam and Zhang, then, was not a departure from the goals of much Chinese avant-garde art, from which it clearly drew inspiration, but an extension of them. If avant-garde artists used the idiom of commercial culture to satirize Mao's legacy, Deng's reforms, and the creeping forces of capitalism, Tam used commercial culture itself to participate in those conversations. The collection must be understood within this broader context. Tam's use of Mao subjected him to the type of ridicule, adoration, and critique that was very much a part of Chinese visual culture at the time. Moreover, it announced loudly what avant-garde artists often only whispered: in repeating Mao's image, they could "fail to repeat loyally," and in the interface between subject and society there is a space for change.[85]

The critic Norman Bryson has written that contemporary Chinese artists work at a time when practices that previously would have been considered dissident or counterrevolutionary are often harnessed for nationalist ends, making it difficult to distinguish between avant-garde and state practices. As such, artists understand that what holds the social together, far more than just state power, is "the myriad acts of self-regulation by which the subject inscribes itself into the social discourse." If, Bryson argues, "the basis of cultural reproduction lies in the subject's own capacity for compulsive repetition and system-building, the significance of aesthetic practices is that it permits those capacities to be deflected or redirected toward the subject's own ends."[86] The Mao collection, in its seemingly endless replication—of images and garments—mirrors this compulsive repetition. But it uses Mao's image not just for indoctrination but also for expression, or at least deflection. Tam may have been naive to suggest that her designs express the "growing freedom of [Chinese] people from Mao's image," but, her aesthetic practice—treading the ambiguous border between self and other, public and private—can wrest the control of image production away from both the state and the artists, and make it accessible to the very subjects whose lives and losses have been shaped by them.

CONCLUSION

In his study of modern history, *The Age of Extremes*, Eric Hobsbawm mused: "Why brilliant fashion-designers, a notoriously non-analytic breed, sometimes succeed in anticipating the shape of things to come better than professional predictors, is one of the most obscure questions in history and, for the historian of culture, one of the most central."[87] Hobsbawm asked this not as an admirer of fashion—his treatment of the popular arts in this text is ambivalent at best—but as one genuinely perplexed about the failure of scholars, politicians, and others to see the emerging developments of our world. "To see the future," one must "look at the past," Hobsbawm later wrote.[88] He was referring here to the importance of history in constructing a perspective about the future, and if we believe fashion theorists, this dictum is precisely why fashion designers seem to always envision the next thing so clearly.

Fashion designers, many scholars have noted, are continually looking to the past, drawing on it, quoting from it. But history in this context has always indexed more than just time. From the birth of modern fashion, designers have culled inspiration from myriad cultural references that have come to stand in for the past—the East is perhaps top among these. These uses of the East have not been limited to Western designers alone. As the example of Han Feng's coolies with which I began this chapter reveal, Asian designers have also conflated history and mythology, place and time. But in their hands, evocations of the East can mean more than just a set of symbols, elements, or styles. So-called Asian forms, images, and icons have become globalized, in fashion and elsewhere. Yet while they have become unmoored from their referent, they still bear the material and historical traces of their origin. Vivienne Tam's Mao collection may in the end simply serve as the exception that proves the rule, but it also demonstrates that it is possible to mark those traces and to forge histories out of icons.

Zhang Hongtu's work is invested, above all, in revealing the personal, intimate, affective relationship of the artist to a global icon. This intimate relationship was forged in the fires of the Cultural Revolution—a time when political allegiance and personal devotion were conflated and contained in the image of Chairman Mao. Zhang sought to expose the connections between national culture, collective memory, personal histories, and private desires, as well as the difficulty or even impossibility of exorcising those histories. If Mao's ubiquitous portraits fostered an imaginative closeness between the Chairman and his subjects—he could not be everywhere, but his images certainly could—Zhang's work highlighted the cost of such an enforced intimacy. His art refuses to accept any distance between personal history and political icon. It refuses to see Mao as only an international icon, detached from the lives of Chinese still affected by his legacy.

Tam's collection helped to complete this narrative. With its absolute proximity to the body, Tam's clothing emphasized more assertively the concept of intimacy expressed in Zhang's work. To see Mao's image draped so closely, and in some cases so provocatively, on the wearer is to be struck by the way that it is made and remade by the human form precisely at the point of contact between the public and the private, between the exposed and the hidden. No longer just a symbol handed down from above to be embraced below, Mao's image is generated, accepted, embellished, or rejected at this point of connection.

This is an intimacy that stands in contrast to the "cultural economy of distance," in Arjun Appadurai's terms, that, as I demonstrated in the last chapter, characterizes Western consumption of non-Western goods.[89] Perhaps it is an enforced intimacy as well, bound up as it is with fashion's own hierarchical demands, but it nonetheless makes central the role of the subject in the production of the image. Zhang implies that all Chinese, himself included, submitted to Mao's authority by investing in this visual icon. Tam's collection may not free people from Mao's image, but it can highlight this history and make visible its imprints on the future. At a time when images freely circulate, unmoored from their historical and social context, this work insists on historical perspective. In doing so, it refuses the logic of distance that seeks to separate here and there, or nation and diaspora, and points to the possibility that Asian images could be more than just a floating signifier. They could serve as resource to narrate historical memories, bolstered—rather than severed—by the process of migration.

To return to Hobsbawm's question, how do fashion designers predict the future so well? They certainly do not do so just by looking at the past. Fashion's history is littered with examples of styles revived, images reused, and materials recycled, but few of these creations can tell us where we're going. What they lack is access not to history, but to historical perspective. Only those who can cull from history its hard-learned lessons, who can keep taut its tension with the present, and who can see their own place in it can give us a perceptive vision of the future. After all, as Hobsbawn also said, "what history cannot tell us is what will happen, only what problems we shall have to solve."[90] Tam and Zhang's collaboration seems to recognize this, for they offer few answers about the future. History here is posited neither as a particular time or place, but as a set of questions that must be continually asked, that must be repeated. To be sure, these are not easy questions to pose, as perhaps those who initially protested this work seemed to sense. In this collection we see the past not as something that can comfortably be left behind, or resurrected in the form of nostalgia, but as close kin to the present. This is the challenge for fashion. To the extent that it can give us a vision of the future, it can do so only by taking up this historical perspective—by seeing in the past not contrast but kinship, not distance but intimacy.

If Asian American designers have been up for the challenge, it is because their diasporic imaginations have been greatly informed by an aesthetic of intimacy. For Tam, this transnational intimacy was articulated through the use of a seemingly recognizable Asian trope, whose apparent visibility hid so much more. But for many other designers, the Asia of their imagination exists both within and beyond these hypervisible signs. Figuring simultaneously as ancestral home and aesthetic resource, as site of production and coveted market, the varied conceptions of Asia and Asian influences in these designers' work at times exceeded the realm of the visual. In the next chapter, I want to examine how Asian American designers expressed this diasporic imagination, informed at once by the affective, the aesthetic, and the economic. What does the East hold for young Asian Americans who are wary of Asian chic, but who nonetheless sense kinship and intimacy with their imagined Asia?

Chapter 5

ASIA ON MY MIND

TRANSNATIONAL INTIMACIES

AND CULTURAL GENEALOGIES

In her roundup of the fall fashion shows of 2004, *Time*'s Kate Betts confessed to a bit of confusion. That year, there were a remarkable number of Asian Americans presenting designs—including such well-known names as Thakoon Panichgul, Derek Lam, and Peter Som—but their presence could hardly be detected in the collections. Contrary to her expectations, these designers betrayed no hint of their Asianness, sending out clothes that looked, as she put it, far "more C. Z. Guest than Suzy Wong." "You could call it an Asian invasion," she postulated, "except that none of these designers would classify his look in such confining geographic and cultural terms, even though each admits that his work is informed by his roots in unexpected ways."[1]

At first glance, Betts's reading of these designers, which set up as question rather than fact any relationship they may have had to their "roots," seems to refuse any easy essentialism. Yet in her attempt to describe these "unexpected" influences, the author dredged up some fairly recognizable tropes of Asianness. She proposed, for instance, that Lam's clothes are shaped by a sense of "Asian propriety and restraint," and that Panichgul's "reserved, almost conservative sensibility reflects his Eastern origins." These designers were described as "very serious," sharing a "demeanor" distinct from the extroverted personalities more common in New York fashion. Betts reasserted the sense of their inherent cultural difference, even as she set out to undermine it. While she acknowledged these designers' refusal to be understood in "confining geographic and cultural terms," she nonetheless articulated an understanding of them drawn from a narrow racial and national imaginary.[2]

These shortcomings highlight the difficulties of writing about culture and aesthetics, especially within a medium so constrained by the demands of the marketplace. I begin with this article not so much to critique it as to acknowledge these challenges and to highlight the crucial questions that it implicitly raises. How should we interpret the ambivalence that Asian Americans have always expressed about their "roots?" What is their relationship to Asia, as a symbolic and material site? How can we talk about an Asian aesthetic without resorting to a reductive racial logic, or to the spectularized images that have dominated Euro-American fashion history? In this chapter, I take up those questions. While my analysis takes me far from the terrain covered by *Time*, it begins with a similar struggle to understand how, in the hypervisible realm of fashion, we read ideas about Asianness that do not rest comfortably on the surface.

Though they did not articulate these questions in this way, my interviewees struggled with them as well. Betts was right to note that Asian American designers did not want to confine themselves culturally or geographically, but this did not mean that culture, history, ethnicity, and nationality were not meaningful in their lives and work. Asia had influenced them in various ways, but when to claim these affinities and when to disavow them, how to mark them and how to erase them, were not questions that they could easily resolve.

To be sure, these designers knew that there was value in their assumed (or prescribed) relationship to Asia, and that a well-placed dragon here and there could land them in the pages of *Vogue* or on the racks at Barneys. This knowledge led many to "do something ethnic," to employ the racialized and gendered tropes that the market so desired. Yet even such apparent capitulations were never straightforward, as my discussion of the occlusions and revelations around Vivienne Tam's Mao collection makes clear. But the designers' understanding of Asia and its influences—informed as it was simultaneously by the affective, aesthetic, and economic—were never contained by these visual tropes alone.

In this chapter, I attempt to tease out the ways (and the places in which) Asian American designers have articulated notions of culture, nation, affinity, and belonging in their work. I explore how they understand their "roots," how these are represented sartorially, and where we might trace their origins. In examining the transnational intimacies that the designers forged with Asia and beyond, I argue that Asian Americans' diasporic imaginations, while manifested in the terrain of the symbolic, were activated by exchanges made in the realm of the material. Just as Asian American designers had been encouraged to articulate an ethnic identity by the benefits won and relationships built with garment producers, they were similarly persuaded to claim a transnational identity by various other material incentives. These subjects forged relationships with Asia in part because they could imagine it as a home, but also in part because they saw it as a burgeoning market. These intimacies were manifested in the symbolic realm not through the use of exotic images and styles, but through a particular approach to design, one that saw clothing as a form of architecture, protecting and enabling the body, rather than dissecting and displaying it. Inspired by the work of avant-garde Japanese designers, particularly the so-called Big Three (Rei Kawakubo, of Comme des Garçons; Yohji Yamamoto; and Issey Miyake), Asian American designers at times sought out forms that could contain rather than exhibit the body. These ideas became their most important Asian influence. Yet, as I demonstrate below, the innovations that Japanese designers brought to Paris had affinities with other sartorial traditions, particularly those from Arab cultures, and thus were perhaps always already polycultural.[3]

By suggesting that Asian Americans were influenced by Japanese cultural formations, then, I do not mean to imply that either of these are discrete or coherent categories. Indeed, in tracing these connections, my aim is less to show how Asian Americans have employed Asian culture—retained, transformed, or acculturated it, to use some common terms for describing its movement—than to raise further questions about the very idea of cultural inheritance, transmission, or genealogy. My investigation into what Asia has meant to these designers, symbolically and materially, has taken me beyond its commonly accepted borders. The transnational intimacies that I have marked here reach both to what we know as Asia and to what we assume is elsewhere. If Asian American designers "inherited" some of their ideas and approaches from the Big Three, do those ideas constitute a type of Asian influence simply because they were formalized by Japanese designers? Where do we mark the boundaries of Asian culture? How do we trace the genealogies of Asian American forms and practices? While I cannot answer all these questions here, I raise them to suggest that the ambivalences my interviewees articulated and *Time* tried to resolve cannot be settled by assuming a notion of an Asian diaspora or Asian world that is disconnected from, to borrow the historian Robin Kelley's formulation, "other streams of internationalism."[4]

FASHIONING HOME

"It's always been easier for me to get attention and sales from Japan," Jen Kao once told me. "For some reason, they just get what I'm doing." Kao had just launched her eponymous label the year before, and though she had garnered some critical attention, she had yet to establish herself in New York's retail outlets. Yet her brand was doing quite well in Japan, where retailers were eager to stock her collections. In defiance of the typical pattern for young designers, who build brand recognition by first selling to local (or online) retail outlets, fledgling Asian American designers like Kao often found that they could sell internationally before even making a dent in the New York market. Indeed, these designers found that some of their most ardent fans and loyal customers came from Asia. Welcomed by a press that covered their collections assiduously, and by governmental and corporate institutions that supported them financially, these designers were in various ways hailed as subjects of a "homeland" to which many had never traveled but from which they gained tremendous material benefits.

As I discussed earlier, the rise of the Asian designer during the mid-1990s coincided with (and was in part enabled by) the passage of the Agreement on Textiles and Clothing (ATC) and the expansion of trade liberalization. During this time, Asian nations anxious about the sped-up demands and downgraded wages required by the era of free trade began efforts to upgrade their garment industries, including establishing fashion schools and other infrastructure, in the hope of transforming Asia from the world's factory to its catwalk. These aspirations, they found, required not just an infrastructural but a cultural overhaul. Against the common perception of Asia as a sartorial backwater, these nations had to remake their image from producers of mass clothing and native costumes into makers of modern, chic fashion. They had, in other words, to rebrand Asia itself.

The results of these efforts are as yet unknown. While firms in Hong Kong and other areas have had some success in own brand manufacturing (OBM), attempts to move up the fashion ladder have been slow and uneven, due in large part to the challenges that Asian designers have faced in gaining acceptance in the centers of fashion. With a few exceptions, Asian designers who have ventured to Paris and New York have found these fashion cities to be less than welcoming. The South Korean brand Y&Kei, for instance, has struggled to find an audience in New York, despite its tremendous popularity in South Korea. Though the brand boasted that its sales reached $110 million in Korea, its first U.S. store, in New York's Soho, had few customers. Attendance at its fashion week presentations has been sparse, and it has received no celebrity endorsements, which in recent years has become key to a brand's success. Gene Kang, one of the brand's two chief designers, admits that in the United States—unlike in Korea—Y&Kei's "clothes don't fly off the shelves, and don't get talked about. I'm not the hot kid on the block." In response to these challenges, the Seoul government recently announced that it would set up a center in Paris to help South Korean designers who are faltering in the international market.[5] During the spring 2010 New York fashion shows, the government launched "Concept Korea: Fashion Collective 2010," a three-day display of works by six Korean designers at the New York Public Library. The goal of the event, cosponsored by the Council of Fashion Designers of America (CFDA), was to increase the global visibility of these designers through their partnership with such influential institutions.

While international fashion has not been quick to embrace Asia's exports, it has been eager to court its consumers. In the last decade, China, Korea, India, Malaysia, and other developing countries in Asia have become coveted new markets for global luxury conglomerates. Investors have in particular extolled the virtues of China, whose burgeoning middle class and increasingly capitalist-friendly government have made the country, in the words of Jonathan Garner, a "global strategist" for Credit Suisse, the new "engine of growth in the global economy."[6] Indeed, many business books have been dedicated to the topic of the Chinese consumer, each more breathless than the next. Garner's tome, for instance, insists that "Chinese consumers have not only woken up and stood up but . . . in increasing numbers they are getting rich and starting to spend. The impact of Chinese consumers on [consumer-oriented] companies is likely to be as significant as the impact of Chinese producers on manufacturing and resources companies in the last 10 years."[7]

Such boosterist rhetoric is typical of these accounts. Though the mantra that Chinese consumption will soon outpace even that of the United States has become accepted wisdom, these claims are not founded on the actual habits of Chinese consumers. Rather, they are based on calculations of their projected spending—on the hopes that their current rate of consumption will continue unabated, and that this currently "marginal force" will soon become the "second-largest economy in the world."[8] If such exuberant numbers do not sell themselves, these kinds of reports are often paired with culturalist narratives that combine China's growing capacity to consume with its long-repressed desire to do so. Living under an authoritarian regime and accustomed to having their "iron rice bowls" (an expression used to describe the job security that most Chinese enjoy) all filled with the same drab content, these subjects are portrayed as particularly enthusiastic consumers.[9] As *Time* put it, "finally allowed to throw off their drab Mao suits," Chinese consumers are "experimenting with what it's like to be free and they will try anything."[10]

These claims—which conflate freedom with consumption—present corporations with both an economic incentive and a moral rationale (should they need one) to pursue new markets, in Asia and elsewhere.[11] Their optimism has sent major luxury firms racing to set up shops in these areas. In recent years, high-end brands like Gucci, Armani, Prada, Versace, and Louis Vuitton have poured resources into Asia, building new flagship stores and filling up shopping malls, all in the hopes of eventually winning the affection and loyalty of these all-important consumers.

To be sure, there has in fact been a growth in income for some in this region. In China, for instance, the per capita income doubled between 1978 and 1990; it increased another 50 percent between 1990 and 1994.[12] And the consumption of domestic goods such as televisions and refrigerators has also greatly expanded. In 1986, 29 percent of Chinese households owned a color television; by 1995, that number had risen to 95 percent, with even higher ownership rates in urban areas.[13] But for the most part, corporations chasing the Asian market have been disappointed by what Elisabeth Croll has characterized as the exaggerated expectations for China's new consumers.[14]

This has certainly been the case with designer fashion. Shiny new boutiques filled with of-the-moment merchandise have attracted more tourists and window-shoppers than they have customers. Far more expensive than even rich Chinese can easily afford, Prada dresses and Armani purses have lingered on the shelves, coveted but not consumed. Even so, Asia remains the great hope for these luxury companies, particularly as declining sales in the West, which dipped even further after the 2008 economic crisis, have made new markets an absolute necessity. With assurances from financial consultants that an Asian shopping boom is just around the bend, these companies are willing to accept their current losses for a future return. In places like China, where capturing even a small percentage of the population would mean selling more than in any other country, the courtship continues as luxury firms wait patiently for the "sleeping giant" (a term first used for China by Napoleon Bonaparte) to awaken.

In the last few years, then, developing countries in Asia have found themselves in the unhappy position of garnering little attention as fashion producers but getting much notice as fashion consumers. While Euro-American corporations have been happy to embrace Asia as a new market, their fashion industry has been less than welcoming to Asian designers. In their struggle to change this situation, Asian governmental and corporate entities increasingly saw Asian American designers, enviably positioned within New York's fashion industry, as useful allies. Located in the West and embraced by its institutions, these designers were seen as insiders whose very presence at the center of fashion could help to rebrand Asia.

As such, Asian institutions have worked hard to forge connections with Asian American designers. They have done so in part by bestowing upon them awards that claim these designers as their own. For instance, David Chu, the Chinese American designer for Nautica, was given a Benefactor Award by the state-run Chinese Fashion Designers Association in 2003. In 2005, the China Fashion Association presented its award for International Fashion designer of the Year to U.S. women's wear designer Vera Wang, the granddaughter of Chinese immigrants. That year, the Hong Kong Design Centre awarded Vivienne Tam—born in Hong Kong and living in New York—the title of World's Outstanding Chinese Designer, which marked her as an "ambassador for Chinese fashion and design throughout the world" and "one of the truly global faces of China." Tam, who is the only fashion designer to have ever won this award, which traditionally recognizes architectural and industrial designers, was chosen because her "success as a designer of Asian background has been an example to young designers in Hong Kong and China."[15]

These awards showcased the work of Asian American designers and marked them as representative of Asian design. They served as evidence not just to the fashion world but to Asian subjects as well that it is possible to move up the fashion ladder. For the crowds gathered in Shanghai to witness Vera Wang accepting her award, her story is "proof," reported one newspaper, "that a designer with a Chinese heritage can have global appeal."[16] The role of these designers, then, was not just to rebrand Asia but to discipline its citizens into a new regime of production. Although there was no such creature as a designer in those sites until just a few decades ago, that function existed, carried out by tailors, sewers, and others who contributed their creative input to the making of clothes. For decades, however, workers, particularly women, were asked to dampen their own creative impulses in order to churn out reproducible, standardized products for transnational firms.[17] As mass manufacturing became more competitive and branded clothing more desirable with the rise of trade liberalization, designers and their creative skills have become a national priority.[18] In this context, Asian American designers stood as a shining example that Asian subjects could and should retrain themselves to meet the changing needs of their government.

Despite the symbolic weight of these events, the awards being handed out were not just symbolic gestures; many of them were monetary prizes that could provide a young designer with a huge financial boost. For instance, in 2005, Samsung Cheil Industries, in a public-private partnership, established the Samsung Fashion Design Fund to "discover and sponsor talented young Korean designers around the world" in order "realize the dream of Korean fashion." The winner receives a cash prize of $100,000 and the accompanying publicity, and there is "an annual event in Seoul to introduce them to Korea." Korean American designers—including Doo-Ri Chung, Richard Chai, Aimee Cho (of Gryphon), and Sonia Yoon (of Bensoni)—have constituted the majority of the recipients.[19] While Chung and Chai were already fairly well established when they were honored by Samsung, Cho and Yoon had been designing for only a few years. When I asked a former Samsung employee (a current Pratt fashion student from Korea) how they were able to garner such recognition at this early stage in their careers, she responded that part of the intention of the fund was to develop new Korean American designers by providing them with the money to jump-start their businesses. But would these funds not be better spent on Korean designers? "Well," she told me, "they see Korean Americans as a better investment. Since they're already here in the New York, it's easier for them to get recognition. And recognition for them means recognition for Korea."

The prizes then suture Asian Americans to Asian states, corporations, and citizens through both material and symbolic means.[20] They hail these designers as Asian subjects who can bring glory to their country and serve as examples to their fellow citizens. By marking them in this way, these institutions are able to convert diasporic peoples into national subjects whose individual achievements can stand in for national victories.[21] The Samsung fund's website makes this link explicit, proclaiming that the fund's goal is not just to recognize design talent but to "develop the individual, the company, and the nation."[22]

This connection is further reinforced by the Asian press, which has been unwavering in its commitment to covering Asian American designers. Asian publications routinely carry stories about them, showcase their collections, and publicize their achievements in accounts that present them as something of local heroes. In doing so, the publications not only expose Asian American designers to new consumers but treat them as national subjects with whom these consumers are encouraged to identify. The designers become more than just another fashionable brand—they become sites of emotional and imaginative investment. When they travel to their "native" country, they are treated like celebrities by fans (and aspiring designers) who want to know how they "made it." The designer Anna Sui, for instance, has said that whenever she visits China, she feels "like a rock star."[23]

This exposure has made it easier for young Asian Americans to enter the retail market in Asia. Many of my interviewees already sold their products internationally, some through Web sites but many through hard-to-reach retail outlets, despite their small-scale operations. Others were eager to market their designs in Asia, confident that they would find a receptive audience since "they already know us over there," as one interviewee told me. In this way, the symbolic claims made on these designers could be translated into material assets, enabling them to receive financial investments, brand recognition, and market exposure in a region that had become fashion's great retail hope. In the race to capture the Asian market, these designers' cultural identities were proving to be an important resource, just as they had in the designers' relationships with garment workers.

For their part, Asian Americans have been quite willing to return this transnational embrace. When offered various prizes, these designers, who ordinarily shy away from public discussions of their cultural background, become quite vocal about the affections they have for their "homeland." In accepting her award from the China Fashion Association, for instance, Vera Wang—born and bred in New York—remarked: "This is very big deal for me emotionally. It really is my roots."[24] Articulating an emotional if not a physical intimacy, these designers often represented Asia as a place to which they were inevitably tied.

Indeed, in our interviews they often presented this "home," forged more through their parents' memories of Asia than their own experiences of it, as something of an emotional touchstone. Interviewees confessed that their parents were far more excited about seeing their names mentioned in the Asian-language press than in the pages of *Vogue*. In this sense, Asia always mattered more. They spoke about feeling an "instant connection" when they visited because they had heard so much about these places from family members. They narrated their desire to open a store in Asia as a journey "back home." This discourse of home pervaded my interviewees' discussions about Asia, imbuing the region with a personal, intimate connection that refused to see it, as the discourse of Asian chic would insist, through the lens of distance.

Of course, these ideas about "home" have long informed the cultural and political imaginaries of many ethnic subjects. Scholars have shown that transnational networks and affiliations of various kinds have become an almost unremarkable part of life under globalization.[25] But home has also always been a complex site; in this case, it was forged not just through affect but also through economics. Asian Americans' interpellation by Asian institutions has garnered them some important economic benefits. Whether they acknowledged or disavowed these benefits, the result is an international presence that is incongruent with their standing in the fashion industry. If, as Jen Kao said, the Japanese "just get what I'm doing," the reasons for this type of reception have everything to do with the performance and the perception of her ethnic identity. In consenting to—even pursuing—those identities, Asian American designers were translating their Asianness into a resource that, whatever else it does and describes, fundamentally works to their economic advantage.[26] While the intimacies articulated by these designers were certainly shaped by their migration histories, cultural memories, familial experiences, and personal desires, they were also activated by material incentives and economic aspirations. It is no coincidence, for instance, that during the same week that Wang accepted her award from the China Fashion Association and spoke those moving words about her roots, she also opened a bridal boutique, The Perfect Wedding, in Shanghai's Pudong Shangri-La hotel.[27]

The discourse of home helps to downplay, or even conceal, these economic dimensions. But it is clear that in expressing their affections for Asia or affiliations with its people, these designers were not just asserting the symbolic importance of home, they were also extracting material value from it. By consenting to be Chinese, Korean, and so on, these designers were entering into a relationship of exchange. For them, the payoff was primarily economic, although the affective returns were also clearly important. For Asian governments and institutions, the benefit is cultural. While Asian states have always been solicitous of their emigrants' overseas dollars, what is notable here is that they have shown extraordinary interests in Asian American designers, who offer them very little in terms of economic return. (Indeed, the designers' success in Asia can only draw revenue from the region.) What these designers can provide, however, is cultural capital, the prestige and status they accrue by virtue of their locations in the West and their embrace by Western fashion institutions. We might think of this, following Juan Flores, as a form of "cultural remittance," though one that does not contribute to the radical cultural changes that he observed.[28] If these Asian Americans are meant to serve as examples for the fashion industry, they also act as models for Asian citizens, who must remake themselves in these designers' image in order to keep up with the demands of global capitalism.

Asian Americans are tied to Asia through this network of exchange, and through the market forces that have linked their fates to the region's. These material networks have helped them transform Asia into a home and themselves into its transnational subjects. Asian American designers have not been artless about when to embrace Asia and when to disavow it, when to perform intimacy and when to enact distance. While they have refused to wear their ethnicities on their sleeves, they have not refused to claim an ethnic identity or to resist the embrace of their "homeland." These decisions, to accept or eschew ethnic and national affiliations, are not determined by utility alone. But nor are they divorced from the terrain of the economic.

Years ago, Stuart Hall pointed out that material circumstances do not just provide the context for understanding symbolic identity; they constitute its very conditions of possibility.[29] This adage has been borne out by the dynamics I have observed here. In some ways, the transnational intimacies that these designers have forged are not so different from the types of exchanges they have enacted with garment workers. In both cases there are interested parties whose sense of their shared identities, real and imagined, encouraged them to build linkages that collapsed the affective and the economic, the familiar or familial and the utilitarian. Just as the exchanges that designers shared with garment workers have been instrumental in the formation of a cross-class affiliation, the benefits reaped (by both parties) has helped to stimulate a transnational connection. In both instances, it was their ethnic identities that brought these designers into the networks of exchange, but it was only through the process of exchange that they came to understand themselves as ethnic or national subjects.

Their performance of a cultural identity, in its ethnicized or transnationalized forms, cannot be divorced from the various material incentives that have made those identities useful. What they reveal is not just that race and ethnicity are social constructs that have material, institutional ramifications, but that material conditions help to constitute what subjects come to know, or claim, as their race, ethnicity, nationality, and so on. Asianness for these designers exists not as a collection of signs to be used or discarded, but as a set of practices that have called those very identities into being, that have materialized them as a resource. In forging intimacies with their roots, these designers were asserting their sense of proximity to this place that was always constructed as somewhere out there. But if the Asia of their imagination was narrated as a cherished home, it was also a burgeoning market; these two were always intimately linked.

ARCHITECTS OF FASHION

But if Asianness was not just a collection of signs, how were these ideas about culture, nation, and identity manifested sartorially, in this most visual realm? Years ago, in one of my very first interviews, the designer Yukie Ohta gave me an unexpected answer to this question. In explaining how she understood the relationship between culture and aesthetics, Ohta told me that she considered her "most Asian quality" the way "I approach design like a math problem." I was bewildered by her reply, not just because it sounded a bit essentialist, but because design seemed as far from a math problem as I could imagine. After all, I was accustomed to hearing designers talk about "inspiration" and "creativity," words that represent their work in a far less analytical light. But Ohta's comment stuck with me because over the years it was repeated by so many other interviewees. Design is "just calculations," Yeohlee Teng told me. "It's all numbers," Selia Yang insisted, adding that her degree in math had been a tremendous help in her design career. "You have to be able to look at the shape and put it into numbers," Yang explained. "Then you have to figure out how to divide the numbers to get the lines you want. It's just doing the math, really." How did these designers come to share such a similarly odd characterization of their work? What did this say about the nature of their "Asian influences"?

It was some time before I understood the significance of Ohta's words. By framing their work in this way, these designers were acknowledging their debt to an important Asian source: avant-garde Japanese designers, particularly the Big Three, who transformed fashion in the 1980s with their "deconstructionist" approach to design.[30] Asian Americans' surprising insistence on seeing design essentially as a math problem can be attributed in part to these influences. Thuy Pham explained to me: "The Japanese designers in the eighties had a distinctively Japanese way of making clothes. They often made clothes on the table, cutting it flat [instead of draping]. I've taken from that technique. You don't really imagine how it's going to fit on the body. And when you throw it on it fits, because it has its own structure and geometry. It's a mathematical way of making clothes. It's like in architecture—you're going after a particular form." The preoccupations that Pham attributes to Japanese designers—this "mathematical way of making clothes," this understanding of clothing as "architecture," this disregard for "how it's going to fit"—would also become a preoccupation for other Asian American designers. And in borrowing their ideas and techniques, some Asian Americans also took up these Japanese designers' different ways of seeing the relationship between clothing and the body, between concealment and exposure.

The appearance of Japanese designers in Paris during the 1980s—the initial shock their clothes provoked and the eventual transformations they engendered—has been well documented.[31] Fashion historians generally begin this history in the 1970s, when Kenzo Takada (of the label Kenzo) set up shop in Paris and won critical praise for his use of mixed prints and folklore-inspired designs. As the first Japanese designer to present at the Paris couture shows and to be accepted by Parisian critics, he paved the way for Kawakubo, Miyake, and Yamomoto. But it was not until the latter arrived in the 1980s that "the Japanese revolution," as the sociologist Yuniya Kawamura has called it, really began.[32] In 1981, Yamamoto and Kawakubo organized a joint show in which they presented shirts with two neck holes and three sleeves; dresses with straight, simple shapes; and oversized coats that could be worn by men or women—all with unfinished seams, irregular hemlines, loosely fitting layers, and asymmetrical shapes. The fashion press initially balked at these creations, which they read as an attack on fashion itself. The French early on referred to the look as "Le Destroy" or, more derisively, as the "Hiroshima Bag Lady."[33] In the United States, it was labeled "post-atom-bomb fashion."[34]

If these designers' creations were not exactly an attack on fashion, they were challenges to some of its fundamental norms. In distinction to much European couture, which has traditionally sought to accentuate the body, these clothes offered a different way of relating to it. With their additional neck holes and sleeves, they refused the primacy of the physical body in dictating the forms of dress. For these designers, there seemed to be no primal, natural body that must be expressed or accentuated by the artifice of clothing. The "fact" of gender, for instance, was not easily represented by their garments, which could often be worn by either men or women. These clothes, moreover, failed to privilege an ideal body, since they did not require one to be of any particular size. (Models for these collections were, however, traditionally thin.) Bumps added onto backs and hips further disguised—or disfigured, according to *Vogue Great Britain*, which dubbed Kawakubo's "bump dress" the "ugliest dress of the year"—the natural body, as if to suggest that it could no longer dictate its exterior covering: instead the two must work together.[35]

These effects later earned the designers the moniker "deconstructionist." But, as Patricia Mears has written, these designers were not actually deconstructing fashion by making luxury items appear worn or shabby, but carefully constructing clothes using innovative materials and techniques.[36] Their attention to the craft of clothing can be seen, for instance, in Miyake's A-POC (a piece of cloth). Produced in 1976, the collection consisted simply of a long tube of jersey from which buyers could cut out a dress, hat, gloves, and socks according to their size, thus minimizing waste while maximizing customization. The ideals of A-POC—the emphasis on the cloth, rather than the design; on variety, rather than normative singularity—became a central preoccupation for avant-garde Japanese designers. Though they were known for using only black, earning them the nickname "crow gang," these designers were always experimenting with new fabric in order to create their new forms. Borrowing in part from the construction of the kimono, they created clothes that required minimal cutting, that eschewed strong lines and silhouettes, and that deemphasized the contours of the body.

Though critics would come around to the Japanese look, these designers' ethnicity continued to frame interpretations of their work. Disparaging remarks about them rarely failed to make use of ethnic, national, or gender stereotypes. But even favorable considerations of their work inevitably drew references to their Eastern sensibility—their fascination with Zen Buddhism, Japanese landscapes, and so forth—that could at times veer into the terrain of cultural essentialism. Critics often saw the strange fit of their clothes in particular as an expression of their cultural proclivity toward modesty, of their desire to hide or deny women's sexuality. "The fashions that have swept in from the East represent a totally different attitude toward how clothes should look from that long established here," wrote one journalist. "The aim is to conceal, not reveal the body."[37]

Such assertions, which rely on racialized and gendered assumptions about so-called Asian values, simplify the ambivalence these designers have always shown toward Western notions of sexuality and sensuality. Kawakubo, for instance, has said: "It bothers Japanese women . . . to reveal their bodies. I myself understand that feeling well, so I take that into account, adding more material, or whatever."[38] Yet this appreciation of women's desire to not reveal the body does not lead her to attempt to conceal it. Rather, she invents shapes and volumes that allow for new modes of embodiment. While her layered and voluminous clothes do discourage any kind of "peekaboo voyeurism," as Barbara Vinken has called it, they are not indifferent to the body.[39] In fact, the relative flexibility of these clothes allows their wearers to engage directly with the body, as the clothes adjust to different sizes, shapes, and preferences. What they do prohibit is the division of the body into individual parts—breasts, waist, legs—that can be isolated, enlarged, lengthened, and displayed.

For much of the history of fashion, Euro-American couturiers have been concerned with staging the body in ways that emphasize certain body parts, largely for erotic effect. Consider for instance the role of the corset in sexualizing the waist, or the bustle in doing the same for the bottom. This staging has not always been done through the exposure of the body, though the showing of increasing amounts of skin is certainly an element of this history. Rather, it has been carried out primarily through the techniques of isolation and immobilization, in which certain parts are emphasized and exhibited in contrast to other parts. Against such a staging of sensuality—in which titillation is manufactured through the concealment of certain parts and the exposure of others—Kawakubo posits, as Vinken has argued, "a body which is not exhibited to the gaze, but rather protected, allowed to remain whole and moveable."[40] The refusal of Kawakubo's garments to isolate, immobilize, emphasize, and exhibit the body for erotic effect is not a denial of sexuality. Rather, it is a presentation of a different notion of sexuality, one not animated by the opposition between naked and clothed, hidden and revealed. For designers like Kawakubo, clothing's primary function is not to render certain parts visible or invisible, thrilling or not, but to give the whole body protection and mobility.

In this sense, design becomes for her and other Japanese designers not a question of appearance or style but a problem of form, of how to construct shapes that can protect and keep whole what they contain. For this reason, the Japanese designers' approach has often been characterized as architectural.[41] Like architects, their aim has continually been, as Susan Sidlauskas has pointed out, to create clothes that "contain and define space."[42] This can be seen in the ways that their creations could at times take on literally the shape of buildings, or drew very directly from particular structures. But more often it is revealed in the ways they functioned as a form of shelter, offering their wearers an exterior surface that contains the body, creating for it a sort of private space in the public domain. One detects this in the shapes of the garments, which are rarely form-fitting. But one senses it perhaps most clearly in the feel of the garments. When worn, they create a peripheral space around the body, framing it with structure, shape, and volume.

These innovations have become some of the hallmarks of the so-called Japanese look, which has had a wide-ranging impact. The deconstructionist approach that they embodied has been taken up by designers all over the world, most prominently by Belgians like Martin Margiela and his group, the Antwerp Six, who are often considered the most direct descendants of the Japanese. Mainstream fashion has also incorporated, on the surface at least, some of their less controversial elements—such as the use of asymmetry and unfinished hems. My aim in offering such a cursory account of these Japanese designers' work is not to suggest that Asian Americans were the only ones to have been influenced by them. Rather, it is to provide context and precedent for the seemingly odd ways that my interviewees have characterized their own work.

That my interviewees admired these Japanese designers is clear; their names were almost always invoked in our discussions. Many, as Thuy Pham has said, saw them as important models.[43] But whether or not they invoked Kawakubo by name, many of them read the body and clothing in a way similar to hers, and had a similar ambivalence about the dialectic of revealing and concealing. They drew from these Japanese designers a way of approaching fashion that would prioritize the whole body, rather than its eroticized parts, and a perspective about sexuality that would deeply inform their process and products, and that would continue to animate debates in contexts much further afield.

The term that my interviewees have used most frequently to describe their work is "architectural." "People who look at my clothes have always described it [sic] as architectural," Thuy Diep told me. "I wasn't trained as an architect, but what I look at naturally are lines and shapes and forms. And I've definitely been thinking about function. Architects are always thinking about the inhabitants, not just the pretty lines, but erecting a building for people to live in. I want to develop that kind of discipline." As Diep's statement suggests, the invocation of architecture here serves at least three purposes. First, it shores up the designers' professional status by creating a relationship to this more disciplined, and therefore legitimated, field. Second, it elevates them above other designers who, presumably, are interested in "just the pretty lines."[44] Third, and most significant, it sutures their work to that of avant-garde Japanese designers, whose creations were an expression of this desire to see clothing not as a disguise or description of what lay beneath, but as a structure that could contain and define the space around it.

Return for a moment to my interviewees' earlier comments about design as a set of calculations. "I used to do a lot of draping, and I still do, but now I'm more fascinated with calculations," Yeohlee Teng told me. Likening her work to that of modern architects like Le Corbusier and artists like Donald Judd, Teng continued: "I think there is a whole school of designers that are minimalistic in their approach, and mathematical in their construction . . . It's a creative design mind. And some of the solutions are calculated mathematically." This can be seen, for instance, in her recent collections, in which she borrows from such geometric forms as the cubes present in Judd's sculptures or in the shape of the recently built New Museum in New York. The resulting "cube dress" retains its form even as it takes on the wearer's own.

Such an approach, Teng explained, allows her to address formal problems in her designs. For instance, when she set out to create a one-size-fits-all collection, instead of draping on models of particular sizes, she employed this mathematical mode to conceive an abstract form that could

Figure 15 Thuy Diep, fall 2009 collection.
Photo by Dan Lecca.

Figure 16 Thuy Diep, fall 2009 collection.
Photo by Dan Lecca.

Figure 17 Thuy Diep, fall 2009 collection.
Photo by Dan Lecca.

Figure 18 Yeohlee Teng, spring 2009 collection, look 26: "White washed silk organza *cube* dress with black *crescents*." Photo by Dan Lecca.

accommodate many different bodies. Teng likened the process to creating a room. "When you go into a room, all rooms are one-size-fits-all," she said. "You could be a three-hundred-pound person, you could be tiny . . . And you would fit in the room. It's the same idea when you try to make clothes that fit everybody." Here the designer was not suggesting that clothes should be made so large that they could literally fit anyone. Rather, she was arguing for an understanding of the relationship between the garment and its wearer in which, like rooms and their inhabitants, neither is defined by the other; instead, each is transformed in the presence of the other. This is the same symbiosis that Kawakubo is after in her work. The result for Teng was a series of capes, dresses, and tops that maintained their formal integrity even as they became remade by each individual wearer. In one sarong, for instance, Teng employed a very simple pattern, cut flat and utilizing almost the entirety of one piece of cloth, to create a skirt that can be adjusted to nearly all bodies. Neither defined by the customer nor disconnected from her, these garments existed in tension with the bodies they dressed.

Figure 19.1 Yeohlee Teng, fall 2009 collection, look 23: "Coal 4-layer *Zero Waste* Sarong with black jersey bodysuit." Photo by Dan Lecca.

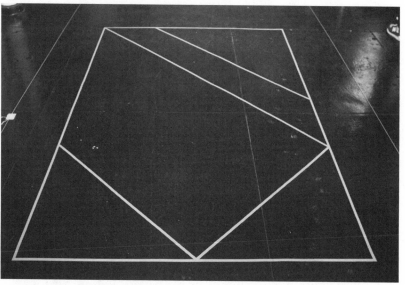

Figure 19.2 Yeohlee Teng, fall 2009 collection, *Zero Waste* Sarong pattern. Photo by Dan Lecca.

One can discern a similar effect in some of Doo-Ri Chung's designs. Chung is known for her use of jersey, a stretchy material that in most cases tends to hug the body. Yet in her hands, the fabric behaves differently. In her construction process, Chung is able to transform this body-conscious material into a fabric that envelopes rather than accentuates. Like Kawakubo, she adds extra material to her dresses, often using yards and yards of fabric. She also eliminates as many seams as possible, so that the cloth drapes and hangs rather than clings. The effect of these "architectural details," as many commentators have described them, is one of volume. Once again, the garment exists not to embellish the body but to form a spatial relationship with it. These dresses are certainly not modest, but neither do they seek to divide and display the body in fetishized parts. There is a fluidity to them that refuses the "erotically staged corporeality" that is common, as Barbara Vinken has said, to Euro-American fashion.[45]

This subtle effect is achieved through Chung's attention to the process of construction, a focus that she shares with many other Asian American designers. While this too may be a product of the Japanese influence, it is probably also, at least in part, informed by their own familial and professional histories. As children, literally and figuratively, of sewers, many of these designers grew up making clothes for both pleasure and profit. This may have instilled in them, as the designer Jean Yu suggested, a certain "sensitivity to construction." Yu explained to me:

I always looked at the construction of the clothes because I was sewing them. It's different than when you're designing on just the surface— stylizing things, which is what most people do. There's a huge difference—well, the outcome may be subtle to some eyes. But for those who know the skill, it becomes quite clear that there's a sensitivity to the construction. You wouldn't fold it this way, as opposed to seaming it this way. Things like that. If you sew, you know. I like to understand something mechanically. And all my stuff is more architectural for this reason, because it's really about understanding the configuration, how it's made—not just, you know, "I want this hemline. I want the sleeves to balloon." It's more than that.

This attention to construction requires a tremendous amount of work, even if that labor is often purposely rendered invisible. In contrast to the exposed seams and unfinished hems that Kawakubo and Yamamoto presented in their early shows, Yu's dresses appear to be virtually seamless.

She achieves this effect by using techniques that minimize cutting and that hide seams, giving the impression that the dress has sprung magically from whole cloth.

If these methods fetishize the commodity—denying the conditions of its production—they also recognize the whole body. Yu's dresses are often cut on the bias (across the grain of the fabric or on a diagonal). Introduced by Madeleine Vionnet at the beginning of the twentieth century, this method of cutting changed the way that designers saw the body: as no longer divided in two (front and back) but as three-dimensional, changing in and through space. Borrowing from Vionnet's technique and from the perspective that she inaugurated, Yu's designs similarly strive to maintain this sense of wholeness and mobility. But echoing the interventions made by the Japanese designers, her clothes also refuse to confine, constrain, or divide the body into its aggregate parts. Yu is able to create clothing that moves both toward and away from the body, that maintains the distinctions between itself and the body, and that strives for a symbiotic relationship with the body.

This effect is, as Yu admits, extremely subtle. As the creator of evening wear and lingerie, Yu's clothes are often characterized as feminine and sexy. These garments are certainly not made for all shapes; they privilege if not an ideal body, then something fairly close to it. But to see her clothes is to observe how even the most revealing garments—the paper-thin lingerie she creates, for instance—seem to encircle the body rather than conform to it. Indeed, even garments meant to constrain—like her brassieres—seem only to rest upon its form. The clothes seem to spiral around their wearer, drawing the viewer's eyes to the body but also to its periphery.

These techniques and approaches have enabled some Asian American designers to rethink the body, or more precisely to rethink, as Kawakubo had, the relationship of body and garment. To be sure, this architectural mode—this desire to think about space and form—has its limits. These designers, like all others, are concerned first and foremost with creating products for a commercial market. If they are invested in questioning assumptions about ideal forms and bodies, and about the function of clothing, these are often secondary to their financial concerns. Nor are these aesthetic interests consistently or universally applied. They are embraced by some designers and ignored by others; apparent in some garments and collections, missing in others. "I don't use [flat cutting] on every garment," Thuy Pham stressed to me. "If I'm making a pair of pants, I want a good fit." Indeed, one of the most successful Asian American designers working today, Philip Lim, admits that he is "not an intellectual designer." "At the end of the day," he said, "it comes down to 'Does it make my butt look good?' "[46]

The influence of the Big Three on these designers is thus inconsistent and subtle. If Japanese designers have been praised by critics and scholars for their creativity and innovation, their clothes have been seen by customers as offbeat and even difficult, suited for only the most fashionably avant-garde. Asian American designers, on the other hand, fit quite comfortably into the contemporary designer market, sending out clothes that are generally stylish and modern, but that pose few of the same challenges for their wearers.[47] Yet if Asian American designers share any Asian influences, they can be detected here, in their thinking about the physical body and its sartorial representation. How they play with that space in between and what these adjustments suggest—that clothes do not just adorn but also shelter bodies, that they cover less than they encase, that they can function not just to divide and display the body but protect it and make it mobile—is what binds this group together, far more than any style, symbol, or icon.

But in what sense were these ideas Japanese? Japanese designers may have deconstructed the dialectic of concealing and revealing and its attendant notions of modesty and sexuality within the world of couture, but those ideas were already being circulated elsewhere. We can find similar gestures in, for example, certain forms of Arab dress, which have long refused the binary between visibility and invisibility, public and private, modesty and immodesty. The so-called Japanese look, then, has connections to these other ways of thinking about body and clothing, seen and unseen. How does our understanding of Asian Americans' cultural influence, heritage, or lineage change when we consider these other traditions and their convergence with what we know of, or claim as, Asian?

HIJAB CHIC?

In the lexicon of clothing, few articles invoke as much political and popular debate as the veil. Though the word "veil" has no single Arabic linguistic reference—it can refer variously to a face cover (*nijab*), head cover (*hijab*), or full body cover (*abaya*, in the Persian Gulf states; chador, in Iran; burqa, in Afghanistan)—in the West it is commonly thought of as singular in practice and meaning. Used in various ways to mark class, status, gender, region, religion, occupation, ethnicity, and so on in many parts of the world, the range of practices that constitute veiling have become fixed onto Muslim women's bodies and reduced to a sign of their religious difference.

While the veil has long stood in the West as a symbol of Islamic oppression, hostility toward this practice has greatly increased in recent years, in the aftermath of the Iranian revolution, the Gulf War, the emergence of the Taliban in Afghanistan, and, of course, the events of September 11, which have all made veiling more visible to Westerners. Veiling in recent years has come to signify Islamic terrorism, the war against which cannot be complete without the unveiling of Muslim women.[48] Though the politics of covering has become highly contested, the public unveiling of women continues to function rhetorically as a sign of liberation, as the countless media images of a burqa-free, "liberated Afghanistan" can attest. In these representations, veiling is rendered incompatible not just with notions of sexual equality but with the exercise of citizenship itself.

Such linkages between gender, religion, and citizenship have made the veil a politically charged symbol and a central preoccupation of state power for both Islamic and non-Islamic nations. While much has been made of the ways in which the Taliban has participated in forced veiling, less has been said about the forced *unveiling* of women. The 1936 outlawing of the chador in Iran, as part of the shah's modernization efforts, for instance, was accompanied by an order for soldiers to forcibly remove the garment from women's bodies. The tensions over the resurgence of the hijab in Turkey, the banning of head scarves in France, and the ongoing legal battles in various parts of Europe and the United States over the cultural rights of immigrants from Muslim-majority nations are all indications that, in various ways, the ability to veil or not to veil has been circumscribed by the state.

Despite the complex negotiations that inform this practice—which mingles "choice" and "compulsion," "expression" and "repression"— veiling continues to be understood through the binaries of modernity and tradition, civilized and barbaric, freedom and oppression.[49] The veil has become, as miriam cooke has argued, "like race, a marker of essential difference," reducing the diversity among Muslim women to a "foundational singularity"—one that can drive both Islamists' attempt to control women's bodies and neo-Orientalists' demand to free the "poor Muslim woman."[50]

In the West, much of what informs popular compassion for the "poor" Muslim woman and animates the desire to "free" her is the assumption that in covering their bodies, these women are also making themselves invisible culturally and politically. Such convictions rely on the belief that visibility is an index of empowerment—that to be unseen or hidden is to be without power, agency, or will.[51] Yet Muslim women's recent unveilings have certainly not led to their liberation, accounts of their new-found freedom to buy makeup and wear fashion notwithstanding. These public unveilings have far more often functioned as a new mask to conceal the operations of war.[52]

Much recent scholarship offers a far more nuanced and complex account of the practices of veiling—the representations of it, the meanings attached to it, the political struggles around it, and so on.[53] My aim here is not to enter into those rich debates, which are beyond the purview of this project. Instead, I am interested in considering how these sartorial traditions instantiate ideas about body and clothing that might intersect with the discourses produced by Japanese designers. The various garments that make up what we have come to know of as "the veil" enact certain ideas about concealment and exposure that resonate very much with the work of the Japanese, and the work of the Asian Americans who were influenced by them. Thinking about how these might all converge would allow us to consider much more carefully and thoroughly the nature and boundaries of these designers' Asian influences. While I do not want to jettison matters of politics, or to underestimate the operations of power at work here, I do want to focus on these formal questions in order to better understand how the veil, as a sartorial object, functions to undermine the very binaries that frame its representation.

There is no doubt that, as many scholars have shown, in many contexts practices of veiling have been used as a means of disciplining women's bodies and of controlling their sexuality. In those instances when veils have been required as a sign of women's religious devotion, sexual modesty, and so forth, veiling relies on a gendered distinction between visibility and invisibility, appearance and seclusion, public and private. Its force as a tool of subjugation demands the ideological maintenance of such boundaries. Yet, as a sartorial form, it does not always uphold these binaries; indeed, in some instances, it can fundamentally challenge them.

Despite popular interpretations, the veil does not actually hide women, reducing them to anonymous figures. Many types of veils only obscure parts of women's bodies. Even full body coverings fail to make women vanish. A woman can be very much be on display in her chador, as when she receives visitors and exchanges greetings outside of the home. Dressed in this manner, she can still be recognized by friends and relatives in the streets, since these garments, which cover her body, do not hide her stature, mannerisms, or other identifying signs.[54] The primary function of these garments, then, is not to make the wearer invisible. Rather, it is to construct space, to enable men and women to create privacy in the public sphere. This privacy is not attained strictly through seclusion or concealment, but through a redrawing of the boundaries of the public. As Alev Cinar has said, this is the "disruptive power of the headscarf." Writing about its re-emergence in Turkey, Cinar argues that the hijab closes off certain spaces, places, and body parts as private, thereby "redefining the constitutive limits of the public."[55] In these contexts, the hijab becomes an articulation of unconventional and nonsecular norms of privacy that challenge the secular norms defining publicness, and that "vests those who draw such boundaries on the body with political agency."[56]

This redrawing of spatial boundaries is not uncommon within an Arab context, as the scholar Fadwa El Guindi has noted.[57] During particular moments of Muslim worship, for instance, faithful individuals can transform any worldly, public place into a sacred, private space by performing the five daily prayers; veils function similarly to define space. El Guindi has likened the veil to *mashrabiyya*, the latticed wood screens and windows in urban Arab architecture, which both guards privacy and enables visibility. Like a mobile mashrabiyya, the veil allows a woman to carry her privacy with her by converting the space around her.[58]

To be sure, in certain contexts, this privacy functions less as a privilege than as a demand. In that sense, women's ability to transform these spaces is always already framed by the necessity of doing so. My point here is not to remove the political stakes involved in veiling as a practice, but only to reorient our thinking about it as a form. Despite the assumption that it works only to secure women's invisibility, the veil seeks less to hide the female body than to contain and define space, to fulfill an architectural function.[59] Indeed, the term "hijab" does not refer to a particular item of clothing for women or men, but rather to a spatial curtain that divides or provides privacy—that has, in other words, an architectural purpose.[60] This understanding of clothing resonates, then, with the ways Japanese designers have thought about their own work. In each case, there is an ambivalence about the distinctions between public and private, covering and concealing. And in each, as noted above, clothing's purpose is to protect rather than exhibit the body.

In some instances, these resonances are discernible visually. Long before hijabs captured international attention (and hysteria), Kawakubo, Miyake, and Yamomoto were constructing clothes that functioned to similarly contain their wearers' heads and bodies. The references to the hijab, though not explicit, are nonetheless clear. Consider, for instance, the collection by Issey Miyake photographed by Irving Penn. Even a cursory glance at the long robes, coats, and dresses, in monochromatic black or white, forming a shell over the models' bodies, will reveal the collection's debt not just to the kimono, but to the chador, hijab, and so on.

In recent years, these references have emerged as a central motif on fashion's runways. The fall 2006 fashion shows were inundated with masks, hoods, hats, and fabric used to cover models' faces in ways that reminded many observers of garments like the chador and burqa. Viktor and Rolf covered their models' faces with masks made of braided hair woven like a lattice, while Vivienne Westwood wrapped yards of fabric around her models' heads. Over the past few years, designer labels from Givenchy and Versace to Galliano and Dior[61] have all dabbled in so-called Arab styles, sending them down the Parisian runway at the same moment that French President Nicolas Sarkozy declared full-body coverings "not welcome" in France.[62]

Like the first blush of Asian chic that emerged over two decades ago, this newest fashion sensation brought mixed reviews. While some critics praised these designers' creativity, others balked, describing the masks, hoods, and so on as "creepy" and "dark." These commentators objected to what they saw as a glorification of war and, more troublingly, as an anti-feminist, if not outright misogynist, impulse. Japanese designers did not escape their attacks. The critic Guy Trebay criticized Yamomoto, whose 2006 fall show featured mannequins wearing hats so large that they covered the model's whole head, for presenting "women with no discernible features."[63] But Trebay saved his harshest words for Jun Takahashi, a designer for the label Undercover. When Takahashi's models came out with their faces entirely wrapped in cloth, and metal chains hanging between their obscured noses and ears, Trebay declared the effect "so sinister" that it made Robert Mapplethorpe's bondage photos look like "Welcome Wagon neighbors." "As disturbing as the chador may be to the eye of many West-

erners," Trebay wrote, "it is not half as troubling as hair masks or head-deforming hats or body bags so demeaning and debilitating that" it made the models appear blinded and confused.[64]

The scholar Ellen McLarney has argued that the appearance of these elements on Parisian runways is an indication of the transformation of the burqa from "an emblem of utter dehumanization to an expression of fashion."[65] Like other markers of foreignness, McLarney suggests, it has become a fetishized commodity, a demonized object redeemed through the culture of consumption. Yet while it is clear that such a process is certainly underway—fashion has proved that it can turn anything into style—the transformation is still not complete.[66] If designers have become enthralled with burqa chic, they have not been able to embrace it without censure. As the above comments reveal, the fashion press at least is still anxious about the designers' ability to transform anything "as disturbing as the chador" into an object of consumer desire. The critiques of these designers' work, in fact, rely on the assumption that the burqa can be seen only as dark and demeaning and that its adoption, in whatever altered form, can be seen only as misogynist. In this sense, it has remained an emblem of dehumanization even as it has become an expression of fashion.

This is not to suggest that these productions do not pose problems, but only that our critique of these objects must not fall back on the same old divisions between the civilized and the barbaric, the modern and the traditional, the free and the oppressed, which have long framed our understanding of them. Although it is fair to argue that fashion designers have commodified these garments, it is not entirely accurate to imply that they had previously been uncommodified—that hijabs existed purely as religious or cultural objects, outside of the domain of fashion and untouched by the forces of capital. The presence of the multibillion-dollar "veiling fashion" industry in Turkey, which has its roots in the reveiling movements across various Muslim-majority nations since the 1970s, is a clear indication that these have long comingled.[67] Moreover, we must be careful to consider how these elements are being used, and what their visibility may suggest. As I have tried to demonstrate throughout this book, people have often forged affinities and connections within domains imagined as quite distinct. For Japanese designers like Yamomoto, Miyake, and Takahashi, this may well have been one of those moments.

While Yamomoto's head-enveloping hats fit well with that year's hijab chic trends, its appearance in 2006 was not unique for this designer. Yamamoto had for decades dressed his models in oversized hats, scarves, and other accessories; these articles were an expression of his long-standing interest in clothing that ill-fit the body. This makes it difficult to argue that he simply appropriated a recently fashionable motif. For his part, Takahashi had long been fascinated with masks. In his 2000 Melting Pot collection, he dressed each model in garments with one textile design and painted the woman's face and head to match—giving the impression of a full body covering. In another collection, he dressed women in a chain-mail head covering reminiscent of European crusades. These images had been a part of his visual repertoire before his controversial 2006 collection, often combined with references to punk and sadomasochism—cultures that have also been commodified. When considered within this larger trajectory, we might read the 2006 collection not just as an example of Takahashi's acts of commodification, but also as his commentary on fashion's ability to turn all cultures into commodities.[68]

This ambivalence is made quite clear when we examine the clothing. For designers like Viktor and Rolf, the masks covering the faces of the models bore no relationship to the garments that adorned their bodies. The dresses and suits in that collection were close-fitting, and shapely in ways typical of most Euro-American couture. The masks, in this instance, served as little more than an exotic accent to the same sartorial fare, creating in the process a dissonance between the veiled and the unveiled. In Takahashi and Yamomoto's collections, however, head coverings and body coverings were of a piece. Yamomoto's hats were as ill-fitting as his clothes. Takahashi's masks blended seamlessly with his garments, producing the impression of a full body covering, just as in his earlier Melting Pot collection.

I do not mean to suggest that these are not appropriative gestures, or that they are not practices of commodification. But I want to consider the possibility that they may also be more than that. As I have tried to demonstrate, avant-garde Japanese designers shared a particular approach to design that saw clothing as an architectural form, which could define and even transform the space around it. While this approach has been characterized as the Japanese look, one can easily draw connections to other forms of dress that similarly meddle with the divisions between public and private, interior and exterior. The recent use of these elements by Japanese designers, then, must be understood within this broader context of collective affinities. Perhaps Yamomoto and Takahashi were just echoing—for shock, style, or profit—the conventions of Arab dress. But, just as plausibly, perhaps they were attempting to articulate a shared language. After all, as the scholars Sunaina Maira and Magid Shilhade have shown in their attempts to theorize the relationship between Arab and Asian American studies, these realms have never been entirely distinct, and we are only beginning to unravel their intellectual, social, and political affinities.[69]

CONCLUSION

To suggest that there may be commonalities, resonances, and even affinities between these forms of dress is, of course, not to deny their differences in terms of cultural contexts, modes of presentation, political implications, economic motives, and so on. Nor is it to suggest a relationship of causality (that Japanese designers drew directly from these sources) or of effect (that shared aesthetic interests result in allied political interests). It is, rather, to ask how we determine the boundaries of culture. Are these productions Asian or something else? Do they shock because they invoke the bodies of Muslim women, or because they were created by Japanese provocateurs? How do we trace the genealogies of these forms and practices?

The scholar Lisa Lowe once wrote that Asian American culture has always been "partly inherited, partly modified, and partly invented."[70] Yet these inheritances and modifications, as Lowe's more recent writings suggest, have drawn not just from Asia but from various other "streams of internationalism."[71] In attempting to map out Asian Americans' material and symbolic relationship to Asia, I too have found myself following trails that led me beyond what has traditionally been thought of as the Asian world. This detour has helped me to see that if Asian Americans' diasporic imaginations are in various ways informed by their "homeland," it was also indebted to influences and affinities that extended beyond its borders.

What, then, did Asia mean to these designers? In one sense, it represented economic interests, a rare opportunity to increase their market presence and financial investments. These benefits provided an incentive for Asian American designers to articulate an ethnic or national identity, invoking the cultural ties and national affiliations normally hidden from their work and from their performance of self. Strategic, creative, utilitarian, and emotional, these invocations of culture tied together the affective and the economic and enabled Asian Americans to see and treat Asia as both home and market.

In this context—in which Asia was as much an economic as a cultural entity, and diasporic identities forged as much from material incentives as from affective bonds—Asian Americans' use of their culture can be seen as expedient, aligning neatly with their own economic interests. This expediency is apparent in their aesthetic treatments as well. Many included signs of Asianness when doing so could lead to press exposure and retail sales. Many more refused to do so, when it could brand them as "only ethnic." As entrepreneurs, these designers were in the business of sales, and their cultural identities were, like all other resources, carefully deployed to bring gains, or at least to increase their chances of survival.

Yet, as I have previously noted, economic relationships for this group have always exceeded the boundaries of the economic, whether seen in the socially binding gift relationships they built with garment workers or here, in their textured articulations of Asianness. While these designers have certainly been willing at times to participate in Asian chic, and to leave unchallenged its Orientalist assumptions, they have also sought to create clothing that could undermine the binaries that have structured notions of the Orient. By framing their work as analytically driven, rather than inspirationally wrought, they once again blurred the distinctions between creative and noncreative, just as they had in their articulation of sewing as central, not marginal, to the production of fashion. Perhaps more importantly, by approaching their work as a problem of structure and form, rather than solely as a question of style, they adopted an understanding of the relationship between body and garment that challenged fashion's dialectic of concealment and exposure, and its attendant expressions of sexuality and sensuality.

The narrative of restraint and reserve that have been used to frame the work of these designers and their Japanese predecessors relies on an understanding of Asians as inherently modest. This construction of modesty as a cultural trait, if not requirement, has of course been essential to representations of Muslim women as well. This has been visualized most potently through their clothing, which purportedly denies not just their bodily visibility but also their sexual freedom and political agency. The ideas about visibility and liberation that frame these conceptions of Arab dress are certainly not limited to it; they have informed discussions about race, gender, and sexuality in various contexts. Narratives about Asian Americans' "racial invisibility," their "sexual hypervisibility," their willingness or lack of willingness to "come out," for instance, all rely on some metaphor of concealment and exposure, even as these are constantly challenged by lived realities. By continuing to question these binaries, Asian Americans' sartorial productions contribute to this refusal to see visibility as the only sign of liberation, sexuality as the only sign of feminism, consumption as the only sign of modernity. They have "inherited" from Japanese designers their approach to the construction of clothing that can accommodate at once containment and exposure, hiding and revealing. Whether or not we want to see that inheritance as Asian depends on how we want to conceptualize the boundaries of the Asian world, whether we want to follow other streams, and when we want to acknowledge affinities. Asian Americans, as I have attempted to show throughout this book, have been quite open in this regard. In an industry built on a logic of distance, they have continually struggled to imagine a world of intimacies.

EPILOGUE

On a warm afternoon in December 2008, I sat down in a New York coffee shop to speak with one of my interviewees. I had not seen her for several months, but she had contacted me with a surprising request: she was interested in applying to graduate school and wanted to hear my thoughts about how to prepare for it. News of the housing crash, gossip about Lehman Brothers, and debates about the economy (was this officially a recession or not?) were demanding our attention in those days. Sitting just blocks away from Wall Street, my interviewee confessed that while she had always liked school—having received a degree in art history from Columbia University—it was the grim economic climate that was nudging her back to academe. "Everyone is struggling to keep their businesses these days," she told me. "Things have always been hard for young designers, but they just got a lot harder. We're not getting credit anymore. Retailers won't stock small labels unless they know they can sell. People aren't really buying. It's been really hard." After years of hustling, she had decided that she needed a break.

If there was ever any doubt that these designers were working in very precarious circumstances, the recent economic crisis has made this clear. Young designers live on credit; at any given time, they either owe money (to investors and factories) or are owed money (by retailers and clients). The credit crunch has made this inherently flexible system much more rigid, and the retail slowdown has made it much more competitive. At a time when even major fashion houses were laying off workers and closing up shop, these small designers had little hope of weathering the storm.

Young designers were of course not the only workers in the industry feeling the sting of the economy. Far more vulnerable were the garment workers, whose livelihood depended on their orders and whose work schedules were dictated by their needs. Long before the Wall Street meltdown, these workers were already in crisis. Overseas competition had forced down their wages and whittled away at their jobs, while increasing real estate prices were driving out the few manufacturers left standing. The recent economic downturn has certainly not helped their lot; conditions of crisis, real or imagined, tend only to further marginalize the already marginal.

If, as I have attempted to show in this book, designers and sewers have both experienced conditions of inequality and precariousness, they do not share them evenly. After all, in these moments of extreme pressure, few garment workers can consider graduate school as a plausible escape hatch. There are many important distinctions between these communities that cannot be undone by my desire to think them together, to highlight the porousness between them and the analogousness between their forms of labor. I have brought these and other seemingly distinct constituencies together—producers and consumers, north and south, creative and non-creative—not because I perceive them as equivalent but because I see them as interconnected.

I have argued that Asian American designers and Asian garment workers have found points of connection and affiliation in spite of, and at times because of, their myriad differences. This is in one sense an axiomatic statement, given the ways that fashion production has always been dependent on garment production—indeed, could not exist without it. And yet while this link has become common knowledge, it has also become obscured by an ever-sharpening division between the designer and the maker of clothing, whose knowledge and expertise are continually downgraded by an economic system that differentiates between skilled and unskilled, head and hand, material and symbolic. This process of splitting demands not just differentiation between tasks and the bodies that perform them, but also disassociation between the whole and the parts, the mind and the body. Under conditions of globalization, it also requires, as Laura Kang has said, a spatial and temporal distancing, whereby manufacturing labor is imagined to be done only out there, in the third world, by women whose conditions of exploitation are seen only as a phase—a relic of the nineteenth century soon to disappear.[1]

These divisions and disassociations shape conditions not just of production but of consumption as well. In this age of multiculturalism, various kinds of otherness have been held up as worthy of our appreciation, admiration, and of course consumption. In the world of fashion, we have seen how Asianness became chic for a time, and how this in-style status enabled Asian American designers to turn their culture into an economic resource. But this fascination with all things Asian was never about an affiliation with its culture, however defined. In fact, these exotic goods were desirable precisely because they existed at a cultural remove—because they could offer consumers passage to the East and at the same time reaffirm their superior positions in the West.

Against this logic of distance, Asian Americans have managed to form intimate ties, materially and symbolically. They have done so by transforming networks of economic exchange into extra-economic relationships, animated by both real and fictive kin, and by valuable and invaluable gifts. These relationships are undeniably provisional and limited, built piecemeal out of conditions not of their own making. We see their fractures in those many instances when assertions of identity, community, friendship, and family are used for utilitarian ends, and most clearly when designers' gains require sewers' losses.

Yet among these fractures there are moments when the designers have forged new ideas, subjectivities, and social arrangements that challenge a market-only ethos, even as they are driven by it. These could not have been constructed, as I have tried to show, outside of the context of material practices and uneven exchanges. But neither could they have been manufactured without an imagination that saw these different modes, images, forms, and constituencies as connected. I have been keen to mark these proximities not because I want to disavow the ongoing fissures, but because I want to highlight the conditions of possibility that they represent.

In recent years, scholars, pundits, technocrats, and cultural critics have all touted our ability to stay connected. Thanks to developments in new technologies, we can have instant Facebook updates and constant Twitter feeds. Yet even as such processes of social networking have diminished the problem of temporal and spatial distance—allowing us to keep up with old friends from far away—they cannot resolve the problem of social and imaginative distance. As the American political discourse of red states and blue states attests, we continue to find it difficult to imagine ourselves as interconnected and our fates as intertwined. This is not just a problem of difference, for even as official multiculturalism has made social differences more palatable, it has not fundamentally challenged the divisions between us and them.

This presumption of distance and disconnection has had the effect of obscuring the circuits that have always linked together culture and labor, material and immaterial, here and there, and a host of other domains imagined as distinct. It has made it even more difficult to see proximity, contact, and affiliation, and to conceive of the conditions under which coalitions might thrive. In writing this account of Asian American designers, I hope to have put pressure on this logic of distance. By highlighting Asian Americans' ability to form material and symbolic connections—to workers and government elites, to histories and icons, to Asian diasporas and "other streams of internationalism"—I hope to have made clear that an aesthetic and architecture of intimacy, for all its erasures and denials, might better serve us all.[2]

As I left my interviewee in December, it occurred to me that the socioeconomic conditions under which I had first observed the subjects of this study had changed in many ways. The emergence of Asian chic and the rise of the Asian designer in the mid-1990s coincided with what is still remembered fondly as the Clintonian boom years. How will the fragile relationships I observed hold up in the face of new economic pressures? The cultural landscape has shifted, too. After two wars in the Middle East, we are now as likely to see stylish burqas (presented, for instance, in Givenchy's 2009 shows) as we are updated cheongsams. How will these changes shape the contours of the cultural economy, and Asian Americans' place in it? Will Asian Americans simply become a reserve army of creative workers, filling the industry's lower ranks and occupying its vulnerable positions, while leaving its hierarchies intact? And the question that nags me most as I conclude this study is: Will the modes and markers of intimacy I saw become a residue of a time gone by, or are they a harbinger of things to come? In other words, is this a narrative of loss or one of emergence?

I suppose the answer is both, since emergence and loss are in many ways constantly intertwined. I was reminded of this by a recent *New York Times* op-ed piece by the prolific writer Barbara Ehrenreich. She pointed out that the recession, having eroded governmental support systems, was leaving people with little more than a "homespun safety net." During this crisis, informal networks of reciprocal giving and support among friends and family have become a first line of defense. But like those shared among marginalized people for decades, these networks were depleting already scarce resources. In helping each other to survive, then, people were also reinforcing their collective vulnerabilities.[3] For many, survival and demise, success and failure have always been linked.

The networks I have highlighted here are in this sense not unique, relying as they do on the same types of informal exchanges, and susceptible as they are to the same kinds of tensions and strains. The architectures of intimacy I see here are thus hardly new. But they serve as a useful reminder, especially in these moments of crisis, that amid the forces that divide, people have always forged connections, assembling coalitions from what they had and what they could imagine.

NOTES

NOTES TO INTRODUCTION

1. Karen Tina Harrison, "The Storefront Ethic Is in Their Blood," *New York Times*, December 17, 2000, Style Desk, 8.

2. Constance C. R. White, "The Rise of Asian Designers," *New York Times*, June 20, 1995, B9.

3. The Ecco Domani Fashion Foundation award was established in 2002. Each winner receives $25,000 to put on a fashion show. The eleven Asian American winners are Alexander Wang, Wayne Lee, Richard Chai, Angel Chang, Jeffery Chow, Derek Lam, Mary Ping, Peter Som, Thakoon Panichgul, Hanuk, and Doo-Ri Chung. The CFDA/Vogue Fashion Fund was established in 2004. Winners receive what the fund's website describes as a "significant financial award" (approximately $100,000) and "business mentoring." The ten Asian American finalists are Philip Lim (twice), Koi Suwannagate, Doo-Ri Chung (twice), Jean Yu, Thakoon Panichgul, Derek Lam (twice), Peter Som.

4. Jones and Leshkowich, "Globalization of Asian Dress," 18.

5. For an incisive account of this shift, see Yúdice, *The Expediency of Culture*. In this work, Yudice argues that the role of culture has greatly expanded in the global era: it now serves a wide variety of instrumental aims, from sociopolitical amelioration to development and economic growth, at the same time that conventional notions of culture—as a model of uplift, distinction, or way of life—have been rendered largely obsolete. Culture no longer refers to any specific content, but serves instead as a resource to use in meeting a variety of goals and as a way to mobilize a range of social actions, including making populations manageable and governable.

6. Florida, *The Rise of the Creative Class.*

7. Ross, *Nice Work If You Can Get It.*

8. Eger, "The Future of Work in the Creative Age."

9. Schoenberger, "Huddled Masses Yearning to Write Java."

10. Tucker, "Byting the Hand That Feeds Us," 14. William Tucker has written that Asian educational systems, which insist on the rote memorization of lessons, have made Asians more suited to the drudgery of programming work. "As a result," he argues, "a kind of international division of labor is taking place. Americans are interested in the more creative aspects of programming, but don't seem to enjoy hard work or drudgery. To a bright young person [from] the Philippines, computer skills are a ticket to a new life. To an American undergraduate, it's a bore" (ibid.). This construction of Asians as technically proficient but lacking in creativity or passion has been reinforced in a variety of contexts, including, as Grace Wang has shown, their representation on such reality television shows as *Project Runway* and *Top Chef* ("A Shot at Half Exposure"). The same claim that Asians lack a culture of creativity has been used to explain why there are so few designers in Asia.

11. For discussions of the formation of an Asian American identity, see, for example, Espiritu, *Asian American Panethnicity*; Wei, *The Asian American Movement*; Takaki, *Strangers from a Different Shore*; Zia, *Asian American Dreams*; and Lee, *Performing Asian America*.

12. See, for instance, Lowe, *Immigrant Acts*.

13. Scholars like Annalee Saxenian (*Regional Advantage*), Richard Florida (*The Rise of the Creative Class*), and Elizabeth Currid (*The Warhol Economy*) have argued that innovation or creativity operates through the informal sharing of information, ideas, and resources within and outside of the workplace by like-minded and complementary workers. These networks are most often formed in places where there is a critical mass of creative people, and when they are encouraged to generate social connections. Currid has applied this idea to her analysis of fashion, art, and music in New York, emphasizing in particular how within these social networks "weak ties"—ties not rooted in strong trust bonds, but between people who are not in close communication with each other—allow creative people such as designers, artists, and musicians to exchange ideas, collaborate, and create economic opportunities. She argues: "The economy of art and culture operates in a constant state of 'hypersocialization,' where weak ties are extraordinarily important" (*The Warhol Economy*, 79). Currid's point— it's who you know—is compelling, but my account shows that in fashion the all-important who can include not just other creative types, but a range of workers who contribute to production of clothing.

14. As I discuss in the following chapters, I treat my interviews as a form of narrative construction that both reflects the reality of my interviewees' experiences and their desire to talk about those experiences in particular ways.

15. Several designers have recently told me that the economic downturn (of which the banking crisis is just one spectacular indication) has affected their businesses in several ways. Young designers are receiving less interest from corpo-

rate investors, are more routinely denied the loans that typically carry them during slow times, and are finding fewer retail opportunities because buyers, facing decreased consumer spending, prefer to sell only established labels.

16. I include in this group Asian designers who were not born in the United States but who have been living in New York for decades. While they are not technically second-generation, they are working in the same professional and cultural milieu as those who are, and they are part of a generation of designers that emerged in a specific historical moment.

17. McRobbie, "Fashion Culture." Angela McRobbie's estimate of the London fashion industry is based on ratios of female to male design graduates.

18. Fashion design has increasingly become a casual, contractual profession, in which workers are primarily self-employed or intermittently employed. McRobbie ("Fashion Culture") has argued that the lack of government protections and regulations in this industry is related to the fact that it is dominated by women.

19. Though men obviously also consume fashion, and though there is an ever-growing men's clothing industry, women are still the primary market for fashion.

20. Lowe, *Immigrant Acts.*

21. In the popular press, "Asian" is used to refer to all individuals from Asia, with little distinction between them in terms of migration histories, cultural locations, national affiliations, and so on. This term is more commonly used than the term "Asian American," though most of the top designers today are not first-generation immigrants and identify themselves as culturally American. The use of the term "Asian" serves to link Asian American designers to an essential Asianness, a move that is reinforced by constant queries regarding the "Asian influences" in their work. However, while such practices of elision are indicative of the operations of Orientalism in this cultural arena, they also reflect the realities of these changed times. In a moment of increased transnational movement and affiliation, it is increasingly difficult to distinguish between various national or ethnic categories and modes of identification. How do we categorize someone like Vivienne Tam, for instance, who was born in China, grew up in Hong Kong before it was handed back to the Chinese, and has lived in New York for the last twenty years? To classify her as either Chinese American/Asian American or as Chinese/Asian would be to dismiss the ways that those identities are lived and negotiated beyond the choice or accident of citizenship, birthplace, residence, and so on, and certainly beyond the juridical distinctions of the citizen-ethnic and the alien-national. In insisting on ethnic or national specificity here, my intent is not to redraw the boundaries that have failed us in so many ways, but only to show how and why national differences matter in this story.

22. For an overview of the history of the international garment trade, see Dickerson, *Textile and Apparel in the International Economy*; Adhikari and Athukorala, *Developing Countries in the World Trading System*; Gereffi, Spener, and Bair, *Free Trade and Uneven Development*; Bonacich, Cheng, Chinchilla, Hamilton, and Ong, *Global Production*; Gereffi and Korzeniewicz, *Commodity Chains and Global Capitalism*; and Rosen, *Making Sweatshops*.

23. The main factors that have kept some buyers—including the small, independent designers in the high-fashion market whom I study here—from producing their goods overseas are the small size of their orders and their need for speedy production. These designers must respond to changing consumer demands quickly and so for the most part produce their goods locally.

24. K. G. Narendranath, "Made in India Brand May Come of Age," *The Economic Times*, August 20, 2004.

25. Goto, "The Production and Distribution Structure in the 'Original Brand' Apparel Industry of Ho Chi Minh City."

26. Appelbaum and Gereffi, "Power and Profits in the Apparel Commodity Chain."

27. A summary of the white paper is available at http://www.vfabric.com/textile/development%20vn.doc. For a discussion of the plan, see Goto, "Industrial Upgrading of the Vietnamese Garment Industry."

28. Ministry of Textiles, "National Textile Policy 2000."

29. Quoted in "Multifiber Pact: China Textile Dominance Spooks Asian Rivals," *Daily Times* (Pakistan), December 19, 2004.

30. Gereffi and Memedovic's *The Global Apparel Value Chain* is a comparative study of developing countries in several regions. It shows that newly industrialized economies (NIES) in Asia, particularly South Korea and China, have led in OBM (own brand manufacturing). The ability to upgrade, the authors demonstrate, depends on several factors—labor supply, wages, land prices, currency revaluation, tariffs and quotas—that vary among countries and regions, and that shape each nation's prospects for moving up the value chain.

31. Keane, *Created in China*.

32. Nadvi and Thoburn, "Vietnam in the Global Garment and Textile Value Chain." For a discussion of the plan, see Goto, "Industrial Upgrading of the Vietnamese Garment Industry."

33. Roger Tredre, "Fashion Craze Sweeps through a New China," *International Herald Tribune*, March 8, 2003; and Edward Cody, "In China, Dreams of Bright Ideas: From Top down, a Push to Innovate," *Washington Post*, June 17, 2006.

34. Many scholars have disputed the claim that non-Western dress is unchanging and requires no aesthetic input on the part of its creators. Antonia Finnane (*Changing Clothes in China*), for instance, has shown the ways that small, often almost imperceptible changes, have long been a part of the history of Chinese

fashion—changes brought about by the emergence of the world trading system, the Cultural Revolution, and later developments.

35. Quoted in Betsy Lowther, "China's Fledgling Designers Eager to Grow," *Women's Wear Daily*, December 1, 2004.

36. Bhachu, *Dangerous Designs*, 106.

37. The director of the Chinese fashion brand Bibin complained: "Take a Western garment we make in our factories, with the same sort of materials, the same worker, the same machines: stick a top-ranking fashion label like Dior on it, and it sells for eight to ten thousand; stick Bibin on it, and you'll get two" (quoted in Finnane, *Changing Clothes in China*, 281).

38. The Asia Fashion Federation is organized by the Japan Fashion Association. See http://www.japanfashion.or.jp/english/index.html.

39. Finnane, *Changing Clothes in China*, 282.

40. See, for instance, Simmel, "Fashion"; Lipovetsky, *The Empire of Fashion*; E. Wilson, *Adorned in Dreams*; Lehman, *Tigersprung*; Crane, *Fashion and Its Social Agendas*; and Kawamura, *The Japanese Revolution in Paris Fashion*. The common assumption that fashion is generally a product of modernized nations has meant that most observers have characterized non-Western countries as having not fashion but garment, dress, costume, and attire—terms used to denote an unchanging sartorial tradition.

41. Hanizah Hashim, "By Design, a New York Link-up," *New Straits Times*, December 21, 1999.

42. Yoon-jung Cho, "Government, Industry Make Moves to Improve Design Standards," *Korea Herald*, September 10, 1997.

43. These schools stress that their curriculum is practical and geared toward giving students know-how to succeed in the design industries.

44. Emily DeNitto, "Parsons Exports Program for South Korean Students," *Crain's New York Business*, April 10, 1995.

45. Betts, "Visions from the East."

46. Hanizah Hashim, "By Design, a New York Link-up," *New Straits Times*, December 21, 1999.

47. Nineteen out of the thirty-four students selected to present during the show were Asian. Asian students also won top honors in the women's, men's, and children's clothing categories.

48. Quoted in Rantisi, "The Ascendance of New York Fashion," 96. When the Nazis occupied Paris in 1940 and effectively shut the city off from the Allies, New York's buyers and manufacturers admitted to being at a loss. The manufacturer quoted in the text commented that before the occupation, "we never had to face reality" (ibid.).

49. Quoted in ibid., 97.

50. American fashion was identified with a particular style—sportswear—rather than a particular American designer. Rantisi notes that it was not until the 1960s that designers really established their own labels and identities; for the most part, until then they worked for large apparel firms. They did not become stars like the couturiers in Paris until fashion publications—especially *Women's Wear Daily*—began treating designers' lives and work as newsworthy and deserving of individual attention (Rantisi, "The Ascendance of New York Fashion," 99).

51. And in the United States, too, we can see the hand of the state, as described in chapter 2.

52. Yu Zhou has characterized the relationship as a two-tiered system, in which garment production is "caught under the fashion runway" (Zhou, "New York").

53. U.S. Department of Labor, Bureau of Labor Statistics, *Occupational Outlook Handbook*, http://www.bls.gov/oco/ocos291.htm (for fashion designers) and http://www.bls.gov/oco/ocos233.htm (for textile and apparel workers).

54. "Young" refers to the amount of time their business has been operating, not to their age, though typically these young designers were in their twenties and thirties.

55. For a discussion of the uses and abuses of discourses of the family within Asian American studies and beyond, see Reddy, "Asian Diasporas, Neoliberalism, and Family"; Martin Manalansan, "Race, Violence, and Neoliberal Spatial Politics in the Global City"; Eng, "Transnational Adoption and Queer Diasporas"; Rodriguez, *Next of Kin*; Stockton, *The Queer Child*; Duggan, *The Twilight of Equality?*; Stacey, *In the Name of the Family*; and W. Wilson, *The Truly Disadvantaged*.

56. Appadurai, *Modernity at Large*, 71.

57. Slavoj Žižek in *The Ticklish Subject* has more provocatively called this version of multiculturalism, which allows consumers to appreciate non-Western culture but to retain it as homogenous, unchanging, and outside of the boundaries of their own culture, as "racism with a distance."

58. Tam, *China Chic*, 90.

59. For discussions of similar processes of intimacy, see Stoler, *Haunted by Empire*, particularly Lowe, "The Intimacy of Four Continents."

60. These fears are exemplified by the ongoing debates about the dangers of deterritorializing or transnationalizing Asian American studies. Some scholars have warned that this transnational turn can gloss over local differences as well as obfuscate the operations of power and privilege within the parameters of the U.S. nation-state. See, for instance, Wong's seminal text, "Denationalization Reconsidered."

61. Friedman, *The World Is Flat*.

62. In fact, many scholars and activists have come to accept these sweated jobs as sometimes the best options for workers in developing countries and in racially stratified developed nations, and have focused their attention on eliminating only the worse abuses of sweatshops. See, for example, Kabeer, *The Power to Choose*.

NOTES TO CHAPTER 1: CROSSING THE ASSEMBLY LINE

1. Peterson, "Doo-Ri Chung."
2. Sue Collins, "In Her Own Words: From Refugee to *Project Runway*," *US Weekly*, March 20, 2006, 120–21.
3. The sociologist Miri Song (*Helping Out*) has written that children in ethnic businesses enter into what she calls a "family work contract," in which there are normative pressures to contribute to the family economy. However, children commonly refer to their labor participation as "helping out," as opposed to paid employment, to distinguish this work from "child labor"—with its pejorative connotations—and to suggest that it has both instrumental or material value as well as moral or symbolic value. One of the main ways that this "helping out" was distinguished from formal employment, of course, is that it is not contingent on remuneration—it is largely unpaid. I raise this issue here to show that the family work contract can function in reverse as well, with parents helping children out. I will return to this notion in more detail in the next chapter, which examines the extra-market interactions between Asian American fashion designers and Asian garment workers as an informal process of helping out.
4. Apparel wholesalers employ 34 percent of the designers. This means that there are almost as many designers who are self-employed as there are designers who earn salaries from larger firms (U.S. Department of Labor, Bureau of Labor Statistics, *Occupational Outlook Handbook*, http://www.bls.gov/oco/ocos291.htm).
5. U.S. Department of Labor, Bureau of Labor Statistics, *Occupational Outlook Handbook*, http://www.bls.gov/oco/ocos291.htm.
6. Wholesalers typically trade in higher volume because they must provide stock for many different retail outlets. They take on a bit more risk because of this higher volume and because they must depend entirely on outside buyers (rather than selling their goods in their own boutiques).
7. Many members of this community eventually migrated to Los Angeles to form the basis of the garment industry there. In fact, a large number of Koreans who are involved in the garment industry in Los Angeles have migrated multiple times, traveling through various parts of Latin America before settling in California.

8. Unless stated, all quotations are from interviews conducted by the author.

9. Rachel Brown, "Coming of Age for Korean Americans," *Women's Wear Daily*, March 19, 2008.

10. Quoted in Chow, "Understated Elegance of Derek Lam."

11. Quoted in Cheakalos, "Tam Time," 149.

12. Jen Kao, "Profile," http://www.jenkao.com.

13. Countless other designers have admitted that their desire to participate in fashion led them to experiment with clothing long before they ever attended fashion school—learning, presumably, by trial and error or by watching their relatives.

14. McRobbie's study of British fashion designers also stressed the importance of design schools in contributing to the fashion industry, both in generating its labor force and in fostering in its designers an understanding of themselves as creative professionals (McRobbie, *British Fashion Design*). See also Frith and Horne, *Art into Pop*.

15. Quoted in Helvenston and Bubolz, "Home Economics and Home Sewing in the United States, 1870–1940," 304.

16. Bhachu, *Dangerous Designs*. For a similar dynamic in the Jamaican context, see Carol Tulloch, "There's No Place Like Home."

17. Park, *Consuming Citizenship*.

18. Many scholars of "second-generation studies" have stressed that the transmission of cultural traditions does not occur unmediated from one generation to another—traditions are not, in other words, simply inherited—and this is certainly true within Asian communities. This body of literature generally suggests that the "new second generation"—as the sociologist Alejandro Portes has called the children of nonwhite, second-wave immigrants (Portes, *The New Second Generation*)—assimilate differently than children of previous immigrant generations. In particular, the literature argues that in addition to failing to integrate because of their race, members of this new second generation often find that there is social and economic value to not assimilating (for example, maintaining cultural and familial networks makes it easier for them to find certain types of jobs, marriage partners, etc.). At the same time, most studies of this generation also suggest that cultural traditions become altered, reinterpreted, and reimagined with each generation, often through their engagement with mainstream culture. See, for example, Maira, *Desis in the House*; Portes, *The New Second Generation*; Min, *The Second Generation*; and Yanagisako, *Transforming the Past*.

19. Denning argues that the formation of "the cultural front"—the extraordinary flowering of arts, entertainment, and thought based on the popular front, the wave of social activism during the Great Depression, represented a radical "laboring of American culture" (Denning, *The Cultural Front*). He uses the term "laboring" to suggest a number of mutually reinforcing phenomena,

including the existence of a strong labor movement; the increased presence of working-class Americans in the arts; the understanding of cultural production as labor, or seeing artists as cultural workers; the struggle for the laboring or social democratization of American culture (xvii).

20. It is not clear to me whether Lee paid her aunt for her labor, and if so, how much. I assume, though, that her aunt did not profit from this exchange and that she was simply helping her niece out.

21. After years of commercial success, Kahng's sales slumped in the mid-90s, and her business declined significantly. But even after she fell out of the spotlight, Kahng continued to design; she still puts out new collections each year.

22. Quoted in Cathy Rose A. Garcia, "Doo-Ri Chung Brings NY Style to Seoul" *Korea Times*, September 29, 2008.

23. Song, *Helping Out*, 11.

24. Song, *Helping Out*.

25. Waldinger, Aldrich, and Ward, *Ethnic Entrepreneurs*.

26. See, for instance, Yoo, *Korean Immigrant Entrepreneurs*; Light and Bonacich, *Immigrant Entrepreneurs*; Light and Bhachu, *Immigration and Entrepreneurship*; and Min, *Caught in the Middle*.

27. Constance C. R. White, "The Rise of Asian Designers," *New York Times*, June 20, 1995.

28. Ibid.

29. The idea of the "creative industries"—those culture-based enterprises that can drive economic development—is commonly attributed to the policies of Tony Blair's New Labour government in England, which provided subsidies to artists, musicians, designers, and other creative entrepreneurs to turn their own obsessions into economically productive activities and their nation into a thriving creative economy. What constitutes a creative industry varies by regions and nations, but the belief that these enterprises can generate jobs and revenues—and good jobs at that—is universal. In the United States, Richard Florida's *The Rise of the Creative Class* (about the importance of creative people to economic development and urban regeneration) and *The Flight of the Creative Class* (about the increasing loss of these people to locations overseas as a result of U.S. domestic and foreign policies after September 11, 2001) have been extremely influential in propagating the idea that cities and nations need to restructure policies and environments to attract this creative class. Cities across the country have signed on to Florida's model, adding bike paths and cafes to their city centers to attract creative types. Editorials about the need to invest in the creative and knowledge sectors, purportedly the fastest growing parts of the U.S. economy, abound in the pages of *The New York Times*, *The Wall Street Journal*, and other publications. A *Business Week* article expresses the typical enthusiasm with this attention-grabbing headline: "The Creative Econ-

omy: Which companies will thrive in the coming years? Those that value ideas above all else" (Peter Coy, August 28, 2000).

30. McRobbie, *British Fashion Design*, 149.

31. McRobbie has made a similar observation, arguing that in the context of British fashion, the gap between the designers and the sewers who make their clothes is not as vast as it appears: "Both groups of workers are emerging out of a culture of unemployment; they are also part of the new low pay economy which has crept into British working life by stealth during and after the Thatcher years; they tend to be urban-based; they work extraordinarily long hours; and they are working in a labour market which traditionally has been gender segregated, with all that entails. They are separated by education and generation, but in all other respects this labour force shares a common cause for improvement and change in the industry as a whole" (ibid., 125).

32. Quoted in Jean Scheidnes, "In the Lim Light," *Daily News Record*, April 23, 2007.

33. McRobbie, *British Fashion Design*, 122.

34. Ibid., 123.

35. Huws, "The Spark in the Engine."

36. Appelbaum and Gereffi, "Power and Profits in the Apparel Commodity Chain"; and Wark, "Fashion as a Culture Industry."

37. For instance, Ellen Rosen has written about the role of the Caribbean Basin Initiative, initiated under the Clinton administration, in the development of the garment industry in the Caribbean (Rosen, *Making Sweatshops*).

38. Skov, "Fashion-Nation," 226.

39. Roger Waldinger (*Through the Eye of the Needle*) has shown that New York's garment industry relies on the dynamics of "spatial agglomeration."

40. Some designers produce their own patterns, but this is relatively rare.

41. Gehlhar, *The Fashion Designer Survival Guide*, 91.

42. Kawamura, *The Japanese Revolution in Paris Fashion*, 147.

43. Shelly Tobin, quoted in ibid.

44. Martha Woodmansee and Peter Jaszi have argued that intellectual property laws rely fundamentally on the notion of an individual genius, a concept that they trace back to the romantic period (Woodmansee and Jaszi, "Introduction," *The Construction of Authorship*, 1–14).

45. Waldinger and Lichter, *How the Other Half Works*, 10.

46. Ibid.

47. Zhou, "New York."

48. Kang, *Compositional Subjects*, 194.

49. In some ways, the desire to render this labor invisible makes perfect sense. After all, fashion, as fashion scholars have defined it, is fundamentally a symbolic production. While it is one of our most labor-intensive cultural forms, it

trades in aesthetic ideals. In order to mobilize consumer desires, it must fetish-ize clothing into abstract ideas about beauty, freedom, romance, novelty, luxury, etc. Fashion advertising relies on this principle. The clothes themselves are rarely the main features in advertisements, but are simply props in a larger play about adventure, mystery, and so on. Given this need to trade in illu-sions, it is hardly surprising that most designers themselves contribute to the fetishization of clothing by distancing themselves from the work behind their garments—probably for more than one reason. This tendency, however, makes my interviewees' comments all the more remarkable.

50. E. Brooks, *Unraveling the Garment Industry*.

NOTES TO CHAPTER 2: ALL IN THE FAMILY?

1. Chin, *Sewing Women*.

2. See, for example, ibid. and Bao, *Holding Up More Than Half the Sky*; Green, *Ready-to-Wear, Ready-to-Work*; Soyer, *Cloak of Many Colors*; Stansell, "The Ori-gins of the Sweatshop"; Stein, *Out of the Sweatshop*; and Waldinger, *Through the Eye of the Needle*.

3. The number of shops actually grew during this period, but New York's share of the industry shrank as a result of competition from other regions of the United States (Waldinger, *Through the Eye of the Needle*).

4. Green, *Ready-to-Wear, Ready-to-Work*, Introduction.

5. Waldinger, *Through the Eye of the Needle*.

6. Green, *Ready-to-Wear, Ready-to-Work*, 2–3.

7. Chin, *Sewing Women*.

8. Proper, "New York"; Waldinger, *Through the Eye of the Needle*.

9. Rantisi, "The Ascendance of New York Fashion," 101.

10. Currid, *The Warhol Economy*. The interest in goods of greater distinction, asso-ciated with a particular designer or brand, has increased in all sectors of con-sumer products, not just in fashion, and has become so prevalent that now we can speak of such a thing as "mass luxury."

11. Bonacich and Applebaum, *Behind the Label*.

12. Rantisi, "The Ascendance of New York Fashion,"103.

13. According to a survey conducted by Rantisi, 60 percent of manufacturers in the garment district make patterns and samples locally; 30 percent perform cutting and 28 percent perform sewing tasks locally. Half of these firms send more than 50 percent of their work overseas, and 30 percent send all their production overseas ("The Ascendance of New York Fashion," 101).

14. Of course, there are exceptions. Designers have to have their knitwear made elsewhere, since that section of the industry has left New York entirely; other parts of their collection may also be hard to produce locally. And some small designers do send their collections overseas. Alice Cheng, for instance, told me

she was fed up with the local manufacturers and now has her production done exclusively in China, despite the fact that it costs more to do so. But this is currently not the most cost-effective or efficient means of production for small-scale operations and is generally used only by mid-sized, fairly stable brands, with department store distribution. I suspect that this will change, as firms in China and elsewhere become more agile at small-batch production, and as New York's garment industry declines further, due to pressures from abroad and from rising rents in the garment district. See also Rantisi, "The Ascendance of New York Fashion."

15. Bao, *Holding Up More Than Half the Sky*, chapters 1 and 3; Chin, *Sewing Women*; and Proper, "New York."

16. Out of 262 garment shops in New York, 111 were violating the 1938 Fair Labor Standards Act. The Department of Labor collected $800,000 in back wages from the shops and fined them $124,715 (Zhou, "New York," 124).

17. Green, *Ready-to-Wear, Ready-to-Work*, 7.

18. Waldinger, *Through the Eye of the Needle*, especially chapter 3, "From Tenement Sweatshop to Global Trade."

19. Chin, *Sewing Women*, 20.

20. Asian American Federation of New York, "Chinatown One Year After September 11th: An Economic Impact Study," April 4, 2002. (Full report available online at: http://www.aafederation.org/research/911Impact.asp.)

21. Chin, *Sewing Women*, 23.

22. Waldinger, *Through the Eye of the Needle*.

23. Bender, *Sweated Work, Weak Bodies*.

24. The story of the factory owner, referred to as "Mr. Siu" by Yu Zhou, is detailed in Zhou, "New York."

25. Likewise, many of the manufacturers, jobbers, and retailers who currently occupy the garment industry's upper echelon are Italian or Jewish Americans, descendants of the immigrants who dominated the lower end of the industry at the beginning of the twentieth century.

26. Bao, *Holding Up More Than Half the Sky*.

27. Zhou adds: "Although some immigrant entrepreneurs have indeed moved in this direction, for the vast majority of the immigrant contractors this strategy is out of reach, although not out of mind" ("New York," 127).

28. Ibid., 114.

29. McRobbie, *British Fashion Design*.

30. Gehlhar, *The Fashion Designer Survival Guide*, 4.

31. My interviewees would not divulge the full names of any of their workers and contractors. The secrecy that attended our discussions about these people was partly because the designers feared jeopardizing them in any way, and partly,

I suspect, because they also feared sharing too much about their business practices—especially those things that gave them any sort of advantage.

32. Some factory owners were born in Asia but had arrived in the United States at a young age (under ten). These owners often followed their parents into the trade, primarily because they felt they did not have opportunities elsewhere (Chin, *Sewing Women*).

33. Certainly "Asian-inspired" was a highly contested term, evoking a range of references and reactions in these designers. I address this issue in detail in the following chapter.

34. McRobbie, *British Fashion Design*, 123.

35. This is quite similar to the relationships formed within the predominantly Jewish garment industry in earlier periods of New York's history, which contributed to the increase of Jewish designers in the fashion industry. The designer Isaac Mizrahi, whose father was a cutter in the garment industry, is one example.

36. See, for instance, Yoo, *Korean Immigrant Entrepreneurs*; Light and Bonacich, *Immigrant Entrepreneurs*; Light and Bhachu, *Immigration and Entrepreneurship*; and Min, *Caught in the Middle*.

37. Social capital is typically described as those resources derived from close interpersonal relationships among individuals, organizations, and communities.

38. Light and Rosenstein, *Race, Ethnicity, and Entrepreneurship in Urban America*.

39. Pawan Dhingra's study of Korean and Indian professionals in the Houston area, *Managing Multicultural Lives*, provides a lucid analysis of how ethnic subjects choose their identities and what work is required to both drive them toward and away from a pan-ethnic identification. I thank Jiannbin Shiao for directing me to this work.

40. Song, *Helping Out*.

41. Here I am reminded of Wenlan Chia's comment that she chooses Chinese vendors over others because she believes, rightly or not, that they will help her more.

42. Jean Yu and Alpana Bawa both maintain their own production staff; Yu's staff shares her studio, located above her shop. These designers did not tell me that they had done this in order to help these sewers; their goal was to maintain better quality control by keeping everything in-house. Nonetheless, they are circumventing the factory system in much the same way as other designers who hire sewers directly.

43. Cited in Zhou, "New York," 118.

44. In the last few years, as the real estate market in New York has boomed, landlords in the garment district have driven up rents or have ceased to renew leases to manufacturers, preferring to transform these spaces into more profit-

able offices and studios. As a result, many manufacturers have been pushed out to Queens, Long Island, and New Jersey, while those that remain are seeing their profits shrink. The CFDA has organized a committee to address this issue, though it has yet to offer any solutions.

45. I did not conduct interviews with sewers for this project, partly because I lack the language skills to communicate with the predominantly Chinese and Korean sewers, but primarily because I was most interested in the ways that designers understood their relationship to these workers. I did, however, observe several of my subjects' interactions with their producers and was able to talk informally to two Vietnamese women during one of my shop visits. The conversation, conducted in Vietnamese, lasted about twenty minutes. In addition, I trailed one designer over the period of two years, observing her as she conducted business with several small manufacturers.

46. Wright, *Disposable Women and Other Myths of Global Capitalism.*

47. Waldinger, *Through the Eye of the Needle.*

48. Korean owners almost exclusively hire Mexican and Ecuadorian immigrants.

49. Chin, *Sewing Women*, 99. Of course, this has not prevented them from fighting for better wages and working conditions, as they did in a massive strike in Chinatown in 1982.

50. Yoo, *Korean Immigrant Entrepreneurs*, 9.

51. Thuy Diep told me: "I don't know if they treat non-Asians differently. But I feel like they hold a different standard with Asians. That's my gut feeling."

52. This was made clear to me by the way designers continually reminded me that "I'm the client" or "I'm the one giving them the job."

53. Mauss, *The Gift.*

54. Godbout and Caillé, *The World of the Gift*, 5.

55. Hence, Marshall Sahlins has suggested, there are different types of reciprocity: "generalized reciprocity," most apparent among family members, where obligation is implicit and indefinite; "negative reciprocity," common among strangers and characterized by suspicion; and "balanced reciprocity," reciprocity that is more or less equivalent (*Stone Age Economics*). See also Alain Testart, "Uncertainties of the 'Obligation to Reciprocate.'"

56. Ostein, Introduction, 7.

57. There are two main camps in the modern study of gifts. The first approach emphasizes gifts' ability to solidify social bonds, and the second stresses gifts' role in exercising power, inequality, and social disintegration. See Ostein, Introduction, for a thorough explication of these two camps.

58. Godbout and Caillé, *The World of the Gift*, 183.

59. Ostein, Introduction, 13. In fact, gifts may actually have very little use value, since they are governed by what David Cheal calls the "principle of redundancy." Presents, he suggests, can in fact give no advantage to their recipients

(if the gift is of no interest to the recipient) and can bring no net benefit (if the value of a gift received is the same as that of a gift given, or is more than is needed, or is something recipients can get for themselves). This is not to say that they have no value, but that they are not governed by a logic of necessity (*The Gift Economy*, 12).

60. Cheal, *The Gift Economy*, 14. Godbout and Caillé similarly argue that gifts have what they call "bonding values," which extend beyond their use or exchange values and are measured according to the gift's "capacity to express, to facilitate, to foster social ties" (*The World of the Gift*, 172).

61. Godbout and Caillé, *The World of the Gift*, 13.

62. Cheal, *The Gift Economy*, 14; Komter, *Social Solidarity and the Gift*, 191. Interdependency does not necessarily mean equality. Interdependent relationships can be those of foes as well as allies, of superior and inferiors as well as of equals.

63. McRobbie, *British Fashion Design*.

64. Terranova, "Free Labor," 38.

65. Sahlins, *Stone Age Economics*.

66. This lack of solidarity may explain why there have been fewer Latino designers, despite the fact that they are also heavily represented in garment production. Perhaps they have not received the help from producers that has been so important for Asian American designers. In this sense, the networks here suffer from the same types of limitations that Aiwah Ong has noted among Chinese in Southeast Asia, where kinship bonds (*guanxi*) have helped to strengthen business networks for some Chinese men, while keeping women and the poor out of business. These bonds therefore create and enlarge opportunities for the few and exacerbate inequalities for the many (Ong, *Flexible Citizenship*).

67. Proper, "New York," 185.

68. W. Brown, *Edgework*, 40 and 45.

69. The term "Asian American" emerged during the late 1960s as both a census category and a defining principle of a coalition-building effort to group together the diverse populations of Asian descent in the United States. But even as it emerged as a conceptual entity, the term's coherence was continually troubled by the heterogeneity of the populations it sought to unite. In the intervening years, this coalition-building principle has been subject to criticism for too often privileging certain narratives and experiences (particularly those of East Asian heterosexual males) and eliding differences of gender, class, sexuality, religion, and national affiliation inherent in such a diverse range of populations. Rather than seeking unity through perceived cultural similarities, scholars like Lisa Lowe (*Immigrant Acts*), Vijay Prashad ("Crafting Solidarities"), and Kandice Chuh (*Imagine Otherwise*) suggest, there is more to be gained in affiliating horizontally, with those individuals and groups

similarly positioned vis-à-vis institutions of power and/or those who share a similar political vision, regardless of their ethnic identity. These scholars call for a community-building effort that is grounded in difference—that makes disparities visible, that doesn't privilege racialization over all other processes of identification, and that opens up affiliations to those who may not look "like us."

70. Many of the designers I interviewed spoke of constantly being asked about how Asian culture is reflected in their design. I take up this discussion in the following chapter.

71. I explore the construction of these designers' identities, particularly in relation to the use of Asian culture in their design, in much more detail in chapter 5.

NOTES TO CHAPTER 3: THE CULTURAL ECONOMY OF ASIAN CHIC

1. DeJean, *The Essence of Style*, 53–55.

2. See, for instance, D. Jacobson, *Chinoiserie*; Oliver Impey, *Chinoiserie*; Meech-Pekarik, *Japonisme Comes to America*; Floyd, "Japonisme in Context"; Martin and Koda, *Orientalism*, 11–13.

3. DeJean, *The Essence of Style*, 54.

4. Most commentators link the emergence of fashion to the Industrial Revolution, which enabled garments to be made rapidly and thus fashion to change rapidly, but the seeds of fashion—as a system of symbolic value—were born at the moment when changes in clothing styles were no longer restricted to the aristocratic elite.

5. Exhibits on the influence of the East on Western dress were launched at the Metropolitan Museum, FIT Museum, Victoria and Albert Museum, and Wadsworth Athenaeum, among others. Popular books on the topic included *China Chic*, by the noted fashion historian Valerie Steele and John Major, and *China Chic*, by the noted fashion designer Vivienne Tam.

6. See, for example, Olivia Barker, "The Asianization of America, But Eastern Influences Do Not Mean Asian-Americans Are Insiders," *USA Today*, March 22, 2001; Julia Szabo, "The China Syndrome: Fashion Embraces Anything Asian, But with a Modern Twist," *Newsday*, March 26, 1998; Wendy Tanaka, "Asian Chic: As the 'Pacific Century' Dawns, Asian Film, Fashion and Food Are Hot," *The San Francisco Examiner*, June 25, 1997; Bob Mackwycz, "Crouching Iron Chef, Hidden Pokemon," *The Toronto Star*, April 1, 2001. In fact, the attention to Asia's influence on American culture prompted *The New York Post* to complain: "Just in time is *The New Yorker*'s spring issue. And, as usual, it's Japanese teens we're asked to check out—because, after all, they supposedly influence everything from cell phones to soft drinks. Call us crazy, but we'd like to read about another culture's influence on trends. Iceland, anyone?" "On the Newsstands," *The New York Post*, March 18, 2002.

7. Yudice, *The Expediency of Culture.*
8. Jones and Leshkowich, "Globalization of Asian Dress," 18.
9. See, for instance, Yoshihara, *Embracing the East*; Tchen, *New York before Chinatown*; Leong, *The China Mystique*; and Klein, *Cold War Orientalism.*
10. Klein, *Cold War Orientalism.*
11. Appadurai, *Modernity at Large*, 71.
12. Kawamura, *The Japanese Revolution in Paris Fashion.*
13. Mears, "Exhibiting Asia."
14. Schweitzer, "American Fashions for American Women."
15. Hoganson, "The Fashionable World: Imagined Communities of Dress."
16. *Vogue* is the fashion standard and, as such, appeals most to fashion insiders. *Harper's Bazaar* is a bit more accessible, with distilled trend reports and fashion advice for both the experienced and novice. *Elle* is the least arcane and is on the border between fashion and lifestyle magazine.
17. I was not able to find eleven issues.
18. Barthes, *The Fashion System.*
19. Bourdieu, *Distinction*, 359.
20. The methodological problem of trying to quantify something like this is, of course, how to avoid the tendency to construct the very thing you are trying to document. My aim was to see how Asian chic was described by these publications, but how would I know Asian chic when I saw it? In order to get around this problem, I went through each set of publications once, pulling out articles and images that used words like "Asian," "Chinese," "Indian," "Oriental," "exotic," and "the East." These images then became my guide. Once I pulled them out, I could compare them to other images and add to my list of "Asian chic" all those I considered close enough to the representative sample, even when they were not explicitly labeled as such. Though this did not entirely eliminate my own interpretative interventions, it did allow me to take my instructions first from the magazines themselves.
21. In spring and fall 1994 there were thirty-seven; in fall 1997 and spring 1998, ninety-three; and in fall 2003 and spring 2004, ninety-four. These numbers indicate a dramatic increase in the amount of articles, images, and so forth that could be found at the end of the decade, as compared to the beginning. Note: Each tally was taken from a twelve-month period. In the case of 1997 and 2003, I counted the twelve months over the course of two different years as the trend seemed to extend beyond the calendar year. Because trends in fashion work in seasons, rather than in calendar years, I felt that tracking contiguous seasons made more sense and allowed me to see more clearly shifts in patterns.
22. "Orient Express," *Vogue*, January 1991, 141.
23. "Moorish Style," *Vogue*, September 1991, 572.

24. "Culture Clash," *Harper's Bazaar*, June 1990, 56.

25. "Indian Summer," *Elle*, January 1990, 126–27; "Squaw Valley," *Elle*, November 1990, 271–75.

26. However, the parameters of this difference were always limited. In fall 1992, for instance, *Elle* advised trendsetters: "Designers all over the world are jumping on board the Orient Express as they look to the Far East for inspiration. Pajamas, opulent silks and satins, and lavish embroidery are some of the basic ingredients in this season's elegant homage to all things Asian." The editorial included images of women wearing fitted cheongsams and tunics embroidered with Chinese calligraphy and beaded dragons, lounging on luxuriously appointed beds, carrying paper umbrellas, and sipping from porcelain teacups. "The East" here is clearly associated with China, and "the Orient" with silks, satins, embroidery, and the sumptuousness and opulence of China's imperial past, but these representations were fairly atypical at the beginning of the 1990s ("Orient Express," *Elle*, October 1992, 205).

27. Cited in A. Brown, "Eastern Exposure," 44.

28. Ibid.

29. Szabo, "Mix Master," 119.

30. *Vogue*, March 1994, 257–63.

31. Ibid., 224–33.

32. As Anne Maxwell has argued, there were differences between colonial photographs, which were widely circulated and created for commercial consumption, and anthropological or ethnological photographs, which were used as objective measures of native people's anatomy and physical features, in that the former were rendered in romantic and sentimental styles to attract and entice consumers. Nonetheless, these depictions were accepted as realistic and as capturing authentic life (Maxwell, *Colonial Photography and Exhibitions*).

33. Martin and Koda, *Orientalism*.

34. Nochlin, *The Politics of Vision*, 33–60.

35. Appadurai, *Modernity at Large*, 71.

36. Ryan, "Orient Express," *Vogue*, May 1997, 103; "Seven Musts of '97," *Vogue*, January 1998, 152.

37. *Elle*, November 2000, 134.

38. *Vogue*, March 2002, 268.

39. *Harper's Bazaar*, December 1999, 156.

40. *Harper's Bazaar*, December 1998, 212.

41. "China Syndrome," *Vogue*, February 1997, 247.

42. "The Buy," *Harper's Bazaar*, January 1997, 140.

43. "Far Eastern Edge," *Elle*, February 1997, 144–45.

44. Sylvia Rhone, quoted in Ryan, "Orient Express," *Vogue*, May 1997, 103.

45. As early as 1993, *Elle*, the first of these three magazines to note the trend in

Eastern influences, directed its readers to find these goods in Chinatown. In a December issue, it jokingly observed: "If Demi Moore had thought of shopping in Chinatown, she'd have saved the fortune she probably spent on the slinky black cheongsam she wore in *Indecent Proposal*." The difference here is that the magazine doesn't characterize one as more authentic than the other—more costume than fashion (Field, "East Meets West . . . Downtown," 112.

46. Applebaum and Gereffi, "Power and Profits in the Apparel Commodity Chain."

47. Xu, "Remaking East Asia, Outsourcing Hollywood."

48. Benjamin, "The Work of Art in the Age of Mechanical Reproduction."

49. To be sure, such tendencies did not die altogether. In 2001, for instance, Donna Karan ran an ad campaign that employed those conventions: a white model is in a native setting, flanked by a woman (presumably) whose face and body is largely obscured by an iconic rice paddy hat. Such representations, however, were no longer the norm by this time—indeed, they were quite rare (*Vogue*, March 2001, 202).

50. "Runway Report," *Vogue*, April 2001, 206–18.

51. The ads at the time showed the same tendencies. An ad for Escada, for instance, showed an image of a woman, hips thrust forward, hair held in a neat bun by decorative chopsticks, carrying a glass of champagne, and wearing a fitted, dragon-printed dress. "It is believed," the accompanying text read, "that those born in the Year of the Dragon are popular individuals, full of life and enthusiasm. Luckily, anyone can adopt this fun-loving spirit. This Escada cheongsam in gleaming satin features a dramatic dragon motif, capturing Eastern exoticism. And just like any slinky dragon lady would expect, the result is fiery hot" (*Vogue*, October 2001, 187).

52. "Runway Report," *Harper's Bazaar*, January 2003, 26.

53. "On the Runway," *Elle*, February 2003, 78–80.

54. Less than a month after September 11, one reporter wrote: "In these times of disturbing news events, the relationship between how you dress and how you feel is more acute than ever . . . In such a chaotic world it's not unusual for people to favor nostalgic items that remind them of home, mothers and seemingly simpler moments, the experts tell us. People want clothes that are unpretentious, like old trustworthy friends" (Jackie White, "Snuggle Up and Hunker Down," *Kansas City Star*, November 4, 2001).

55. Cohen, *The Asian American Century*.

56. "Runway Report," *Harper's Bazaar*, January 2003, 20; "Point of View," *Vogue*, January 2003, 113; "Orient Express," *Elle*, October 2003, 156.

57. "Chinoiserie," *Harper's Bazaar*, March 2003, 84.

58. Vivienne Tam, Donna Karan, Michael Stars, Miu Miu, Blumarine, Roberto Cavalli, Shirin Guild, Saks Fifth Avenue (MaxMara), Prada, Gucci, Dior, Cartier, Victoria's Secret, Custo, Neiman Marcus (Akris), Guess, Follies.

59. "Buy, Keep, Store," *Harper's Bazaar*, August 2003, 96.

60. Bourdieu, *Sociology in Question*, 138.

61. Fashion historians like Valerie Steele, for instance, have written that one cannot criticize fashion's appropriations of the East as mere fantasy, because fashion is about fantasy. Steele writes: "[It] is necessary to realize that fashion is not *about* the accurate historical reconstruction of past styles. To say that fashion involves the creation of fantasies is not a valid criticism, although it is certainly true that the fantasies expressed in fashion may be subject to critical deconstruction." Steele and Major, *China Chic*, 70.

62. Gopinath, "Bollywood Spectacles."

63. Quoted in Howell, "Eyeing the East," 222.

64. M. Jacobson, *Roots Too*, 25.

65. Quoted in Prashad, *The Karma of Brown Folk*, 64.

66. Betts, "Dreaming of Cherry Blossoms," 73.

67. Everything from national identity cards (known as Real IDs) to recycling and the price of fish has been debated in the context of how it will help or hinder the U.S. need to "stay competitive with China." See, for instance, this statement issued by the office of Senator Lamar Alexander of Tennessee, a Republican: "We need to make sure that we don't create an unfunded mandate with Real ID. Currently it is an $11 billion unfunded mandate on state governments over the next five years. What does that mean? It means higher property taxes, higher tuition costs, less funding for higher education so we can stay competitive with China and India, less money for lower classroom sizes and less money for rewarding outstanding teachers" (Alexander, "Real ID").

68. Bush, "State of the Union."

69. Bush, "Remarks."

70. Cited in Paul Steinhauser, "Americans See China as Economic Threat," http://www.cnn.com/2009/US/11/17/obama.china/index.html. For a full account of the poll, see: http://www.pollingreport.com/china.htm.

71. Ibid.

72. Steele and Major, *China Chic*.

73. "Look to the East," *Elle*, October 1992, 256.

74. This association was made most obvious by the high-end firms like the jewelers H. Stern, Fred Leighton, and Cartier. In 1997 Fred Leighton put out a gold and diamond griffin brooch priced at $32,000; in 2003 Cartier advertised a special collection of jewelry called "le baiser du dragon" (the kiss of the dragon), employing similar images of dragons and so on in diamonds and platinum. For Fred Leighton, see *Harper's Bazaar*, September 1997, 437; for H. Stern, see *Elle*, April 1999, 221; and for Cartier, see *Elle*, June 2003, 107.

75. "The Lush Life," *Elle*, October 1996, 279.

76. "All the Raj," *Vogue*, June 1999, 184.

77. "Nouveau Boho," *Elle*, December 2004, 123.

78. Sykes, "Slouching towards Bohemia," 636.

79. Charnin, "Memoir of a Hip Hippie," 146.

80. D. Brooks, *Bobos in Paradise*.

81. Here I am referring to Prashad's reformulation of W. E. B. Du Bois's question: "How does it feel to be a problem?" To South Asians and Asian Americans, who have continually been seen as a model minority, to be emulated by others, Prashad asks, "How does it feel to be a solution?" (*The Karma of Brown Folk*, viii).

82. Clifford, "Collecting Ourselves," 266.

83. Leshkowich and Jones, "What Happens When Asian Chic Becomes Chic in Asia?"

84. Ibid.

85. Biographical statement, available on her Web site: http://www.viviennetam .com.

86. Tam, *China Chic*.

87. Francine Parnes, "Vivienne Tam's East-Meets-West Fashion Philosophy," *New York Daily News*, August 13, 2000.

88. Meredith Etherington-Smith, quoted in Skov, "Fashion-Nation," 220.

NOTES TO CHAPTER 4: "MATERIAL MAO"

1. Steele and Major, *China Chic*, 96.

2. Rosemary Feitelberg, "Butterfly Effect: A Filmmaker and His Designer Pal Put on a Show," *Women's Wear Daily*, May 22, 2006, 58.

3. See, for more information, "About," at http://www.hanfeng.com.

4. Cheng, "Skin Deep," 59.

5. "Anna Sui: A Fashion Gypsy, She's Been All Over Asia and the Far East in Search of Sartorial Inspiration," *Vogue*, June 2002, 185.

6. Quoted in Sally Singer, "That Touch of Mink," *Vogue*, July 2002, 92.

7. These passages were taken from http://www.anandjon.com, a Web site that is no longer accessible.

8. Quoted in Sykes, "Zen on a Hanger," 268.

9. "Power and Influence: South Asian Americans," *Newsweek*, March 22, 2004.

10. Jon was arrested in March 2007 on charges of rape and was found guilty in November 2008. On August 31, 2009, he was sentenced to fifty-nine years in prison.

11. Huggan, *The Postcolonial Exotic*, 28. In his study of the institutional dimensions of postcolonial literature, from publishing houses to the Booker Prize, Huggan suggests that postcolonial cultural producers work at a site of "discursive conflict" between their "oppositional practices"—which attempt to break down ideas about their inherent exoticness—and the transmission of those

practices in a market that capitalizes on otherness. These discursive conflicts, which Huggan calls the "postcolonial exotic," inevitably produce a "pathology of cultural representation" of which "strategic exoticism" is both a symptom and a response, so that signs of cultural differences are at once made visible and commodifiable (ibid.).

12. This was before she moved to the meatpacking district.

13. Lehman, *Tigersprung*, xx.

14. This is not unlike Louis Vuitton's use of the coolie image in its 1994 ads for a luggage collection, though in those ads the coolie is kept safely in the past, while for Feng coolies are also a part of the present.

15. Lehman, *Tigersprung*, xx.

16. Tam, *China Chic*, 308.

17. Schrift, *Biography of a Chairman Mao Badge*, 56.

18. Schrift, *Biography of a Chairman Mao Badge*; Michael Dutton "Stories of the Fetish."

19. Schrift, *Biography of a Chairman Mao Badge*, 72; also quoted in Barmé, *Shades of Mao*, 40.

20. Schrift, *Biography of a Chairman Mao Badge*, 73.

21. Dutton, "Mango Mao," 177.

22. Schrift, *Biography of a Chairman Mao Badge*, 147. Schrift documents numerous testimonies of this nature. A witness at a mass rally, for instance, recounted the following telling scene of a man donning his badge for the first time: "Carefully, he unfolded the paper to reveal a large pin with the image of Mao on it. Suddenly, he became nervous. Then, opening his shirt, he bared his chest . . . His little fingers trembled feverishly as he held the sacred object. He turned his back again, and, bowing deeply before Mao's poster, addressed it. 'Mao, you are like a god to me, and I will do all in my power to please you. Accept the prayer of your humble servant' " (115).

23. Barmé, *Shades of Mao*, 9.

24. Dutton, "Mango Mao," 183.

25. Barmé, *Shades of Mao*, 35.

26. Ibid., 48.

27. See, for instance, Schell, *Mandate of Heaven*; Baranovitch, *China's New Voices;* Wu, *Remaking Beijing*; Dutton, *Streetlife China*; Barmé, *Shades of Mao*.

28. In an article about the appearance of an inordinate amount of Mao knick-knacks in Huaihua County, in western Hunan Province, *The People's Daily* wrote that "in analyzing the phenomenon, we can see that the inhabitants of Huihua have a deep admiration for the leaders of the Chinese Revolution, and especially for Chairman Mao as well as for Communist and socialist values" (quoted in Schell, *Mandate of Heaven*, 282).

29. The art historian Wu Hung has suggested that developments in Chinese con-

temporary art outside of the direct sponsorship of the party—often termed avant-garde or nonofficial art—should rightly be called experimental art, for "avant-garde art" overestimates its aesthetic radicalism and "nonofficial art" overestimates its political radicalism (Wu, *Exhibiting Experimental Art*).

30. Critical appropriations of Mao have been a part of Chinese contemporary art for several decades (Wang Keping's sculpture of Mao recreated as a winking Buddha from 1978 is an early example) but became much more widespread and prominent after 1989, following the events at Tiananmen Square. The manipulation of Mao's image that took place in this period was part of a larger process of demystifying political symbols—including Tiananmen and Tiananmen Square, the Great Wall, and the Chinese written language—that began in the late 1970s, with the beginning of post–Cultural Revolution art.

31. For a discussion of this painting, see Lin, "Those Parodic Images," 114.

32. Quoted in Dal Lago, "Images, Words and Violence," 35.

33. Chang Tsong-zung, quoted in Wu, *Transience*, 20.

34. The label "double kitsch" was first applied to this style by the critic and historian Gao Minglu. This brief overview of cynical realism and political pop draws heavily on Wu, *Transience*; Gao, "Toward a Transnational Modernity"; Sullivan, *Art and Artists of Twentieth-Century China*.

35. Lu, "Art, Culture, and Cultural Criticism in Post-new China," 119.

36. Sullivan, *Art and Artists of Twentieth-Century China*, 278.

37. See, for instance, Liu Xiabo, "The Specter of Mao Zedong" (276–82), and Sun Jingxuan, "A Specter Prowls Our Land" (121–28), translated pieces included in Geremie Barmé's *Shades of Mao*.

38. Dal Lago, "Personal Mao," 52.

39. Wu has written that artists of this generation give us works that "strike us with a psychological dimension rarely seen in contemporary Chinese art" (*Transience*, 53).

40. Quoted in Yee, "An Interview with Zhang Hongtu," 3.

41. Olesen, "Breaking Free, Flying High."

42. Tam, *China Chic*, 89.

43. Ibid., 90.

44. Barmé writes that enthusiasm for Mao waned in direct proportion to the state's promotion of him as an official icon (*Shades of Mao*, 5 and 15–16).

45. Tam, *China Chic*, 90.

46. Ibid.

47. Andrews, *Painters and Politics in the People's Republic of China*.

48. Wu, *Transience*, 17–22.

49. Quoted in Schell, *Mandate of Heaven*, 290.

50. Yee, "An Interview with Zhang Hongtu," 3.

51. Wu Hung, *Transience*, 45.

52. Yee, "An Interview with Zhang Hongtu," 3.

53. Because of these comparisons, the painting was removed from an exhibit organized by the Congressional Human Rights Foundation and Senator Edward Kennedy on the ground that it was offensive to Christians. Zhang responded: "Eight years ago, I moved to the United States from China in order to have freedom to paint. Should I now move from the United States?" (quoted in Barmé and Jaivin, *New Ghosts, Old Dreams*, 409).

54. Benjamin, "Madame Ariane," 98–99.

55. Wu, *Transience*, 29.

56. Liu Xiaobo, "The Spectre of Mao Zedong," translated piece included in Geremie Barmé's *Shades of Mao*, 276.

57. Quoted in Schell, *Mandate of Heaven*, 291.

58. For instance, the art historian Xiaoping Lin has written: "The Chinese masses and avant-garde artists in the 1990s treat the image of Chairman Mao as a 'floating' or arbitrary iconic sign that has little to do with its historical context or reality, just as Andy Warhol did with the same icon in his work" ("Those Parodic Images," 114). See also Lu, "Art, Culture, and Cultural Criticism in Post-new China."

59. Quoted in Tam, *China Chic*, 92.

60. Quoted in ibid., 94.

61. Dal Lago has persuasively argued that by infusing these solemn images with the tint of low culture, Li has vulgarized Mao and transformed him into a truly popular icon ("Personal Mao," 58).

62. Mao's sexual exploits were perhaps most vividly recounted by his physician (Li, *The Private Life of Chairman Mao*).

63. Quoted in Schrift, *Biography of a Chairman Mao Badge*, 117–18.

64. Quoted in Barmé, *Shades of Mao*, 21.

65. Wu, *Transience*, 45.

66. Gao, "Toward a Transnational Modernity," 29.

67. Tam, *China Chic*, 88.

68. Ibid.

69. Ibid., 90.

70. Debra Gendel, "Mao, Mao, Mao—How Do You Like It?," *Los Angeles Times*, November 7, 1994; Khan and Wilkins, "China Chic"; Hahn, "Vivienne Tam."

71. Fionnula McHugh, "How Cool Is Mao? Is It Hip or Just Flip to Flaunt Mao's Image on T-shirts?," *South China Morning Post*, June 4, 1995, Sunday magazine, 22.

72. Ibid. Zhang has said that there have been similar treatments of his work in Hong Kong: "In Hong Kong they see it only in political terms. A couple of students from the mainland came to my show there. They signed their names in the visiting book, but when they came out they scratched them out. It wasn't

a criticism; they were afraid that someone might find out they'd been to see this 'dangerous' stuff. I felt really sad" (quoted in Tam, *China Chic*, 94).

73. E. Wilson, *Adorned in Dreams*, 2.

74. Ibid.

75. This is not to say, of course, that those who displayed Mao's image were always loyal to his ideas, but only to suggest that this was a primary vehicle in which to express publicly their feelings of loyalty.

76. Quoted in Tam, *China Chic*, 94.

77. The classic example is Hebdige, *Subculture*. See also F. Davis, *Fashion, Culture, Identity*; Bernstock and Ferriss, *On Fashion*; Crane, *Fashion and Its Social Agendas*; Barnard, *Fashion as Communication*; and Entwistle, *The Fashioned Body*.

78. Hollander, *Seeing through Clothes*, 311.

79. Butler, *Bodies That Matter*.

80. Wu has suggested that Zhang's use of these images reveals his ambivalent relationship to Hong Kong. Looking at Hong Kong from across the Pacific Ocean, Zhang is an outsider whose visual vocabulary is informed by the stock images of the global media, which posit the handing over of Hong Kong as an already predetermined media spectacle. Projected from external locations, whether Britain or China, these images represent Hong Kong without an intrinsic history or an internal space—as symbol of the tug of war between British colonialism and Chinese nationalism. At the same time that Zhang uses these tropes, he voices a deep skepticism about this published history. His T-shirts pose questions and highlight contradictions without resolving them (Wu, "Afterword 'Hong Kong 1997' ").

81. For a thorough treatment of the relationship between counterculture and cool, see Frank, *The Conquest of Cool*.

82. Mimi Avins, "Translating China's Classics," *Los Angeles Times*, May 21, 1998.

83. Burgin has defined the "popular preconscious" as "those ever-shifting contents which we may reasonably suppose can be called to mind by the majority of individuals in a given society at a particular moment in history; that which is 'common knowledge' " (*The End of Art Theory*, 58). Though Burgin does not address this point directly, one can assume that this preconscious does not cease once a subject has migrated to another society. Therefore, diasporic subjects may have more than one popular preconscious, or may have a popular preconscious that differs from that of their host society. Luz Calvo has convincingly argued that subaltern artistic practice will make use of "what I might call a post-colonial preconscious that is distinct from the 'common knowledge' of the society at large and that the subaltern's specialized knowledge produces a particular kind of viewing pleasure for those who 'get it' " (Calvo, "Art Comes for the Archbishop," 216).

84. Dutton, "Stories of the Fetish," 264.

85. Butler, *Bodies That Matter*, 124.

86. Bryson, "The Post-ideological Avant-garde," 58.

87. Hobsbawm, *The Age of Extremes*, 178.

88. Hobsbawm, "To See the Future, Look at the Past," *Guardian* (London), June 7, 1997.

89. Appadurai, *Modernity at Large*, 71.

90. Hobsbawm, "To See the Future, Look at the Past," *Guardian* (London), June 7, 1997.

NOTES TO CHAPTER 5: ASIA ON MY MIND

1. Betts, "Visions from the East."

2. Ibid. The narratives of reserve and restraint Betts presented, for instance, hewed closely to popular depictions of Asian Americans as model minorities: quiet and high-achieving students, diligent if robotic workers, emotionally reserved even if (in the case of women) sexually knowledgeable.

3. The concept of the "polycultural" was first articulated by Robin Kelley ("People in Me") and was elaborated upon by Vijay Prashad (*Everybody Was Kung Fu Fighting*, especially 65–69).

4. Kelley, "How the West Was One."

5. Quoted in Serafin, "Lost in Translation," 30.

6. Garner, *The Rise of the Chinese Consumer*, xii.

7. Ibid.

8. Ibid., 4. As even Garner admits, "currently, in U.S. dollar terms, Chinese consumers are only a marginal force in global consumption spending." But using what is called the "purchasing power parity" (PPP) rate, which measures not dollars spent but the quantity of purchases and thus the rate of spending, analysts can generate rosier data to support their projections (ibid.).

9. Lisa Rofel (*Desiring China*) has argued that these discourses were not produced only externally, but internally as well, in the ways that young people equated consumption with cosmopolitanism. Desiring subjects, with appropriate aspirations and longings, were as important to a post-Mao China as they were to transnational corporate speculators.

10. Beech, "The Rebel Returns," 51.

11. We see very similar discourses used in the context of Afghanistan.

12. D. Davis, *The Consumer Revolution in Urban China*, 1–2.

13. Ibid., 2.

14. Croll, *China's New Consumers*.

15. This description is available at http://www.hkdesigncentre.org/en/awards/wocd2005.asp.

16. Suzy Menkes, "Taking China: Vera Wang's Long March," *International Herald Tribune*, November 8, 2005.

17. In her study of the Hong Kong fashion industry ("Fashion-Nation"), Lise Skov has argued that, in fact, for decades design input on the part of local workers has been very much discouraged. The role of these workers was to simply reproduce and carry out designs generated in the West.

18. For a discussion of the national push toward the creative sectors in China, see Keane, *Created in China*.

19. "Award Details," http://samsungfashionpos.com (accessed June 4, 2009).

20. This process is very specific to particular ethnicities and nationalities: Korea supports Korean American designers, China supports Chinese American designers. There is no cross-national affiliation, and no articulation of "Asia" or "Asian" as a coherent geographic or cultural identity. In using the terms "Asia" and "Asian American" here, I do not mean to suggest otherwise, but only to show how the same process is being played out at various sites in "Asia" and among various ethnic subjects constructed as "Asian Americans."

21. Individual ignominy affects the nation as well. When the designer Anand Jon was brought to trial on dozens of counts of rape, the Indian consul general in San Francisco wrote to the California attorney general's office to express the Indian government's concerns involving Jon's case.

22. "What is SFDF," http://samsungfashionpos.com (accessed June 4, 2009).

23. Quoted in Syl Tang, "China's Designs on Global Chic," *Financial Times*, October 8, 2005.

24. Quoted in Suzy Menkes, "Taking China: Vera Wang's Long March," *International Herald Tribune*, November 8, 2005.

25. See, for instance, Gopinath, *Impossible Desires*; Rhacel Parreñas and Siu, *Asian Diasporas*; Anderson and Lee, *Displacement and Diasporas*; Chang, *Envisioning Diaspora*; R. Smith, *Mexican New York*; and Flores, *The Diaspora Strikes Back*.

26. Yudice, *The Expediency of Culture*.

27. Suzy Menkes, "Taking China: Vera Wang's Long March," *International Herald Tribune*, November 8, 2005.

28. Flores, *The Diaspora Strikes Back*.

29. Hall, "Race, Articulation, and Societies Structured in Dominance."

30. While the term "deconstruction" was first applied to the work of the Belgian designer Martin Margiela, the concept had already been practiced by avant-garde Japanese designers. Fashion historians credit the 1981 joint show by Kawakubo and Yamamoto with formalizing elements of deconstruction, whose precedents they traced to the London punks in the 1970s. For an account of this history see, Mears, "Fraying the Edges."

31. See, for example, Kondo, *About Face*; Craik, *The Face of Fashion*; Kawamura, *The Japanese Revolution in Paris Fashion*; and Mears, "Exhibiting Asia."

32. Kawamura, *The Japanese Revolution in Paris Fashion*.

33. Quoted in Mears, "Exhibiting Asia," 99.

34. Quoted in Vinken, *Fashion Zeitgeist*, 99.

35. Cited in Kawamura, *The Japanese Revolution in Paris Fashion*, 142.

36. Mears, "Fraying the Edges," 34.

37. Bernadine Morris, "From Japan, New Faces, New Shapes," *New York Times*, December 14, 1982.

38. Quoted in Kawamura, *The Japanese Revolution in Paris Fashion*, 137.

39. Vinken, *Fashion Zeitgeist*, 103.

40. Ibid., 103.

41. It was in fact in examining the work of Kawakubo that Brooke Hodge, curator of the exhibit Skin and Bones: Parallel Practices in Fashion and Architecture, "was struck by visual similarities between clothing design and architectural structure" (Hodge, "Skin + Bone," 11).

42. Sidlauskas, *Intimate Architecture*. Though many Western designers have been similarly interested in these issues—Cristobal Balenciaga and Madeleine Vionnet, to name just two—fashion historians credit Japanese designers with articulating this vision most coherently and forcefully.

43. Asian American designers share some biographical commonalities with these Japanese designers, too. Like a number of the Asian Americans, Kawakubo had no formal training in design. And like many others, Yamamoto was the son of a dressmaker whose first career choice was not fashion. (At the behest of his mother, Yamamoto studied law; he received a degree but never practiced.)

44. No doubt there is a certain amount of anxiety hidden in these types of statements—anxieties about the seriousness of their profession, its legitimacy as field of knowledge, its status as low culture, and so on—that has long plagued fashion designers. For instance, the couturier Charles Frederick Worth, who is known for having shifted the role of the dressmaker from a technician executing an outfit of the client's selection to a creator who designed individual creations, struggled to have people see his work as art and him as an artist. He used rare fabrics and elaborate decorations to reinforce the idea that fashion could be on par with sculpture and painting. Worth also surrounded himself with artists in order to secure his legitimacy as an artist. Asian American designers may have experienced this even more acutely, since their intimate relationships to garment workers has, as I noted in chapter 1, at times threatened to undermine their professional status and their creative identity. On this issue of fashion designers as artists, see M. Davis, *Classic Chic*.

45. Vinken, *Fashion Zeitgeist*, 100.

46. Quoted in Robin Givhan, "The Emperor's New Clothes. Seriously," *Washington Post*, February 6, 2007.

47. In comparing these two groups, Betts wrote, "Whereas Japanese designers like Rei Kawakubo of Comme des Garçons and Yohji Yamamoto, who emerged in the Paris fashion scene in the early 1980s, were about pushing the boundaries of fashion and making radical statements on the runway—all black palettes, jackets with three sleeves—this new group looks generally to more classical and conservative muses" ("Visions from the East").

48. McLarney, "The Burqa in Vogue."

49. See, for instance, Moalem, *Between Warrior Brother and Veiled Sister*.

50. cooke, "Deploying the Muslim Woman," 91 and 93.

51. The relationship between visibility and politics has, of course, always been far more complex. Scholars working in various contexts have shown that struggles for inclusion, representation, and appearance have not always proven to be empowering, nor has being unseen, hidden, or "in the closet" been only marginalizing and disempowering. See, for instance, Berlant, *The Queen of America*; S. Smith, *American Archives*; Wexler, *Tender Violence*; McAlister, *Epic Encounters*; Kang, *Compositional Subjects*; and Casper and Moore, *Missing Bodies*.

52. See, for instance, Butler, *Precarious Life*.

53. See, for instance, Jarmakani, *Imagining Arab Womanhood*; Moalem, *Between Warrior Brother and Veiled Sister*; Sedghi, *Women and Politics in Iran*; Haddad, "The Post-9/11 *Hijab* as Icon"; and Williams and Vashi, "Hijab and American Muslim Women: Creating the Space for Autonomous Selves."

54. El Guindi, *Veil*, 93.

55. On the same page, Cinar writes: "By delineating that which is private, the headscarf delimits the public gaze" ("Subversion and Subjugation in the Public Sphere," 903).

56. Ibid.

57. El Guindi, *Veil*, 93.

58. Ibid., 95.

59. For instance, in their attempt to revive the burqa, pop critics have recently asserted its value as an object that allows women to see but not be seen. As Joan Juliet Buck, the former editor-in-chief of French *Vogue*, wrote: "I can see you, you can't see me . . . I'm safe and I'm free" (McLarney, "The Burqa in Vogue," 14).

60. Hadimioglu, "Black Tents."

61. Stefano Tonchi, "From Paris: Designers Look East," *The New York Times* blog, June 29, 2009 (http://themoment.blogs.nytimes.com/2009/06/29/design ers-look-east).

62. Quoted in Amy Odell, "John Galliano, Carolina Herrera, Nina Ricci, and More

Design Fancy Abayas." These versions of the abaya ranged in price from $5,500 to $11,150. The first batch were given as gifts to Saks Fifth Avenue's most faithful Saudi clients, with ready-to-wear versions, retailing for around $2,500, rolled out in September.

63. Guy Trebay, "Women Masked, Bagged and, Naturally, Feared," *New York Times*, March 1, 2006.

64. Ibid.

65. McLarney, "The Burqa in Vogue,"14.

66. There are obvious resonances between this and the development of Asian chic.

67. Gokariksel and Secor, "New Transnational Geographies of Islamism, Capitalism, and Subjectivity."

68. McLarney advances this argument, recognizing the ambiguities in Takahashi's project: "As a Japanese designer, Takahashi occupies an ambiguous cultural position between Orient and Occident. By packaging the burqa as a product, even as an artistic commodity, he ties worlds together through shared consumer values. His punk burqas simultaneously evoke resistance and submission, dominance and subjection, liberation and repression in the same semiotic field of his clothing. An avant-garde rebel of the fashion industry, Takahashi himself embodies these contradictions, playing with the field but also against it. This is the process by which hegemonic discourses succeed 'in framing all competing definitions within their range' (Hebdige 1979, 16). Takahashi seems to say: people wear different masks; the gaze disciplines our body; power relations are woven into the very garment we wear" ("The Burqa in Vogue,"19). This ambivalence, I would argue, is made more palpable by the clothes themselves.

69. Maira and Shilhade, "Meeting Asian/Arab American Studies."

70. Lowe, *Immigrant Acts*, 65.

71. Lowe urged for an understanding of both the contacts between colonized peoples and the "forgetting" of these crucial connections, the recognition of which would enable the reconstruction of "a global past in which Asia emerges within and independently of a European modernity built on African slavery, in which Asian contract labor in the Americas is coterminous with the emancipation of African slaves" ("Intimacies of Four Continents," 205).

NOTES TO EPILOGUE

1. Kang, *Compositional Subjects*, chapter 4.

2. Robin Kelley, "How the West Was One."

3. Barbara Ehrenreich, "Is It Now a Crime to Be Poor?," *New York Times*, August 8, 2009.

BIBLIOGRAPHY

LIST OF INTERVIEWEES

Note: Name of Designer (Name of Label or Affiliation)

Alpana Bawa (Alpana Bawa)

Angel Chang (Angel Chang)

Charles Chang-Lima (Charles Chang-Lima)

Alice Cheng (A. Cheng)

Wenlan Chia (Twinkle)

Shin Choi (Shin Choi)

Yvonne Chu (Yvonne Chu)

Thuy Diep (Thuy)

Kelima K. (Kelima)

Gemma Kahng (Gemma Kahng)

Soojin Kang (Liz Claiborne, graduate of Parsons)

Jen Kao (Jen Kao)

Elizabeth Kim (name changed at request of interviewee)

Eugenia Kim (Eugenia Kim)

Ga-Hyun Kim (freelance designer, graduate of Savannah College of Arts and
    Design)

Olivia Kim (fashion publicist, Laforce + Stevens)

Carrie Lee (name changed at request of interviewee)

Diana Lee (Philip Lim)

Jussara Lee (Jussara Lee)

Wayne Lee (Wayne)

Sara Ma (name changed at request of interviewee)

Patricia Mears (curator FIT museum)

Sehti Na (Sehti Na)

Yukie Ohta (Yukie Ohta)

Mary Pham (name changed at request of interviewee)
Thuy Pham (United Bamboo)
Yeohlee Teng (Yeohlee)
Calvin Tran (Calvin Tran)
Margie Tsai (Margie Tsai)
Jennifer Wang (Wang's)
Selia Yang (Selia Yang)
Jean Yu (Jean Yu)

REFERENCES

Adhikari, Ramesh, and Prema-chandra Athukorala, eds. *Developing Countries in the World Trading System: The Uruguay Round and Beyond*. Northampton, Mass.: Edward Elgar, 2002.

Alexander, Lamar. "Real ID." *Federal News Service*, March 1, 2007.

Anderson, Wanni, and Robert G. Lee. *Displacement and Diasporas: Asians in the Americas*. New Brunswick, N.J.: Rutgers University Press, 2005.

Andrews, Julia F. *Painters and Politics in the People's Republic of China, 1949–1979*. Berkeley: University of California Press, 1994.

"Anna Sui: A Fashion Gypsy, She's Been All Over Asia and the Far East in Search of Sartorial Inspiration." *Vogue*, June 2002, 185.

Appadurai, Arjun. *Modernity at Large: Cultural Dimensions of Globalization*. Minneapolis: University of Minnesota Press, 2008.

Appelbaum, Richard, and Gary Gereffi. "Power and Profits in the Apparel Commodity Chain." In *Global Production: The Apparel Industry in the Pacific Rim*, edited by Edna Bonacich, Lucie Cheng, Norma Chinchilla, Nora Hamilton, and Paul Ong, 42–62. Philadelphia: Temple University Press, 1994.

Asian American Federation of New York. "Chinatown One Year after September 11th: An Economic Impact Study," April 4, 2002. (Full report available online at: http://www.aafederation.org/research/911Impact.asp.)

Bao, Xiaolan. *Holding Up More Than Half the Sky: Chinese Women Garment Workers in New York City, 1948–1992*. Urbana: University of Illinois Press, 2001.

Baranovitch, Nimrod. *China's New Voices: Popular Music, Ethnicity, Gender, and Politics, 1978–1997*. Berkeley: University of California Press, 2003.

Barmé, Geremie R. *Shades of Mao: The Posthumous Cult of the Great Leader*. Armonk, N.Y.: M. E. Sharpe, 1996.

Barmé, Geremie R., and Linda Jaivin. *New Ghosts, Old Dreams*. New York: Times Books, 1992.

Barnard, Malcolm. *Fashion as Communication*. New York: Routledge, 2002.

Barthes, Roland. *The Fashion System*. Translated by Matthew Ward and Richard Howard. Berkeley: University of California Press, 1990.

Beech, Hannah. "The Rebel Returns." *Time*, February 28, 2005, 51.

Bender, Daniel E. *Sweated Work, Weak Bodies: Anti-Sweatshop Campaigns and Languages of Labor.* New Brunswick, N.J.: Rutgers University Press, 2004.

Benjamin, Walter. "Madame Ariane: Second Courtyard on the Left." In *One-Way Street,* translated by Edmund Jephcott and Kingsley Shorter, 98–99. London: New Left Books, 1979.

——. "The Work of Art in the Age of Mechanical Reproduction." In *Illuminations,* edited by Hannah Arendt. Translated by Harry Zohn, 217–52. New York: Schocken, 1968.

Berlant, Lauren. *The Queen of America Goes to Washington City: Essays on Sex and Citizenship.* Durham, N.C.: Duke University Press, 1997.

Bernstock, Shari, and Suzanne Ferriss, eds. *On Fashion.* New York: Routledge, 1994.

Betts, Kate. "Dreaming of Cherry Blossoms: At Dior, Galliano's Geishas Have a Message." *Time,* February 5, 2007, 73.

——. "Visions from the East: Four Young Asian Designers Steal the Spotlight at New York's Fashion Show." *Time,* September 27, 2004, 64.

Bhachu, Parminder. *Dangerous Designs: Asian Women Fashion the Diaspora Economies.* New York: Routledge, 2004.

Bonacich, Edna, and Richard Appelbaum. *Behind the Label.* Berkeley: University of California Press, 2000.

Bonacich, Edna, Lucie Cheng, Norma Chinchilla, Nora Hamilton, and Paul Ong, eds. *Global Production: The Apparel Industry in the Pacific Rim.* Philadelphia: Temple University Press, 1994.

Bourdieu, Pierre. *Distinction: A Social Critique of the Judgment of Taste.* Translated by Richard Nice. London: Routledge, 1984.

——. *Sociology in Question.* Translated by Richard Nice. London: Sage, 1993.

Brooks, David. *Bobos in Paradise: The New Upper Class and How They Got There.* New York: Simon and Schuster, 2000.

Brooks, Ethel. *Unraveling the Garment Industry: Transnational Organizing and Women's Work.* Minneapolis: University of Minnesota Press, 2007.

Brown, Alix. "Eastern Exposure." *Harper's Bazaar,* August 1994, 44.

Brown, Wendy. *Edgework: Critical Essays on Knowledge and Politics.* Princeton, N.J.: Princeton University Press, 2005.

Bryson, Norman. "The Post-Ideological Avant-Garde." In *Inside Out: New Chinese Art,* edited by Gao Minglu, 51–58. San Francisco: San Francisco Museum of Modern Art, 1998.

Burgin, Victor. *The End of Art Theory: Criticism and Postmodernity.* Atlantic Highlands, N.J.: Humanities Press, 1986.

Bush, George W. "Remarks at Parkland Magnet Middle School for Aerospace Technology in Rockville, Maryland." Public Papers of the President, April 24, 2006.

——. "State of the Union: American Competitiveness Initiative." White House Documents and Publications, January 31, 2006.

Butler, Judith. *Bodies That Matter: On the Discursive Limits of Sex*. New York: Routledge, 1990.

———. *Precarious Life: The Powers of Mourning and Violence*. London: Verso, 2004.

"The Buy." *Harper's Bazaar*, January 1997, 140.

"Buy, Keep, Store." *Harper's Bazaar*, August 2003, 96.

Calvo, Luz. "Art Comes for the Archbishop: The Semiotics of Contemporary Chicana Feminism and the Work of Alma Lopez." *Meridians* 5, no. 1 (2004): 201–24.

Casper, Monica, and Lisa Jean Moore. *Missing Bodies: The Politics of Visibility*. New York: New York University Press, 2009.

Chang, Alexandra. *Envisioning Diaspora: Asian American Artists Collective*. New York: Timezone 8, 2009.

Charnin, Jade Hobson. "Memoir of a Hip Hippie." *Harper's Bazaar*, October 1998, 144–48.

Cheakalos, Christina. "Tam Time." *People*, November 23, 1998, 149–50.

Cheal, David. *The Gift Economy*. New York: Routledge, 1988.

Cheng, Anne. "Skin Deep: Josephine Baker and the Colonial Fetish." *Camera Obscura* 69, vol. 23, no. 3 (2008): 35–79.

Chin, Margaret M. *Sewing Women: Immigrants and the New York City Garment District*. New York: Columbia University Press, 2005.

"China Syndrome." *Vogue*, February 1997, 246–52.

"Chinoiserie." *Harper's Bazaar*, March 2003, 84.

Chow, May. "Understated Elegance of Derek Lam: Fashion Designer Skips Eastern Flair for Viennese Luxe." *AsianWeek*, June 4, 2004. http://www.asianweek.com/2004/06/04.

Chuh, Kandice. *Imagine Otherwise: On Asian Americanist Critique*. Durham, N.C.: Duke University Press, 2003.

Cinar, Alev. "Subversion and Subjugation in the Public Sphere: Secularism and the Islamic Headscarf." *Signs* 33, no. 4 (summer 2008): 891–913.

Clifford, James. "Collecting Ourselves." Reprinted in *Interpreting Objects and Collections*, edited by Susan M. Pierce, 266. New York: Routledge, 1994, 258–68.

Cohen, Warren I. *The Asian American Century*. Cambridge: Harvard University Press, 2002.

Collins, Sue. "In Her Own Words: From Refugee to *Project Runway*." *US Weekly*, March 20, 2006, 120–21.

cooke, miriam. "Deploying the Muslim Woman." *Journal of Feminist Studies in Religion* 24, no. 1 (2008): 91–99.

Coy, Peter. "The Creative Economy: Which Companies Will Thrive in the Coming Years?" *Business Week*, August 28, 2000, http://www.businessweek.com/2000/00_35/b3696002.htm.

Craik, Jennifer. *The Face of Fashion: Cultural Studies in Fashion*. New York: Routledge, 1993.

Crane, Diana. *Fashion and Its Social Agendas: Class, Gender, and Identity in Clothing*. Chicago: University of Chicago Press, 2000.

Croll, Elisabeth. *China's New Consumers: Social Development and Domestic Demand*. New York: Routledge, 2006.

Currid, Elizabeth. *The Warhol Economy: How Fashion, Art, and Music Drive New York City*. Princeton, N.J.: Princeton University Press, 2007.

Dal Lago, Francesca. "Images, Words and Violence: Cultural Revolutionary Influence on Chinese Avant-Garde Art." In *Chinese Art at the Crossroads: Between Past and Future, Between East and West*, edited by Wu Hung, 32–40. London: Institute of International Visual Arts, 2001.

——. "Personal Mao: Reshaping an Icon in Contemporary Chinese Art." *Art Journal* 58, no 2. (1999): 46–59.

Davis, Deborah S. "Introduction." In *The Consumer Revolution in Urban China*, edited by Deborah S. David, 1–25. Berkeley: University of California Press, 2000.

Davis, Fred. *Fashion, Culture, Identity*. Chicago: University of Chicago Press, 1994.

Davis, Mary E. *Classic Chic: Music, Fashion, and Modernism*. Berkeley: University of California Press, 2006.

DeJean, Joan. *The Essence of Style: How the French Invented High Fashion, Fine Food, Chic Cafes, Style, Sophistication, and Glamour*. New York: Free Press, 2005.

Denning, Michael. *The Cultural Front: The Laboring of American Culture in the Twentieth Century*. London: Verso, 1996.

Dhingra, Pawan. *Managing Multicultural Lives: Asian American Professionals and the Challenge of Multiple Identities*. Stanford, Calif.: Stanford University Press, 2007.

Dickerson, Kitty. *Textile and Apparel in the International Economy*. New York: Macmillan, 1991.

Duggan, Lisa. *The Twilight of Equality? Neoliberalism, Cultural Politics, and the Attack on Democracy*. Boston: Beacon, 2003.

Dutton, Michael. "Mango Mao: Infections of the Sacred." *Public Culture* 16, no. 2 (spring 2004): 161–87.

——. "Stories of the Fetish: Tales of Chairman Mao." In *Streetlife China*, edited by Michael Dutton, 239–71. Cambridge: Cambridge University Press, 1998.

——, ed. *Streetlife China*. Cambridge: Cambridge University Press, 1998.

Eger, John M. "The Future of Work in the Creative Age." May 2004. http://www.culturalcommons.org/comment-print.cfm?ID=17.

El Guindi, Fadwa. *Veil: Modesty, Privacy, and Resistance*. New York: Berg, 1999.

Eng, David. "Transnational Adoption and Queer Diasporas." *Social Text* 21, no. 3 (2003): 1–37.

Entwistle, Joanne. *The Fashioned Body: Fashion, Dress, and Modern Social Theory.* Cambridge: Polity, 2000.

Espiritu, Yen Le. *Asian American Panethnicity.* Philadelphia: Temple University Press, 2003.

"Far Eastern Edge." *Elle*, February 1997, 138–48.

Field, Veronica. "East Meets West . . . Downtown." *Elle*, December 1993, 112.

Finnane, Antonia. *Changing Clothes in China: Fashion, History, Nation.* New York: Columbia University Press, 2008.

Flores, Juan. *The Diaspora Strikes Back: Caribbean Latino Tales of Learning and Turning.* New York: Routledge, 2008.

Florida, Richard. *The Flight of the Creative Class: The New Global Competition for Talent.* New York: HarperCollins, 2007.

——. *The Rise of the Creative Class and How It's Transforming Leisure, Community, and Everyday Life.* New York: Basic, 2003.

Floyd, Phylis Anne. "Japonisme in Context: Documentation, Criticism, Aesthetic Reactions." Ph.D. diss., University of Michigan, 1983.

Frank, Thomas. *The Conquest of Cool: Business Culture, Counterculture, and the Rise of Hip Consumerism.* Chicago: University of Chicago Press, 1997.

Friedman, Thomas L. *The World Is Flat: A Brief History of the Twenty-First Century.* Updated and expanded ed. New York: Farrar, Straus and Giroux, 2006.

Frith, Simon, and Howard Horne. *Art into Pop.* London: Methuen, 1987.

Gao, Minglu. "Toward a Transnational Modernity." In *Inside Out: New Chinese Art*, edited by Gao Minglu, 15–40. San Francisco: San Francisco Museum of Modern Art, 1998.

Garner, Jonathan. *The Rise of the Chinese Consumer: Theory and Evidence.* Chichester, England: Wiley, 2005.

Gehlhar, Mary. *The Fashion Designer Survival Guide: Start and Run Your Own Fashion Business.* Rev. ed. New York: Kaplan Business, 2008.

Gereffi, Gary, and Miguel Korzeniewicz, eds. *Commodity Chains and Global Capitalism.* Westport, Conn.: Praeger, 1994.

Gereffi, Gary, and Olga Memedovic. *The Global Apparel Value Chain: What Prospects for Upgrading by Developing Countries?* Vienna: UN Industrial Development Organization, Strategic Research and Economics Branch, 2003.

Gereffi, Gary, David Spener, and Jennifer Bair, eds. *Free Trade and Uneven Development: The North American Apparel Industry after NAFTA.* Philadelphia: Temple University Press, 2002.

Godbout, Jacques T., in collaboration with Alain Caillé. *The World of the Gift.* Translated by Donald Winkler. Montreal: McGill-Queen's University Press, 1998.

Gokariksel, Banu, and Anna J. Secor. "New Transnational Geographies of Islamism, Capitalism, and Subjectivity: The Veiling-Fashion Industry in Turkey." *Area* 41, no. 1 (2008): 6–18.

Gopinath, Gayatri. "Bollywood Spectacles." *Social Text* 23, nos. 3–4 (fall–winter 2005): 157–70.

———. *Impossible Desires: Queer Diasporas and South Asian Public Cultures.* Durham, N.C.: Duke University Press, 2005.

Goto, Kent. "Industrial Upgrading of the Vietnamese Garment Industry: An Analysis from the Global Value Chains Perspective." Ritsumeikan Center for Asian Pacific Studies working paper, http://www.apu.ac.jp/rcaps/modules/webpublication/content/07-1_RCAPS_WP.pdf.

———. "The Production and Distribution Structure in the 'Original Brand' Apparel Industry of Ho Chi Minh City: Knowledge-Intensive Functions and the Internationalization of Production and Distribution." In *The Transformation of Vietnam's Industry during the Period of Transition: Development Led by the Growth Domestic Enterprises,* edited by Mai Fujita, 105–36. Institute for Developing Economies (Chiba, Japan, 2006).

Green, Nancy L. *Ready-to-Wear, Ready-to-Work: A Century of Industry and Immigrants in Paris and New York.* Durham, N.C.: Duke University Press, 1997.

Haddad, Yvonne Yazbeck. "The Post-9/11 *Hijab* as Icon." *Sociology of Religions* 68, no. 3 (fall 2007): 253–67.

Hadimioglu, Cagla. "Black Tents." *Threshold* 22 (summer 2001): 18–26.

Hahn, Lorraine. "Vivienne Tam." CNN.com. October 20, 2005.

Hall, Stuart. "Race, Articulation, and Societies Structured in Dominance." In *Black British Cultural Studies: A Reader,* edited by Houston Baker, Manthia Diawara, and Ruth Lindenborg, 16–61. Chicago: University of Chicago Press, 1996.

Hebdige, Dick. *Subculture: The Meaning of Style.* New York: Routledge, 1981.

Helvenston, Sally I., and Margaret M. Bubolz. "Home Economics and Home Sewing in the United States, 1870–1940." In *The Culture of Sewing: Gender, Consumption and Home Dressmaking,* edited by Barbara Burman, 303–26. New York: Berg, 1999.

Hobsbawm, Eric. *The Age of Extremes: The Short Twentieth Century, 1914–1991.* London: Joseph, 1995.

Hodge, Brooke. "Skin + Bones." In *Skin + Bones: Parallel Practices in Fashion and Architecture,* edited by Brooke Hodge, 10–21. London: Thames and Hudson, 2006.

Hoganson, Kristin. "The Fashionable World: Imagined Communities of Dress." In *After the Imperial Turn: Thinking with and through the Nation,* edited by Antoinette M. Burton, 260–78. Durham, N.C.: Duke University Press, 2003.

Hollander, Anne. *Seeing through Clothes.* New York: Avon, 1975.

Howell, Georgina. "Eyeing the East." *Vogue,* May 1994, 220–24.

Huggan, Graham. *The Postcolonial Exotic: Marketing the Margins.* London: Routledge, 2001.

Huws, Ursula. "The Spark in the Engine: Creative Works in the Global Economy." *Work, Organisation, Labour, and Globalisation* 1, no. 1 (2006–7): 1–12.

Impey, Oliver R. *Chinoiserie: The Impact of Oriental Styles on Western Art and Decoration*. London: Oxford University Press, 1977.

"Indian Summer." *Elle*, January 1990, 126–27.

Jacobson, Dawn. *Chinoiserie*. London: Phaidon, 1993.

Jacobson, Matthew Frye. *Roots Too: White Ethnic Revival in Post–Civil Rights America*. Cambridge: Harvard University Press, 2006.

Jarmakani, Amira. *Imagining Arab Womanhood: The Cultural Mythology of Veils, Harems, and Belly Dancers in the U.S.* New York: Palgrave Macmillan, 2008.

Jones, Carla, and Ann Marie Leshkowich. "The Globalization of Asian Dress: Re-Orienting Fashion or Re-Orientalizing Asia." In *Re-Orienting Fashion: The Globalization of Asian Dress*, edited by Sandra Niessen, Ann Marie Leshkowich, and Carla Jones, 1–49. Oxford: Berg, 2003.

Kabeer, Nalia. *The Power to Choose: Bangladeshi Garment Workers in London and Dakha*. New York: Verso, 2002.

Kang, Laura Hyun Yi. *Compositional Subjects: Enfiguring Asian/American Women*. Durham, N.C.: Duke University Press, 2002.

Kawamura, Yuniya. *The Japanese Revolution in Paris Fashion*. New York: Berg, 2004.

Keane, Michael. *Created in China: The Great New Leap Forward*. New York: Routledge, 2007.

Kelley, Robin. "How the West Was One: The African Diaspora and the Remapping of American History." In *Rethinking American History in the Global Age*, edited by Thomas Bender, 123–48. Berkeley: University of California Press, 2002.

——. "People in Me." *Colorlines* 1, no. 3 (winter 1999): 5–7.

Khan, Riz, and Stacey Wilkins. "China Chic: More to the East Than the Exotic." CNN International, December 19, 2000, Transcript # 121900cb.k18.

Klein, Christina. *Cold War Orientalism: Asia in the Middlebrow Imagination, 1945–1961*. Berkeley: University of California Press, 2003.

Komter, Aafke E. *Social Solidarity and the Gift*. Cambridge: Cambridge University Press, 2005.

Kondo, Doreen. *About Face: Performing Race in Fashion and Theater*. New York: Routledge, 1997.

Kwong, Peter. *Chinatown, New York: Labor and Politics*. New York: Monthly Review Press, 1979.

——. *The New Chinatown*. New York: Hill and Wang, 1996.

Lee, Josephine. *Performing Asian America*. Philadelphia: Temple University Press, 1998.

Lehman, Ulrich. *Tigersprung: Fashion in Modernity*. Cambridge: MIT Press, 2000.

Leong, Karen. *The China Mystique: Pearl S. Buck, Anna May Wong, Mayling Soong and the Transformation of American Orientalism*. Berkeley: University of California Press, 2005.

Leshkowich, Ann Marie, and Carla Jones. "What Happens When Asian Chic Be-comes Chic in Asia?" *Fashion Theory* 7, nos. 3–4 (September 2003): 281–99.

Li, Zhisui. *The Private Life of Chairman Mao*. Translated by Tai Hung-Chao. New York: Random House, 1996.

Light, Ivan, and Parminder Bhachu. *Immigration and Entrepreneurship: Culture, Capital, Network*. Piscataway, N.J.: Transaction, 2004.

Light, Ivan, and Edna Bonacich. *Immigrant Entrepreneurs: Koreans in Los Angeles, 1965–1982*. Berkeley: University of California Press, 1991.

Light, Ivan, and Carolyn Rosenstein. *Race, Ethnicity, and Entrepreneurship in Urban America*. New York: Aldine de Gruyter, 1995.

Lin, Xiaoping. "Those Parodic Images: A Glimpse of Contemporary Chinese Art." *Leonardo* 30, no. 2 (1997): 113–22.

Lipovetsky, Gilles. *The Empire of Fashion: Dressing Modern Democracy*. Princeton, N.J.: Princeton University Press, 1994.

"Look to the East." *Elle*, October 1992, 256–78.

Lowe, Lisa. *Immigrant Acts: On Asian American Cultural Productions*. Durham, N.C.: Duke University Press, 1996.

——. "The Intimacies of Four Continents." In *Haunted by Empire: Geographies of Intimacy in North American History*, edited by Ann Laura Stoler, 191–213. Durham, N.C.: Duke University Press, 2006.

Lu, Sheldon Hsiao-peng. "Art, Culture, and Cultural Criticism in Post–New China." *New Literary History* 28, no. 1 (1997): 111–33.

"The Lush Life." *Elle*, October 1996, 279–85.

Maira, Sunaina. *Desis in the House: Indian American Youth Culture in New York City*. Philadelphia: Temple University Press, 2002.

Maira, Sunaina, and Magid Shilhade. "Meeting Asian/Arab American Studies: Thinking Race, Empire, and Zionism in the U.S." *Journal of Asian American Studies* 9, no. 2 (June 2006): 117–40.

Manalansan, Martin. "Race, Violence, and Neoliberal Spatial Politics in the Global City." *Social Text* 23, no. 3–4 (fall–winter 2005): 141–55.

Martin, Richard, and Harold Koda. *Orientalism: Visions of the East in Western Dress*. New York: Metropolitan Museum of Art, 1994.

Mauss, Marcel. *The Gift: The Forms and Reasons for Exchange in Archaic Societies*. Translated by W. D. Halls. New York: Routledge, 1990.

Maxwell, Anne. *Colonial Photography and Exhibitions: Representations of the Native and the Making of European Identities*. London: Leicester University Press, 2000.

McAlister, Melanie. *Epic Encounters: Culture, Media, and U.S. Interests in the Middle East, 1945–2000*. Berkeley: University of California Press, 2001.

McLarney, Ellen. "The Burqa in Vogue: Fashioning Afghanistan." *Journal of Middle East Women's Studies* 5, no. 1 (winter 2009): 1–23.

McRobbie, Angela. *British Fashion Design: Rag Trade or Image Industry?* London: Routledge, 1998.

——. "Fashion Culture: Creative Work, Female Individualization." *Feminist Review* 71, no. 1 (2002): 52–62.

Mears, Patricia. "Exhibiting Asia: The Global Impact of Japanese Fashion in Museums and Galleries." *Fashion Theory* 12, no. 1 (March 2008): 95–119.

——. "Fraying the Edges: Fashion and Deconstruction." In *Skin + Bones: Parallel Practices in Fashion and Architecture*, edited by Brooke Hodge, 30–37. London: Thames and Hudson, 2006.

Meech-Pekarik, Julia. *Japonisme Comes to America: The Japanese Impact on the Graphic Arts, 1876–1925.* New York: Abrams, 1990.

Min, Pyong Gap. *Caught in the Middle: Korean Communities in New York and Los Angeles.* Berkeley: University of California Press, 1996.

——, ed. *The Second Generation: Ethnic Identity among Asian Americans.* Walnut Creek, Calif.: Altamira, 2002.

Ministry of Textiles. "National Textile Policy 2000," http://www.worldjute.com.

Moalem, Minoo. *Between Warrior Brother and Veiled Sister: Islamic Fundamentalism and the Cultural Politics of Patriarchy in Iran.* Berkeley: University of California Press, 2005.

"Moorish Style." *Vogue*, September 1991, 569–76.

Nadvi, K., and J. Thoburn. "Vietnam in the Global Garment and Textile Value Chain: Impacts on Firms and Workers." *Journal of International Development* 16, no 1. (January 2004): 111–23.

Niessen, Sandra, Ann Marie Leshkowich, and Carla Jones, eds. *Re-Orienting Fashion: The Globalization of Asian Dress.* Oxford: Berg, 2003.

Nochlin, Linda. *The Politics of Vision: Essays on Nineteenth-Century Art and Society.* New York: Harper and Row, 1989.

"Nouveau Boho." *Elle*, December 2004, 123.

Odell, Amy. "John Galliano, Carolina Herrera, Nina Ricci, and More Design Fancy Abayas." *New York*, June 29, 2009, http://nymag.com.

Olesen, Alexa. "Breaking Free, Flying High: Zhang Hongtu's Journey from Maoism to Modern Art." Virtualchina.com, December 9, 1999. (URL no longer available.)

Ong, Aihwah. *Flexible Citizenship: The Cultural Logics of Transnationality.* Durham, N.C.: Duke University Press, 1999.

"Orient Express." *Elle*, October 2003, 156.

"Orient Express." *Elle*, October 1992, 205–10.

"Orient Express." *Vogue*, January 1991, 141.

Ostein, Mark. Introduction. In *The Question of the Gift: Essays across Disciplines*, edited by Mark Ostein, 1–41. New York: Routledge, 2002.

Park, Lisa Sun-Hee. *Consuming Citizenship: Children of Asian Immigrant Entrepreneurs.* Stanford, Calif.: Stanford University Press, 2005.

Parreñas, Rhacel S., and Lok C. D. Siu, eds. *Asian Diasporas: New Formations, New Conceptions.* Stanford, Calif.: Stanford University Press, 2007.

Peterson, Holly. "Doo-Ri Chung: Rising from the Basement to the Big Time." *Newsweek,* December 26, 2005, 92.

"Point of View." *Vogue,* January 2003, 109–29.

Portes, Alejandro, ed. *The New Second Generation.* New York: Russell Sage Foundation, 1996.

Prashad, Vijay. "Crafting Solidarities." In *A Part, Yet Apart: South Asians in Asian America,* edited by Lavina Dhingra Shankar and Rajini Srikanth, 105–26. Philadelphia: Temple University Press, 1998.

——. *Everybody Was Kung Fu Fighting.* Boston: Beacon, 2001.

——. *The Karma of Brown Folk.* Minneapolis: University of Minnesota Press, 2001.

Proper, Carl. "New York: Defending the Union Contract." In *No Sweat: Fashion, Free Trade and the Rights of Garment Workers,* edited by Andrew Ross, 173–92. New York: Verso, 1997.

Rantisi, Norma. "The Ascendance of New York Fashion." *International Journal of Urban and Regional Research* 28, no. 1 (March 2004): 86–106.

Reddy, Chandan. "Asian Diasporas, Neoliberalism, and Family: Reviewing the Case for Homosexual Violence in the Context of Family Rights." *Social Text* 23, no. 3–4 (2005): 101–19.

Rodriguez, Richard T. *Next of Kin: The Family in Chicano Cultural Politics.* Durham, N.C.: Duke University Press, 2009.

Rofel, Lisa. *Desiring China: Experiments in Neoliberalism, Sexuality, and Public Culture.* Durham, N.C.: Duke University Press, 2007.

Rosen, Ellen Israel. *Making Sweatshops: The Globalization of the U.S. Apparel Industry.* Berkeley: University of California Press, 2002.

Ross, Andrew. *Nice Work If You Can Get It: Life and Labor in Precarious Times.* New York: New York University Press, 2009.

"On the Runway." *Elle,* February 2003, 78–80.

"Runway Report." *Harper's Bazaar,* January 2003, 18–27.

"Runway Report." *Vogue,* April 2001, 206–18.

Ryan, Kimberly. "Orient Express." *Vogue,* May 1997, 99.

Sahlins, Marshall. *Stone Age Economics.* Chicago: Aldine, 1972.

Saxenian, Annalee. *Regional Advantage: Culture and Competition in Silicon Valley and Route 128.* Cambridge: Harvard University Press, 1994.

Schell, Orville. *Mandate of Heaven: A New Generation of Entrepreneurs, Dissidents, Bohemians, and Technocrats Lays Claim to China's Future.* New York: Simon and Schuster, 1994.

Schoenberger, Karl. "Huddled Masses Yearning to Write Java." *Industry Standard*, May 8, 2000, 175–94.

Schrift, Melissa. *Biography of a Chairman Mao Badge: The Creation and Mass Consumption of a Personality Cult.* New Brunswick, N.J.: Rutgers University Press, 2001.

Schweitzer, Marlis. "American Fashions for American Women: The Rise and Fall of Fashion Nationalism." In *Producing Fashion: Commerce, Culture, and Consumers,* edited by Regina Lee Blaszczyk, 130–49. Philadelphia: University of Pennsylvania Press, 2008.

Sedghi, Hamideh. *Women and Politics in Iran: Veiling, Unveiling, and Reveiling.* Cambridge: Cambridge University Press, 2007.

Serafin, Tatiana. "Lost in Translation." *Forbes Asia,* May 7, 2007, 30.

Sidlauskas, Susan. *Intimate Architecture: Contemporary Clothing Design: Giorgio Armani, Gianfranco Ferre, Krizia, Stephen Manniello, Issey Miyake, Claude Montana, Ronaldus Shamask, Yeohlee Teng.* Cambridge, Mass.: Committee on Visual Arts, 1982.

Simmel, Georg. "Fashion." *American Journal of Sociology* 42, no. 6 (May 1957): 541–58.

Singer, Sally. "That Touch of Mink." *Vogue,* July 2002, 92.

Skov, Lise. "Fashion-Nation: A Japanese Globalization Experience and a Hong Kong Dilemma." In *Re-Orienting Fashion: The Globalization of Asian Dress,* edited by Sandra Niessen, Ann Marie Leshkowich, and Carla Jones, 215–41. Oxford: Berg, 2003.

Smith, Robert. *Mexican New York: Transnational Lives of New Migrants.* Berkeley: University of California Press, 2006.

Smith, Shawn Michelle. *American Archives: Gender, Race, and Class in Visual Culture.* Princeton, N.J.: Princeton University Press, 1999.

Song, Miri. *Helping Out: Children's Labor in Ethnic Businesses.* Philadelphia: Temple University Press, 1999.

Soyer, Daniel. *Cloak of Many Colors: Immigration, Globalism, and Reform in the New York City Garment Industry.* New York: Fordham University Press, 2005.

"Squaw Valley." *Elle,* November 1990, 271–75.

Stacey, Judith. *In the Name of the Family: Rethinking Family Values in the Postmodern Age.* Boston: Beacon, 1996.

Stansell, Christine. "The Origins of the Sweatshop: Women and Early Industrialization in New York City." In *Working-Class America: Essays on Labor, Community and American Society,* edited by Michael H. Frisch and Daniel J. Walkowitz, 78–103. Urbana: University of Illinois Press, 1983.

Steele, Valerie, and John Major. *China Chic: East Meets West.* New Haven, Conn.: Yale University Press, 1999.

Stein, Leon. *Out of the Sweatshop: The Struggle for Industrial Democracy.* New York: Quadrangle, 1977.

Stockton, Kathryn Bond. *The Queer Child: Growing Sideways in the Twentieth Century*. Durham, N.C.: Duke University Press, 2009.

Stoler, Ann Laura, ed. *Haunted by Empire: Geographies of Intimacy in North American History*. Durham, N.C.: Duke University Press, 2006.

Sullivan, Michael. *Art and Artists of Twentieth-Century China*. Berkeley: University of California Press, 1996.

Sykes, Plum. "Slouching towards Bohemia." *Vogue*, September 1999, 634–40.

———. "Zen on a Hanger." *Vogue*, March 1999, 267–68.

Szabo, Julia. "Mix Master." *Harper's Bazaar*, January 1994, 119–24.

Takaki, Ronald. *Strangers from a Different Shore: A History of Asian Americans*. Rev. ed. Boston: Back Bay Press, 1998.

Tam, Vivienne, with Martha Huang. *China Chic*. New York: Reagan, 2000.

Tchen, John Kuo Wei. *New York before Chinatown: Orientalism and the Shaping of American Culture, 1776–1882*. Baltimore: Johns Hopkins University Press, 2001.

Terranova, Tiziana. "Free Labor: Producing Culture for the Digital Economy." *Social Text* 18, no. 2 (summer 2000): 33–58.

Testart, Alain. "Uncertainties of the 'Obligation to Reciprocate': A Critique of Mauss." In *Marcell Mauss: A Centenary Tribute*, edited by Wendy James and N. J. Allen, 97–110. New York: Berghahn, 1998.

Tucker, William. "Byting the Hand That Feeds Us." *American Spectator*, May 1998, 24–27.

Tulloch, Carol. "There's No Place Like Home: Home Dressmaking and Creativity in the Jamaican Community of the 1940s and 1960s." In *The Culture of Sewing: Gender, Consumption and Home Dressmaking*, edited by Barbara Burman, 111–28. New York: Berg, 1999.

U.S. Department of Labor. Bureau of Labor Statistics. *Occupational Outlook Handbook*. 2010–11 edition, 2009, http://www.bls.gov/oco.

Vinken, Barbara. *Fashion Zeitgeist: Trends and Cycles in the Fashion System*. Translated by Mark Hewson. Oxford: Berg, 2005.

Waldinger, Roger. *Through the Eye of the Needle: Immigrants and Enterprise in New York's Garment Trades*. New York: New York University Press, 1986.

Waldinger, Roger, Howard Aldrich, and Robin Ward. *Ethnic Entrepreneurs: Immigrant Business in Industrial Societies*. Newbury Park, Calif.: BookSurge, 2006.

Waldinger, Roger, and Michael Lichter. *How the Other Half Works: Immigration and the Social Organization of Labor*. Berkeley: University of California Press, 2003.

Wark, Mackenzie. "Fashion as a Culture Industry." In *No Sweat: Fashion, Free Trade, and the Rights of Garment Workers*, edited by Andrew Ross, 227–49. New York: Verso, 1997.

Wei, William. *The Asian American Movement*. Philadelphia: Temple University Press, 1993.

Wexler, Laura. *Tender Violence: Domestic Visions in an Age of U.S. Imperialism.* Chapel Hill: University of North Carolina Press, 2000.

Williams, Rhys H., and Gira Vashi. "Hijab and American Muslim Women: Creating the Space for Autonomous Selves." *Sociology of Religions* 68, no. 3 (fall 2007): 269–87.

Wilson, Elizabeth. *Adorned in Dreams: Fashion and Modernity.* New Brunswick, N.J.: Rutgers University Press, 2003.

Wilson, William Julius. *The Truly Disadvantaged: The Inner City, the Underclass, and Public Policy.* Chicago: University of Chicago Press, 1987.

Wong, Cynthia Sau-ling. "Denationalization Reconsidered: Asian American Cultural Criticism at a Theoretical Crossroads." *Amerasia Journal* 21, nos. 1–2 (2005): 1–27.

Woodmansee, Martha. "On the Author Effect: Recovering Collectivity." In *The Construction of Authorship: Textual Appropriation in Law and Literature,* edited by Martha Woodmansee and Peter Jaszi, 15–29. Durham, N.C.: Duke University Press, 1994.

Woodmansee, Martha, and Peter Jaszi. "Introduction." In *The Construction of Authorship: Textual Appropriation in Law and Literature,* edited by Martha Woodmansee and Peter Jaszi, 1–14. Durham, N.C.: Duke University Press, 1994.

Wright, Melissa. *Disposable Women and Other Myths of Global Capitalism.* New York: Routledge, 2006.

Wu Hung. "Afterword 'Hong Kong 1997': T-shirt Designs by Zhang Hongtu." *Public Culture* 9, no. 3 (spring 1997): 415–25.

——. *Exhibiting Experimental Art.* Chicago: Smart Museum of Art, 2000.

——. *Remaking Beijing: Tiananmen Square and the Making of Political Space.* Chicago: University of Chicago Press, 2005.

——. *Transience: Chinese Experimental Art at the End of the Century.* Chicago: Smart Museum of Art, 1999.

——. "Introduction." In *Chinese Art at the Crossroads: Between Past and Future, Between East and West,* edited by Wu Hung, 8–16. London: New Art Media, 2001.

Xu, Gang Gary. "Remaking East Asia, Outsourcing Hollywood," http://archive .sensesofcinema.com/contents/05/34/remaking_east_asia.html.

Yanagisako, Sylvia. *Transforming the Past: Kinship and Tradition among Japanese Americans.* Stanford, Calif.: Stanford University Press, 1985.

Yee, Lydia. "An Interview with Zhang Hongtu." In exhibit pamphlet for Zhang Hongtu: Material Mao, Bronx Museum of the Arts, 1995.

Yoo, Jin-Kyung. *Korean Immigrant Entrepreneurs: Network and Ethnic Resources.* New York: Routledge, 1998.

Yoshihara, Mari. *Embracing the East: White Women and American Orientalism.* New York: Oxford University Press, 2002.

Yúdice, George. *The Expediency of Culture: Uses of Culture in the Global Era*. Durham, N.C.: Duke University Press, 2003.

Zhou, Yu. "New York: Caught under the Fashion Runway; Immigrant Enterprises in the Garment Industry of New York." In *Unravelling the Rag Trade: Immigrant Entrepreneurship in Seven World Cities*, edited by Jan Rath, 113–34. Oxford: Berg, 2002.

Zia, Helen. *Asian American Dreams: The Emergence of an American People*. New York: Farrar, Straus, and Giroux, 2001.

INDEX

Sun, Zixi, 143
sweatshop, 19, 215 n. 62; reemergence of, 26, 69; reliance on immigrant labor in, 70

Takada, Kenzo, 181
Takahashi, Jun, 195–98, 238 n. 68
Tam, Vivienne, 24, 34, 39, 135, 139, 175, 211 n. 21; biography of, 39–40, 146; collaboration with Zhang Hongtu of, 24, 156–65; use of Asian chic by, 130
Teng, Yeohlee, 100, 180, 185–88
thick solidarity, 65, 93
trade policies, 10–11, 67
Tran, Calvin, 92
trends: setting of, 104, 121. *See also* Asian chic, Burqa chic
Tsai, Margie, 83, 137–38
Tucker, William, 210 n. 10

veiling, 192–193; as space making, 194
Vietnam, 11, 12, 212 n. 27
Vionnet, Madeleine, 103
visibility, 237 n. 51; politics of, 191–95, 197, 200–201, 237 n. 51
Vogue (magazine), 225 n. 16; promotion of American designers and, 18

Wang, Guangyi, 144
Wang, Jingsong, 143
Wang, Vera, 34, 100, 175, 177–78
Wang sisters (Jennifer and Sally), 40, 58, 63–64, 75, 79–82, 84
women, 7–8, 70–72, 84–85; as garment industry labor force, 71; politics of body of, 192–95, 204; as sewers, 41–42, 63–64
World Trade Organization, 10

Yamomoto, Yohji, 195–98
Yang, Selia, 57, 59, 180
Yoo, Jin-Kyung, 88–89
Yu, Jean, 39, 189, 221 n. 42
Yu, Youhan, 143
Yúdice, George, 101, 209 n. 5
Yves Saint Laurent, 104, 107–9, 125, 131

Zhang, Hongtu: biography of, 145–48; collaboration with Vivenne Tam of, 24, 156–65; Hong King T-shirts and, 163–64, 233 n. 80; use of Mao Zedong's image by, 148–56

Thuy Linh Nguyen Tu is an assistant professor of
Social and Cultural Analysis at New York University.
She is the editor, with Mimi Thi Nguyen, of *Alien
Encounters: Popular Culture in Asian America* (2007) and,
with Alondra Nelson, of *Technicolor: Race, Technology,
and Everyday Life* (2001).

Library of Congress Cataloging-in-Publication Data
Tu, Thuy Linh N.
The beautiful generation : Asian Americans and the
cultural economy of fashion / Thuy Linh Nguyen Tu.
p. cm.
Includes bibliographical references and index.
ISBN 978-0-8223-4890-0 (cloth : alk. paper)
ISBN 978-0-8223-4913-6 (pbk. : alk. paper)
1. Asian American fashion designers. 2. Fashion—
United States—Social aspects. 3. Fashion—Economic
aspects—United States. I. Title.
TT504.4T8 2011
746.9'208995073—dc22   2010035871